Africa's Dependency Syndrome:
Can Africa Still Turn Things around for the Better?

Nkwazi N. Mhango

Langaa Research & Publishing CIG
Mankon, Bamenda

Publisher:
Langaa RPCIG
Langaa Research & Publishing Common Initiative Group
P.O. Box 902 Mankon
Bamenda
North West Region
Cameroon
Langaagrp@gmail.com
www.langaa-rpcig.net

Distributed in and outside N. America by African Books Collective
orders@africanbookscollective.com
www.africanbookscollective.com

ISBN-10: 9956-762-11-3

ISBN-13: 978-9956-762-11-8

© Nkwazi N. Mhango 2017

Table of Contents

Acknowledgements

This volume would not have seen the light of the day had my wife Nesaa not stood by my side. I wholeheartedly acknowledge her immense and unconditional help and support. So, too, my brother, friend and mentor, Prof Sean Byrne did a lot to convince me that I can still churn wealth materials. My brother Prof Munyaradzi Mawere as well kept on bugging me to write even more. Prof Jessica Senehi also encouraged me a lot not to mention Brothers, Sirili Akko (Arusha-Tanzania); and Salih Hassan Ibrahim (Winnipeg, MB, Canada) who always want to be the first to read my books. Langaa Publishers have always been instrumental in my writing. Our children Ng'ani (Nyanyi), Nkuzi (Kuji) and Nkwazi Jr., (Genius) have always inspired me to do more. I, therefore, disingenuously acknowledge and appreciate all who in a way or another contributed to making me who I am today.

Preface

This book is intended to act as a wakeup call, if not an eye opener, for African countries to take their destiny into their hands. It aims at encouraging Africans to negate the dependency they have been forced to accept as true while it is a hoax based on the propensities and resources Africa boasts having. Mhango [*forthcoming*] argues that dependency in some cultures, especially collectivistic ones, is wealth based on Social Capital Theory under which "social relationships among people" can be productive resources" (Coleman 1988 cited in Chiu, Hsu and Wang 2006: 1875). However, the same is vice versa in individualistic culture. Although it is not the first book to have embarked on such a journey, I believe it will add up to the call for Africa to turn things around for the better so that it can do away with pointless dependency while it actually sits on humungous resources of high value (Mhango 2015; 2016). In my journey to addressing the problems that Africa has faced for many decades, I am showing where the said problems lie and what should be done to turn things around for the better based on the present opportunities such as investing in science and technology, the rise of China and India, and competition these emerging powers are going to cause. However, there is a caution here that the coming of China and India may end up exacerbating exploitation if Africa is not going to play its cards smartly.

The difference this book makes is the fact that the author is optimistic that Africa will one day turn things around for the better. And the difference the book is the fact that the author exclusively and specifically shows how Africa can turn things around. However, this will not be a walk to the park. It needs a lot of soul searching, commitment and high moral authority for African leadership to start thinking like dignified humans-cum-creatures. For, in many African cultures, nobody should live on charity or handouts from someone without having any means or plans to reciprocate or returning the charity. It is from this backdrop, among others, that Africans never know any social assistance provided by the government. Instead, they are the ones that offer social assistance to the government through their taxes and labours that many corrupt Africa mumbo jumbos spend without any gist of accountability or remorse.

As argued, this volume is different from many books that have addressed the issue of Africa's dependency. While many scholars have appointed one or a few particular issues to address, this book takes a multifaceted approach of addressing many issues in one volume. While many scholars such as Walter Rodney, Kwame Nkrumah, Julius Nyerere, Didia Dal, Munyaradzi Mawere, Francis Nyamnjoh and many more have addressed one side of the coin by blaming colonialism on everything on foreign causes of its destabilisation, underdevelopment, poverty and whatever ills Africa faces, this book, to the contrary, blames both sides namely the colonial powers and African governments that took over after colonialism for the quandaries Africa has been in. Eme (2013) notes that the approach the so-called international community—led by the United Nations (UN)—was more or less a treatment of symptoms instead of causes, and the gap gradually widened between the so-called developed and less developed countries of this world (p. 118). Ironically, despite this anomaly being known for a long time, nothing has ever been done to address it. Instead, it has been reinforced and internalised so as to become the new normalcy if not the *sine qua non*e of development—that has never been actualised—for Africa.

To do justice for both sides so that they can see their contribution to the quandaries Africa is in historically, I have decided to implicate both sides not just because I wanted to do so. It is because of the roles they intentionally or unintentionally played in creating the cleft stick for Africa this volume addresses. This is why it is stated from the outset that Africa needs to venture into both sides of the divide when it comes to its anguishes and stumbling blocks in its efforts to turn things around for the better. Essentially, this approach helps the duo to see their culpability or the role they played so as to accept liability; and thus, thereby help each other by working together to address the problem they both created either by commission or omission. On the one hand, there are problems that are purely colonial that caused Africa's underdevelopment, dependency and poverty. While, on the other hand, there are some causes and problems that are purely African either committed intentionally or otherwise all depending on how one looks at them epistemologically based on the true history of Africa. You can divide these problems in two categories namely external and internal or inflicted and self-inflicted ones. So, too, the said problems can be divided into three typologies namely economic, political and social. For, if we critically examine the concepts of development, dependency and underdevelopment, we find that Africa has never depended on the West. Instead the reality is vice versa. This is so if we avoid manipulative politics that has become the *realpolitik* of the current world where lies are made truth and vice versa. If anything, this is the line of logic Africans need to know. Again, how will they know this and why? They need to teach each other the reality about their predicaments so that they can see the problem in its true colours. Knowing this reality will encourage them to ask very crucial questions: Why should they depend on us but tell us the opposite? If our dependency is a myth, does it mean we can demystify it and move forward just like others humans and societies in Europe and Asia did?

This volume strives for justice for Africa and anybody else. The underlining philosophy is that charity always begins at home. One needs to do justice for him or herself before extending it to others without forgetting that everybody is required to treat others the way he or she would like to be treated. This is why; justice is the centre stage in spite of not being discussed extensively. Therefore, to avoid blaming without showing how things can be made right, this book has avoided the categorisation of issues based on their externality on internality. Instead, this volume addresses every issue by touching on both sides at a go. Nevertheless, it does not mean that those who categorise African quandaries based on the above categories are wrong. What matters most is the intention or spirit of doing so. It is the matter of choice; and, in the main, it depends on how doable one approach is compared to others. In principle, this book bases primarily on intersectionality of the issues based on interdisciplinary deconstruction.

In addressing the traps that Africa is caught and stranded in, the book challenges African countries to wise up and take their destiny in their hands. So, too, the book challenges the international community to accept their contribution in pushing Africa to where it is today. By exploring all such possibilities and realities, I still believe that Africa can still turn things around for the better. This is an easy thing to do. Nonetheless, when it comes to how to do it, there are many possibilities of which one is not to do. Again, why should Africa fail to turn things around while it has all potentials and potentialities? For me, Africa has to turn things around due to many reasons that this book will enumerate and discuss. Therefore, the major question one needs to ask is: How will Africa turn things around? The book answers the question. However, it does not prescribe the timeframe it will take for Africa to turn things around given that it took a long time for Africa to reach where it is now. Again, the book generally urges African countries to become self-reliant by thinking big and revisiting its history, behaviour, systems, structures and whatnot. How will they do this? The book proposes to African countries to divorce the tendency of dependency that aid rich countries have always extended to them without allowing them to stand on their legs is the panacea for their development. Actually, the book is putting a finger on the crux of striking issues that Africa faces. In the main, the book questions Africa's dependency while it sits on humungous and much-needed resources. Although many have asked the same question, the book does so in different way by exploring many important areas that Africa needs to address and round for the better future of its people.

Abbreviations

A.D–Anno Domino
ACP–African Caribbean and Pacific
AfDB–African Development Bank
AIDS–Acquired Immunodeficiency Syndrome
ANC–African National Congress
ATO–African Trade Organisation
AU–African Unity
BBC–British Broadcasting Corporation
CAR–Central African Republic
CBC–Canadian Broadcasting Corporation
CNN–Cable News Television
CPR–Cardiopulmonary resuscitation
CPR–Control Profit and Resources
DCI–Director of Criminal Investigations
DPO–Director of Police Operations
DRC–Democratic Republic of Congo
EEC–European Economic Commission
ESAP–Economic Structural Adjustment Policies
FAO–Food and Agriculture Organisation
FBI–Federal Bureau of Investigation
FOCAC–Forum on China–Africa Cooperation
GBV–Gender Based Violence
GDP–Gross Domestic Product
GLR–Great Lake Region
GNP–Gross National Product
HIPC–Heavily Indebted Poor Countries
HIV–Human Immunodeficiency Virus
ICC–International Criminal Court
IDG–International Development Goal
IFF–Illicit Financial Flows
IFI–International Financial Institutions
IIRO–International Islamic Relief Organization

IMF–International Monetary Fund
ISIL–Islamic State in Iraq and Levant
IT–Information Technology
ITO–International Trade Organisation
ITU–International Telecommunications Union
KHRC–Kenyan Human Right Commission
MCC–Millennium Challenge Corporation
MDG–Millennium Development Goal
MNC–Multi-Nationals corporations
MNFI–Multi-National Financial Institutions
MNH–Muhimbili National Hospital
MPI–Migration Policy Institute
NGO–Non-Governmental Organisation
PEV–Post-Election Violence
PhD–Doctor of Philosophy
SSA–Sub-Saharan Africa
TNT–Trinitrotoluene
TRIP–Trade-related Aspects of Intellectual Property Rights
UK–United Kingdom
UNCTAD–United Nations Conference on Trade and Development
UNDP–United Nations Development Program
UN–United Nations
USSR–Union of Soviet Socialist Republics
US–United States
WB–World Bank
WTO–World Trade Organisation
WW–World War

Chapter 1

Aid Dependency and Aid Vicious Circle

To kick off the discussion in the discourse, this book starts by defining the term dependency in order to enable the readers to be in the big picture. To this volume, dependency is any chronic behaviour affecting a person or society so as to force it perpetually to succumb to depending on someone or society to address his, her or its needs and sometimes problems in order to develop. As per Dependency theory, Max-Neef (1991: 38 cited in Matunhu 2011) argues that development emanates directly from the actions, expectations, and creative and critical awareness of the protagonists themselves but not otherwise. However, experience shows that sometimes can emanate from outside after the protagonists plunder others the same way the West did to Africa so as to under-develop it (Rodney 1972 cited in Matunhu *Ibid.*); and thereby develop Europe. Europe's internal thrust enabled it to seek development outside Europe. Again, given that there are no countries left to colonise, Africa needs to look inside itself and colonise and utilise its immense resources for its development. In a simple parlance, dependency can be defined as the antithesis of independence.

On his side, Dos Santos (1970 cited in Andrews and Okpanachi 2011) maintains that dependency is a situation in which the economy of certain countries is conditioned by the development and expansion of another economy to which the former is subjected. In his definition of dependency, Dos Santos goes further so as to incorporate knowledge and its sources in assessing and bringing development. Therefore, when we address Africa's dependency on the West, we need to incorporate many things so as to cover all spheres of life. This is

1

why this volumes tackles the problem by categorising it in three facets namely, economic, political and social.

Furthermore, in addressing Africa's dependency that is hinged on aid, this book emphasises the importance for Africa to do things by itself instead of allowing or letting others do so for it. Since attaining their political independence, many if not all African countries have, over and above, depended and lived on aid that rich countries–mostly Western–have extended to them (Moss, Pettersson and Van de Walle (2006). Most of the African countries have their budgets, elections and other development projects are always supported by mainly rich Western countries. This is because, for many years, Africa has been depending on aid the donors extend to it. Primarily, those extending aid to Africa most of them are the same that benefit from its resources sold at cheap price or illegally in areas facing conflicts. Despite receiving aid for a long time, Africa is still relatively poor. This means that aid is not working; and it will never work shall Africa keeps doing things *in situ*. Berg (1997, 2000 cited in Moss, Pettersson and Van de Walle *Ibid.)* observe that aid has had negative effects on local institutions, especially "when aid flows reach 5 percent of GDP, which would mean that the overwhelming majority of states in the region are negatively affected" (p. 19). This is exactly what has been going on in Africa for a long time now. And, it is obvious that those extending aid do so not just because of altruistic motives but ulterior self-sustaining ones. No fisherman puts the bait on hook for the love of fish. He does so for the love of the fish's flesh but not otherwise. Essentially, any economic growth that is not reflected in the lives of common people is as good as non-existent so to speak.

Aid has never worked for Africa; and if it did, it did not deliver the expected results to say the least. Interestingly, when such statistics is provided, many Africans whose countries are featured in it go haywire celebrating such a *milestone* that cannot be reflected on the lives of those they rule with discretion and ineptness. To pragmatically turn things around, Africa seriously needs to abandon its despicable tendency of depending on aid while it sits on huge resources of many kinds. Some scholars blame Africa's dependency on poor government, especially the lack of strong institutions of governance. This is partly true, however. Basically, we need to unearth one crucial reality that many scholars do not mention or tackle in discussing Africa's dependency, deficiency and inefficiency resulting from poor governance and the lack of competent and accountable leadership. This is nothing but the holes colonial governments left abaft after handing over the reins of powers to newly independent African countries. Bräutigam and Knack (2004) disclose that soon after gaining their independence some African countries experienced balance of payments problems which forced them to borrow from the IMF to cover shortfalls in foreign exchange (p. 259) due to the gaping holes their colonial master caused and left behind. What made things harder and worse for Africa is the fact that the exploitative world system remained unchanged even after African countries acquired their political independence which means they were not free economically.

Essentially, Africa started on the wrong foot by accepting to partake of "financial folly", (Reinhart and Rogoff 2009) which is self-explanatory. What actually happened was nothing but changing colonial systems that ceased to be manned by direct colonial agents. This is why calling many corrupt post-colonial governments colonial tools does not aim at belittling them or ignoring a small contribution visionary African leaders of the time made. However, compared to what was envisaged and expected, Africa scored poorly and minimally. Thomson (2016) argues that post-colonial consequences of being incorporated into this international political system kept on haunting Africa up until now. Practically, by accepting to be incorporated to a

3

colonial and exploitative system, Africa became the part and parcel of its own exploitation. For, it became the accomplice to the crime it was supposed to fight to see to it that it was redressed for all ills colonialism cause Africa. The dependency that followed thereafter is the result of Africa to fail to disentangle itself from the very system that authored its problems.

Due to the callowness and euphoria of attaining the independence, post-colonial African leaders did not agitate to have their countries reimbursed for the economic dearth and miseries colonial rules caused and left abaft at the time they relinquished their colonies. The failure to demand that Africa be redressed turned the independence many African countries were having a good time about in the 60s meaningless, especially for the *hoi polloi* that have suffered from various manmade miseries ever since. Had African countries sought redress, the independence of their countries would become meaningful. Instead, they confidently embarked on monkey see monkey do; namely believing that they would prevail the same way their former colonial masters did without underscoring the means and reasons behind such a success that was not reflected on the lives of their ever suffering people. If you look at the tools or engines of economies such as infrastructure, manpower and sound environment, all were badly amiss. Take the Central African Republic (CAR), for example. It did not have even a single university at the time it attained independence (Bloom, Canning and Chan 2006) not to mention paved roads. How could such a country–that later was marred with maladministration resulting from *coup d'états*–would pull itself out of such a limbo without necessarily been helped or redressed by those who exploited it under colonialism so as to author the vulnerability the country has been in ever since?

The CAR represents many African countries whose independence ended up becoming a loss. For, it does not add up to think that such a country would do much better without any systemic capital. Further, how the country with none or dilapidated infrastructure would make it to prosperity without fundamentally changing or overhauling the whole system it inherited from its colonial masters? Once again, who would do so while those who plugged the gap sought their personal glories even if they come by vending their brothers and sisters? And, this is essentially the typical replica of many African countries. How does one expect such a country to excel like its former colonial master, France that went on perpetually destabilising and exploiting it? What makes the West to share the big part of blames is the fact that it kept on benefiting from its colonial system so as to turn it into an international or world system under capitalistic neoliberal policies that have seen Africa cascading even further down compared to how it was soon after gaining independence.

We may blame African countries today simply because we are precocious enough to. Again, when you compare the effects of their take [s], especially allowing their countries and economies to totally depend on aid and handout, there was something terrible wrong with the leadership in these countries that allowed their countries to keep on serving the economy of the mother country (Hopkins 2014) while theirs were continuously starving and tanking. For the desire of serving the economies of their mother countries, African countries did not end up being exploited but they also shunned each other when it comes to do business (Mhango 2015). I do not think that for African countries to trade among themselves does need experts from their colonial masters. It is the matter of making the right decision and seeing the loss the lack of inter-trading habit among African countries has caused. Historically though, African countries used to trade among themselves when Africa was still one entity before being divided and partitioned in 1884 in Berlin. This is why long distance trade such as the medieval Trans-

Saharan trade (Wright 2007) or City State-Long Distance Trade is not new concept (Mitchell 2002:288, 2005 cited in Kim and Kusimba 2008). Although such details are now decaying in history books, they have something to teach for Africa when it comes to having self-confidence in turning things around. Furthermore, such networks that existed and throve before the introduction of colonialism can act as the launching pad for Africa to turn things around by re-establishing intra and inter trade among African countries.

When it comes to the culpability and responsibility for Africa's miseries, it takes two to tango. There is no way we can blame African countries only without implicating those who took them for a ride. Let us say that agitating for being redressed would not succeed due to the archaic nature of the international systems. What if they had agitated to change the market arguing that instead of being given aid, they must be given fair prices for their produces? If anything, this is the mistake Africa needs to learn from; and turn around if it wants to turn things around.

There is no way Africa can go on depending on aid while it lets its produces to be bought at exploitative prices under the current international market led by the World Trade Organisation (WTO) which is renowned for reinforcing the exploitation of Africa under which some countries have less standing and benefits (Goldstein, Rivers and Tomz 2007). For Africa to turn things around, it needs to either renegotiate the terms of the WTO or deconstruct and overhaul it if not to form its own African Trade Organisation (ATO) that will give it the edge and means of playing a crucial role in international trade due to having resources the whole world needs and depends on. Better with fair trade than generous aid given for the intention of self-serving for those offering it. In this capitalist world, nothing is for free. By being made to depend on aid, African economies will never stand on their feet. As mentioned above, many African governments run their business depending on

6

foreign aid. They have never asked themselves what will happen shall donor countries stop offering aid to their countries. And if you look at what donor countries rob Africa and what they get, Africa is at loss.

This chapter has purposely started with question on the evaluation of aid and the way it does not help African economies to grow in economic terms (Rajan and Subramanian 2008). This issue is important among others. For, it helps us to gauge if the economies of African countries have grown due to receiving aid or what is likely to keep on happening if the manner and trend of seemingly extending aid to these countries continues. So, too, it helps us to devise the way by which to help Africa out of dependency and poverty resulting from the status quo as colonial drives enshrined it in the international system. Such a take helps us to envisage what is to happen to Africa shall things remain the same. Also, knowing what will happen will help African countries to start thinking about the less travelled road out of their impasse-cum-predicaments shall they decide, plan and wish to so, chiefly when they consider that aid can either come to an end anytime or can be used for more exploitation of Africa all depending on the needs of the donors but not the needs of Africans.

Whether aid has worked or not, it is subject to discussion. On the other hand, Africa's poverty and economic backward speak volume as to what worked and what did not. Ojo (2016) invokes endogamous theory to show how aid has never brought any desired development to African countries arguing that "systemic corruption and vampirism, utter disregard for democratic ideals, and the 'sit-tight syndrome" (p. 129) political instability and pervasive civil wars have rendered African states economically and technologically immobile since independence so as to perpetually depend on aid extended by their former colonial masters. Therefore, the theory does not link aid to growth. If anything, what aid has always done to Africa is causing a lot of dependency, exploitation and underdevelopment despite sitting on immense reserves of resources. This is obvious due to the fact that even when it comes to defining assessing and gaging if there is growth in Africa or not, the same donors have an upper hand. Ironically, donors assess and define everything to make what is reported, in the main, so as to make everything to totally depend on how donor countries want it to look like for their interests as opposed to the interests of Africa. In in many cases as we will show later, donors' verdict lines with their conclusion[s] even if and when such a verdict is detrimental and wrong. This is the danger which Africa faces after allowing donors to define and evaluate it as they deem fit based on their plans. Mhango (2017) queries the rationale for Africa to allow the same criminals that enslaved and colonised it to "justly and judiciously define" its development based on their exploitative neoliberal policies that have never worked for Africa which he terms the madness of its kind or just a tall order. Africa needs to change this. It is only animals that we are able to freely define without fearing that they can complain that doing so lacks their contributions. When it comes to humans, the situation is the opposite. We need to involve them in any process that involves them.

Whether aid is a causal force behind growth in some Africa economies or not it is subject to discussion. It is noteworthy to realise that, at individual country level, the case is always differently positive and negative depending on how the country abides by the conditions donor countries stipulate. However, in the main, many African economies have always performed poorly due to exploitative and harsh conditions donors put on aid. Evidentially, this is why the donor community has always referred to itself as the First World while they refer to African countries as the Third World. The coining of the first and the third world has become an albatross in Africa's neck due to the fact it has made it believe that it is poor despite sitting on humongous precious resources not to mention forcing it to internalise and normalise such an anomaly. Thus, strive to become at least the second world. With such mind-set and practise, there has never been a time Africa contemplated about joining the first world in anything. This is psychologically detrimental and destructive. For, it makes Africa's priorities weaker not to mention goals. African sage has it that when you intend to go for hunting, never aim at killing a rabbit or a rat; instead, aim at killing a wildebeest or a buffalo so that you can have excessive meat to lend others. So, by believing that Africa is a third world, the donor community has made it to aim at hunting for the rabbits and rats but not wildebeest and buffaloes the same donor community does. With such a mind-set, Africa has never aimed higher than disentangling itself from its superimposed third world artificial, degrading and deceptive status. If we face it, how, for example, the countries that have no resources except exploitative colonial institutions such as Belgium and Switzerland become the first world while the giants of resources such as Angola and the DRC become the third world? What type of logic and calculus are we using to come to such injudicious conclusion? While such fallacy is reinforced and internalised, those committing such a crime are priding themselves of being the *founders*, *guardians* if not *pontifices maximus* of human rights in which equality and equity are cardinal parts. Does this make sense and do justice really? Radelet (2006) maintains that there is no relationship between aid and growth in many African countries despite aid being pumped into African countries for over five decades. Again, who benefit from such aid? Moyo (2009) maintains that aid money has benefited corrupt leaders who take is as easy money they can easily squander. Even though, the spirit of extending aid has never been to benefit common peoples as an anonymous Western official cited in Tan-Mullins, Mohan and Power (2010) notes that Western countries are not a donor, we are a poor country so we can't really afford to give grants, on the other hand we want to trade and that would benefit everyone.

At one time, Uganda, despite being hijacked by a despot dictator, was the darling of the West simply because, apart from succeeding in duping them, it toed the line according to their *diktat* (Munene 2010: and Bompani 2017). This enabled Ugandan long time undemocratic rule to get away with murder. Whatever Museveni did from fighting HIV/AIDS, modernising the economy of Uganda to stabilising the country, was applauded as successful even if it was doubtful as it later proved to be after the fallout with his masters who sought other stooges to use in robbing Africa.

Museveni was praised for *wisely* spending donors' money. For example, according to Mwenda (2006), in the year 2005, Uganda government spent 11 percent of its annual budget, or US$200 million, on the military of which about 20 percent of that amount, or US$40 million, was lost to corruption while only 20 percent went to education. Nevertheless, if we consider how Uganda at the time reported was the darling of the West, chances are that such findings were aimed at showing how donor money implicationally performed its *miracles* to the country even if in reality the situation told a very different story. Miedema (2010) notes that Museveni's relationship with donors was pivotal in giving them nearly free rein over the policy and budget-making processes, the donors left him a free hand or sometimes even gave him a helping hand with his military plans which still goes on under the global war on terror.

To assess if aid works or not, we need to consider long time effects to the country touted to have *performed* miraculously. Before buying into the findings of the said report, we need to assess and evaluate Uganda's performance before and after receiving the said aid. Essentially, what made such aid been regarded as well utilised is the fact that the country in question served the covert interests of the donor countries. For example,

Whitaker (2010) discloses that some former British colonies that have experiences some terrorist attacks have become good allies of the US whereby they receive at least US $135 million annually in US economic and military assistance annually which the regimes used for their political survival. The US does not fail such allies in anything be it legal or illegal, acceptable or unacceptable provided that they toe its line as it has been in the case of Rwanda and Uganda which invaded the DRC in 1996 (Lawson 2007) and the US kept mum. There was no way these invasive countries could be held accountable due to the fact what they are doing in the DRC is the only role left for many African governments namely to provide contractual legality that legalises the extraction work of the transnational companies (Ferguson 2006). This is why interpersonal relationship between the heads of the three countries has never been affected by this crime committed by two against another country. For them, personal interests are more important than those of the populace. This is because in many instances some are country was run by a series of complex "power relationships" and regional "big men" (Dunn cited in Cook 2010: 399) maintained by imperialism and neo-colonialism (Mhango 2016b) which is why invasive countries have never been punished or being reprimanded by the champions of human rights and democracy.

Further, Lawson maintains that aid for three decades had achieved little in terms of growth and democratization. Under the guise of aid, some strongmen such as Museveni were able to outwit the West by even cooperating with their enemies as it was in the case of Libya. It is an open secret that Museveni, for example, has been able to serve two masters namely the West by keeping his friendship with former Libyan strongman, Muamar Gaddafi as he maintained his close ties with Western leaders. Thanks to this trick, at one time, Museveni became the "darling of the West" under *Pax Musevenica* (Campbell 2007) which guaranteed him the power to lord it over Ugandans without

11

necessarily embarking on democratic rules. Due to this lethal alliance hinging on exploiting of Africa's resources by using African stooges, there was no way the West could fail their ally in Uganda that they badly needed at the time, especially when the DRC was on the verge of collapsing after the West turned its back on another long-time venal dictator Mobutu Seseseko in Zaire then the DRC at the time. Essentially, when it comes to alliance with Africa and the West, what matters is nothing but the interests of the latter as opposed to the interests of the former. This is why aid has never pulled Africa out of misrule and poverty. It is because of this double standard that many African countries have internalised for their peril. Again, if there is anything that Africa needs to radically and practically address is nothing but this sort of toxic relationship or alliance.

More on why Uganda became a good ally of the West, it is because it allowed Museveni to become Uganda's de facto ruler after banning his opponents (Tidemand 2013) knowing that the West would not touch him or force him to embark on true democratic rule. Once again, this shows exactly how the West behaves when it has its interests to safeguard. Democracy becomes the thing of the past if not insignificant for a country or a leader who is ready to safeguard such dubious interests as this case indicates. Apart from being a double standard, allowing Museveni to rule Uganda for as long as he deems fit without fully introducing true multiparty policies that many African countries are forced to introduce, contradicts the whole way the West has been dealing with noncompliant African regimes or countries as far as true democratisation is concerned.

Ironically, the West truly knows that undemocratic rules are corrupt through and through due to the lack of checks and balances. Despite this been known, they still pour aid to such countries knowing that such money will be misappropriated and squandered. How can such funds survive or deliver without accountable and transparent government in the first place? Try to compare how Museveni was treated preferentially with what happened when his ally, Gaddafi, decided to become a good boy to the West. He was removed from the list of leaders who support terrorism. However, this had a price tag on it. Gaddafi had to cough over US$2.7 billion (Mupepi 2016) to an escrow account at the Bank of International Settlements in Basel (Murphy 2003) also see Tandon (2011). Despite agreeing to pay such huge sum, Gaddafi seemed to have been forced to pay for the crime he claimed to not have committed. Emerson (2004) maintains that Gaddafi was *ripped off* after claiming that evidence presented in the case that saw one Libyan Megrahi was fabricated; and thus he was innocent. Ironically though, Gaddafi went ahead pooh-poohing the judgment that ordered the families of the victims to be granted US$700 million in damages (p. 488). After realising that Gaddafi was forced to buy his innocence from the West, go further and compare with what transpired after he did the opposite that led to his toppling and later demise. Put it in mind; the US–that leads the West in this business of safeguarding their interests in Africa–has neither permanent allies nor permanent foes except permanent interests. Nonetheless, Rice (2008) in trying to show that US's realism policies are not controversial notes that the US had permanent allies, especially those it shares values with. Rice faults Lord Palmerston who said that nations have no permanent allies.

After showing the double standard and controversies regarding how the West deals with poor countries, let us explore if aid brings development to recipient countries. In addressing the major question, I will, *inter alia*, explore the conditions or strings attached to aid, what donors expect out the aid extended, and above all, how the aid is used or misused. This becomes important area to explore due to the fact that almost every powerful country has vested covert and overt interests in Africa. To the contrary, Africa has interests in these countries but it does not have any viable strategies to realise its interests in these countries. So, too, despite having interests in the donor countries, Africa does not have equal footing to advocate and defend its interests the same way latter does *vis-à-vis* Africa.

When it comes to having interests to be secured and safeguarded in Africa for foreign rich countries, it goes without saying; the West is not alone. Currently, China and India are making inroads to Africa in their concerted efforts and strategies to share African cake. They too are offering "aid" in order to entice Africa. The assumption is that they are trying to help Africa out while to the contrary they are plundering its resources as we will see in the new scramble for Africa in chapter four. These countries have recently worked aggressively to see to it that they win leverage in Africa by convening conferences with Africa to discuss how they can *help* Africa. Many African leaders who like to be helped, seized this opportunity some to entrench themselves in power after the West either shunned or fell out with them while others go there hoping they can get more handouts. To see to it that their strategies succeed, they duo are oft-extending less-conditional aid to Africa in order to win the hearts and minds of African rulers who are the only ones who decide who should have sphere of influence on them or not. This is why we call this the second scramble for Africa after the first that ushered colonial rule in Africa. My assumption is that given that there is no equal and equity, reciprocity and parity in this relationship, chances are that the donors are likely to benefit while the recipients lose in the name of aid as it has been the case for Africa in dealing with Western countries. Africa needs to learn a lesson from the first scramble that left it burgled, plundered, vandalised and underdeveloped.

Many examples show that neither Africa nor the donors have ever been able and ready to learn from their mistakes and quandaries provided that this game of deceit has always been their source of income and power over others. For, donors keep on playing the same game by simply changing the rules while Africa keeps on repeating the same mistakes that saw it become dependent on its former colonial masters. What transpired recently in Tanzania speaks volume. The American Millennium Challenge Corporation (MCC), an independent U.S Government foreign aid agency, decided not to endow Tanzania with the aid it had previously promised it. As usual, the MCC found a pretext in democracy as if Tanzania was the first country to rig the elections. How many dictatorship the US is currently protecting? However, Tanzania did something unexperienced before. In hitting back, which is rare for many African countries, Tanzanian government urged its people to end dependency on donors. It seems; the new president John Pombe Magufuli who is renowned for working hard and cutting unnecessary expenses in government expenditure has decided to turn things around. If African leaders could take a leaf from Tanzania, chances of turning things around are higher now than ever before. The *Guardian* (1 April, 2016) observes that:

> The country won a five-year MCC grants package worth $698 million for water, roads and power projects back in 2008. But the award of the second round of grants was initially deferred due to corruption concerns, and has now being shelved over the Zanzibar polls.

Although we do not condone or support election fraud that Tanzania is accused of to have occurred in Zanzibar, we applaud Tanzania's courage of the mad that enabled it to see the problem many African countries see but either ignore or fear to confront it head on. Essentially, what Tanzanian government, just like any poor country, thought was aid from the MCC seems to be more verbal than practical just like the project that gave birth to all this namely the Millennium Development Goals (MDGS). Küpçü (2005: 96 cited in Bäckstrand 2006) notes that "most partnerships have unbalanced representation and are led by Northern governments, international organizations and predominantly Washington-based NGOs" (p. 301). The unbalance such partnerships bear result from the fact that their terms are exploitative and vague in nature all tailored to serve the interests of the donors. Importantly, this imbalance found in the partnership between Western countries, their NGOs and African countries shows how such inducements can work on the favour of donors even when their terms are not clearly stated or promised kept. For example, Hulme (2009) notes that while the International Development Goals (IDGs) set targets for the developing world, the same do not set the targets for the rich countries. This means that rich countries are not duty bound for the failure of the IDGs or there is no legal force to force them to meet their obligations of live up to their words thanks to having no targets set for them. This is why aid has ended up producing "unbalanced process" (Nicolai, *et al.*, 2014) but not envisaged development. In the example adduced above, although Tanzania was trying to defend its way of conducting elections, we think African countries need to learn how to say no to aid that does not accommodate or serve their interests. They need to reject the conditionality on aid straightaway if they want such aid to help them meet their goals or force the IDGs and the MDGs or aid serve their interests but not those of the donors. I understand that donors as well, have their goals they want to achieve by extending aid to poor countries, have been in place for many decades. Again, if we ask, what has been achieved compared to what was expected, we find that donors have always got away with murder otherwise African countries which make a big chunk of developing world would have already developed. If indeed donors want to help Africa as they have always maintained, there must be equity and justice that are aimed at equally benefiting both sides. Instead of putting high premiums on aid, African countries need to manage their resources well so that they can end abusive and degrading aid.

Another ideal example is what transpired in Libya in since 2011. Western countries created pretexts of punishing their arch-rival Muamar Gaddafi who before had decided to mend the fences without knowing that doing so would engineer his demise. Gaddafi was toppled and later summarily killed in the same year. Although Gaddafi did not depend on aid, the West still forced him to embark on democratisation of his country which was not a bad idea if it were done in a good and right way. Looking at two cases in Libya, Uganda and Tanzania, I can argue that donor community wanted to use such conditions of democracy and other inducements to have sort of powers to control these countries something that is replicated almost in all Africa countries. If you consider Tanzania, for example, for the country that produces tanzanite, gold, and other precious minerals in tonnes, what is $698 million if it manages its resources accountably and reasonably? It takes a doofus to allow others to rob her or him while such a person keeps on complaining while evidencing the plundering of such minerals. Tanzania that was slammed with such a denial of already promised aid produces natural gas; it is the home of Lake Victoria, the largest national park in Africa, Serengeti and many more among resources that the country is endowed with. The *Guardian (Ibid.)* quoted Tanzanian president Magufuli as saying "we have to stand on our own ... Tanzania will persevere" after the MCC denied his country the monies. If this is not out of anger, many African leaders need to think this way so that they can counteract such manoeuvres responsibly and creatively in order to fully pull their countries out of wanton dependency and beggarliness. However, we must make one observation that Africa should not bank too much or solely depend on the commitment or the probity of single person (president). Instead, it needs to create and strengthen public institutions. This way, it is very easy for Africa to say no to donor countries; and thereby initiate the era of equally negotiating the way it must relate with them.

Ironically, when donor countries default on their promises the way some African default on their promises for democracy no punitive measures are taken against them simply because blessed is the hand that giveth than the one that taketh; one may argue. Another fact that helps donors to get away with murder is the fact that they do not deal with Africa solely individually. They act as a group that also use strong institutions such as IFIs to pass their agendas. So, too, recipients have no authority whatsoever to question their donors which emanates from colonial legacy. One would think that donor countries that preach and teach Africa democracy would so, too behave democratically so as to lead by examples. Africa needs to radically and systematically change this anomaly-cum-anathema that has always put it in the corner. More fundamentally, Africa, if indeed wants to become free and prosperous, needs to think out of aid-dependency box; and stop living on handouts while it is sitting on immense untapped resources. There is no way Africa can achieve any economic development by depending on subjective but not objective aid. For, aid now is draconically untoward for Africa.

Aid That Has Never Worked

There are some questions that we need to ask *vis-à-vis* aid that Africa has been receiving since independence. Has aid ever worked for Africa or added the burden to the future of Africa? If it did, why has Africa remained poor despite receiving billions of dollars? Is aid given as aid or something else? Who benefit from such aid between the donors and recipients? There are some reasons as to why aid has never, and it will never, if things are not turned around. First of all, donors are like gods who should not be faulted or questioned whenever they do things contrary to what they either preach or promise. Besides defaulting, and not living up to their words, donors apply various lulls, rules and ruses to dupe poor countries depending on what works well for the former but not the latter. Also, they apply double standards in delivering their aid as they use it to exploit those they extend it to. An ideal example to show how donor countries exploit poor countries can be drawn from the whole project known as the Heavily Indebted Poor Countries (HIPC) that the World Bank (WB) initiated in 1996 aimed at cancelling debts for the HIPCs of which many are in Africa. If you look at HIPC's *modus operandi*, you find that it was more a hoax if not a ruse to pull poor countries in more debts than a serious commitment to alleviate or uproot poverty in poor countries. How do you cancel debts by offering new ones with the same conditions that forced you to cancel the old ones? How do you of loans to finance debts and call these tools of means of making economy grow or pull a poor country out of poverty while you adding more causes of poverty? Fosu (1996) cited in Malik, Hayat and Hayat (2010) examines the relationship between economic growth and external debt for the sample of sub-Saharan African countries for the period 1970-1986. The study reveals that on average a high debt country faces about one percentage reduction in the GDP annually; also see Noman and Stiglitz (2015). Such findings show how aid has not worked for the interests of recipient countries but instead, it worked for the donors. Abuzeid (2009) maintains that the massive influx of massive amounts of aid to receiving countries has caused more harm than good. This needs to be drastically and practically changed shall Africa aspire to develop meaningfully. For how long will Africa depend on aid while it is sitting on immense reserves of precious resources of all kinds?

There is evidence to support the failure of aid to Africa. When donor countries found that aid did not work for the interests of Africa, for example, to maintain the *status quo*, they introduced debt cancellation which also did not assuage the problem. As we go, this move is likely to be more disastrous for Africa than aid itself. For example, Moyo (2009) articulates that debt cancellation by adding more debts–not to mention serving the debts–creates and perpetuates vicious debt circle for African and other poor countries. Such a situation has over and above been enhanced by corrupt and myopia regimes that have ruled Africa for a long time without either learning or turning things around for the better. To do away with this, the donor community decided to tie debt cancellation to good governance. Such a moral undertaking nevertheless did not relieve Africa the burden of dept. Moyo (*Ibid)* argues that aid did not work even where it was not stolen. Instead, it became unproductive due to the fact that one hand was cancelling the debts while the other was adding more of the same. Despite knowing such stark truth that loans that service debt cannot pull their countries out of poverty, African leaders up until now have kept on getting such aid with conditions provided that either they get their cuts or are able to stay in power. On their part, donors too still pump more money to already failed projects due to the fact that they are sure that recipient countries will one day pay in the future even if and when they know too well that it will not work (Easterly and Easterly 2006). When it comes to what to do, Berg (2000) paints a grim picture arguing that moneylenders and their recipients are hard to learn a lesson [s] from the past experience due to the fact that it is hard to kill failed ideas of the past which have always been the practices of both parts in this vicious-aid circle. Therefore, Africa needs to abandon the dependency on aid by turning into the plans of action that minimise its reliance on foreign aid shall it aim at turning things around in the foreseeable future (Taiwo 2011). As it is the title of their book, the *West's efforts to aid the rest have done so much ill and so little good.* This is obvious. No way would Africa turn things around while it was working on old failed ideals and practices.

To turn things around, all parts in aid pact need to use new ideas and practices to see to it that past mistakes are not repeated or ignored. You can see this on good governance that the West introduced in Africa. Did it have any roots in Africa? So, too, Africa was not prepared for this new undertaking. Muller (2011) defines good governance as a process or activity that allows individuals, the societies or organisations to make their own important decisions, whom to involve and how it should be done with defined policies based on their aspirations, desires, needs, plans and targets. However, the report of the *Commission on Global Governance 2* (1995 cited in Esty 2006) maintains that good governance means different things in different contexts however the concept basically revolves around decision making. Therefore, there is no one agreed principles either of governance or good governance (Kaufmann, Kraay and Mastruzzi 2011). For the purposes of this book, governance is understood as the autonomous ability for the members of community, society, group or whatever to have an upper hand on the business of their lives based on their accepted, plans, principles, rubrics, interests and goals among others.

After exploring governance and good governance, we need to ask ourselves simple questions: Are African countries allowed making their own important decisions for their intended economic and political interests based on their principle, rules, plans and whatnots? Are they allowed to choose who should be involved and who should not in the process? Do they have any inputs in many programmes they are forced to fulfil under the pretext of the international community? What happens is like giving someone a gift; and thereby the giver prescribes some proscriptions of how to use the gift. However, to the contrary, aid is not a gift. But if we look at the meaning of aid or help, it is supposed to be directed where the problem is as far as the recipient[s] is concerned. So, too, for the aid to become meaningful, the intention of the receiver must be accommodated. It is no secret that Western countries have always offered aid to the projects they are interested in as opposed to the recipients'. When it comes to decision making, Africa needs to be part and parcel of failure to which, it must boycott such aid. Democratic decision making is one of the requirements of the rule of law and democracy in general. To the contrary, when it comes to good governance, Africa receives a straightjacket without any input in the designing and making of the policies and projects aid has always been directed to. I think this is where the failure starts. Always, aid that African countries have received is determined by those who extend it to them. As I will indicate later, some donor countries force their recipients to hire their home companies to deal with the projects such aid fund. Such practices, apart from doubling the burden, are likely to direct the process which denies the recipient the power to decide what is important for her or him. Due to their desperations, despite knowing the dangers aid creates, African leaders receive the same just hoping that things would change in the future.

We cannot blame African rulers alone. It takes two to tango. Donors have their fair share of blames for investing in the lossmaking holes. What do they expect when they sink millions of dollars in such unthankful holes? The answer is obvious even to a bird. Zaire, then the Democratic Republic of Congo (DRC) under Mobutu's kleptocratic regime provides an ideal example of how debts have become a burden to many African countries. The situation becomes even worse due to the fact that such rulers, apart from squandering the said monies, spend them on feeding and keeping their private armies for the purpose of remaining in power unconstitutionally. They do not fear anything given that nobody can force them to act responsibly, especially if they safeguard and serve donors' interests. Furthermore, Uganda provides an ideal example. Currently, Uganda has two types of armies, the national and the private one manned by the son of the president. Museveni has been in power for over three decades. And chances are that he wants to pass the baton on to his son, Keinerugaba Muhoozi. Due to oft-shakeups in the ranks whereby old guards are falling now and then, many think that he does so all aimed at paving the way for his son who Izama and Wilkerson (2011) note that Colonel Muhoozi currently is the commander of the Special Forces Group which is the elite group forming a backbone of Ugandan military; and that controls most of its heavy weapons which include aircraft and artillery) plus its intelligence know-hows. "He has quietly become the regime's top securocrat, with responsibility for his father's safety as well as key installations such as the oil facilities" (p. 75) which arguably puts him ahead of others as far as succession in Uganda is concerned.

Museveni has been playing his cards covertly and overtly depending on what works well for him and his family, especially using Ugandan military; he has turned into a private one. He knows how the same military can turn tables on him shall it decide to say enough is enough. However, this is not possible now in Uganda. For the military that has brutalised Ugandans for over three decades know that without backing the president who welcomes it to the dining table it can lose its opportunity to enjoy the national cake, especially if the same president falls and a democratic government takes over. The two are always binding together due to this fear of losing their positions. To succeed in getting services from the army and other arms of the state, rulers allow political, administrative and military elites to manipulate and use state powers for their personal gains (Tagri and Mwenda 2013). The situation becomes worse once such abuses of power and corruption is normalised as it is currently in many African countries where military elites are untouchable simply because they can use their guns and influence to silence whoever stand in their way. Kohn (1997) maintains that there are possibilities for the executive induce and use corrupt army to overturn the constitution or coerce the legislature to swing it its way as it has always been in Uganda under Museveni who has never understood or used the separation of power. Again, still Museveni' government gets budgetary support from the donors. And, essentially, it is this support that has kept many corrupt regimes in power. Stop helping them so that their citizens would make them accountable.

Arguably, when corrupt and despotic regimes use the military to control the reins of power, chances for national institutions to become white elephants as it is now in Uganda are high. This is why even in the so-called developed democracies such as the US and France civilian control of the military has been a concern (Kohn, *Ibid:* 1) which Museveni does not want to happen in Uganda under his long-time undemocratic rule. For, he knows–as well as other African despots do–that if the legislature, which is made up of civilians controls the military, his days would be numbered. He, too, knows too well that when biased military intervene in any political setting it may tip the balance of power (Wood, Kathman and Gent 2012) either way, so as to make those clinging on it unsure of what can happen. If such a military turn tables, it may mean the demise of the *status quo*, especially in the countries that have been under despotic rule for a long time like it has been in Uganda under Museveni since 1986. We witnessed this in Burkina Faso recently not to mention Tunisia. For such despots, change is unwelcome due to the fact that it can sweep them out of power; and thereby exposes closets full of skeletons accumulated for a long time. And, this is obvious for the rulers who have been in power without exercising any rule of law or democracy. Such rulers are afraid of their armies despite depending on them. This is why they keep on change its top brass in order to create frictions and mistrust within the army. Africa needs to change this situation by forcing long time despots out of office so that democracy can take place in such countries. However, the democracy that we advocate here must have no strings attached to it as it has been.

Despite being able to control their armies by using civilian institutions thereby knowing how despots can use the army to lord it over the civilians, donor countries such as France, the US and others have never done anything to stop such an imposition in Africa. They know; if they stop despots who protect their interests they could create some possibilities for democratic and stable governments as we have seen in Tanzania to come and deny them the opportunities they enjoy under despots. Likewise, despots such as Museveni and many more know that donors do not like them; but they need their services the same way despots need theirs. Due to the nature of their demands and needs, the duo use each other to see to it that everybody get what one needs and wants from another even if and when doing so means sacrificing the whole citizens of countries despots mismanage as it has been in many high-handed countries in Africa and elsewhere. And this is why donors have never done anything to coax or force African despots to introduce true democracy let alone foiling their plans of staying in power even longer, for example, donors know that Museveni wants to pass a baton to his son or protégé all depending on who will safely safeguard his interests after vacating from power. This does not mean that donor countries do not know the dangers such a project can cause to the country and the region in general. They know everything save that shall any chaos breakout; they will still sell arms if not to pick up another stooge to safeguard their interests. Again, the devil that you know is better than the one you do not know.

Fight Corruption Tied on Aid

Moreover, there is another aspect of lossmaking in this corruption resulting from selfishness and self-services that many African presidents and their appointees enjoy. Ironically, in some countries, such power abuses are backed by constitutional provisions. Aged and sick government officials are always accompanied by their doctors, relatives not to mention who's who that go to see them in hospitals they are oft-admitted. Furthermore, apart from paying for their medical and lodging expenses, governments pay for their air tickets and those of those who accompany them which in most cases are in the first class not to mention being paid *per diem*s for the whole time they spend in hospital abroad where they go to seek better medical services after sabotaging the same in their countries.

I submit that the war on corruption should be a top-down approach for the high and the mighty and down-up for the grassroots. I think by this approach, Africa will be able to quickly and decisively thwart vice that is one of things that have kept Africa down. In some country corruption is untouched as if it has been legalised through the backdoor. Governments that cannot take on corruption are themselves inept and corrupt. So, too, such government cannot serve the people but instead those forming them serve themselves on the expenses of the pauperised majority. Lambsdorff (2003) argues that corruption is likely to lower the productivity of capital due to a variety of channels. For, it renders affected governments incapable or unwilling to achieve public welfare which has always been lacking in many African countries since they gained independence. To turn things around, Africa needs to create conducive environment for checks and balances and accountability that will force governments to deliver. For, if they do not, they will be kicked out. It is only through accountable and responsible leadership that Africa can move forward. The developed countries reached the apogee by only introducing such a type of leadership. There is no miracle about their development.

Generally, in Africa, as it has been for presidents, many ministers and who is who have been in power for decades intermittently. Many presidents like to work with some of their loyal and reliable consigliore, courtiers, praise singers, and bum lickers. Biya provides an ideal example. He came to power when the United States (US) was under Ronald Reagan. *Depuis lors*, the US has had five presidents including Reagan and Obama have served as presidents of the US; and almost all of them served two terms except for the two terms in Office. Soon Obama will wrap his term in office. This means the seventh president must be added to the list of US presidents that served while Biya is still in office. You can conclude that Biya will vacate the office of president in a casket for sure till death do him part with his beloved power. The same goes with other longest serving African presidents such as Denis Sassou-Nguesso (Congo), Idris Derby (Chad), Isayas Afwerki (Eritrea), Paul Kagame (Rwanda), Robert Mugabe (Zimbabwe), Jose Eduardo dos Santos (Angola), Theodoro Obiang (Equatorial Guinea), Yoweri Museveni, and Omar Bashir (Sudan). Due to the fact that such rulers have been in power for a long time, also, most of their ministers have been in government for long time if they did not fall out with their bosses. Such ministers are Emerson Munangagwa who is now the Vice President to Mugabe, and has been in the government since 1980; Philémon Yang Muna, Cameroon's current Prime Minister, who has been in government since 1975; and Raymond Zephyrin Mboulou, Minister of Interior of Congo Republic who has been around for a long time, among others.

Another recent example can be drawn from South Africa where President Jacob Zuma faced the music after it came to light that more money was spent on the upgrading of his private homestead in Nkandla, his home village in January 2013. When the Public Protector ruled that Zuma had to pay back the extra money, Zuma refused for over three years up till April 2016 when the Constitutional Court of South Africa ruled out that Zuma breached the constitution along with the parliament full packed with members from his party that illegally exonerated him using their majority in the house. Island (2011) argues that in May 2009, a security assessment of Zuma's Nkandla residence in KwaZulu-Natal was done by state security. State security personnel recommend improvements of around R27.9m. By June 2010, R77m from other programmes directed to the Nkandla security upgrades. Nowhere in Western countries president's private homestead can be upgraded while there are state houses. In South Africa, this money-sinkhole has been going on even before Nelson Mandela came to power. The *Guardian* (November 29, 2013) reports the 215m rand spent on Zuma's home is in stark contrast to state money spent on improving the security of previous presidents, FW de Klerk, South Africa's last white president, who left office in 1994, received 236,000 rand (£14,179) for upgrades to his house, while 32m rand (£1.9m) was spent on Nelson Mandela's home. Again, this is a drop in the ocean of grand corruption in South Africa as far as Zuma is concerned. For, the *Telegraph* (4 April, 2016) shone light on Zuma's opulence. It reports that "more woes are heaped onto South Africa's president Jacob Zuma with the mention in the leaked Panama Papers of a multi-million rand oil deal in the Democratic Republic of Congo involving his already controversial nephew, Khulubuse Zuma," who is said to be one of South African richest persons simply because he is the nephew to president Zuma. By stashing such millions abroad, Zuma and company denied many jobs to South Africans. On the same day, the *Daily Maverick* (4 April, 2016) reports that "in June 2015, a South African court found Zuma liable as chairman in the collapse of a gold mining company that led to more than 5,000 job losses."

Donor countries default their pledges due to the fact that they know that recipient countries have no moral authority to question them. They know how the rulers, not the leaders, of poor countries do the same to their citizens. Refer to how many poor countries pass budgets that they do not fulfil to the letter thanks to having much discretionary powers not to mention corruption they mainly partake in.

In a nutshell, if Africa puts a stop on the megalomaniac spending geared by rust for power and selfishness, and bad governance, chances of turning things for the better are high. It only requires Africa to take decisive steps, especially through learning from its bitter history of colonialism, neo-colonialism and exploitation in general as perpetrated either by foreign or local colonialists. The lessons gotten from such an experience will help Africa to boot its dictators out of offices so that competent and democratically-elected leader could come in and turn things around for the better. I will address one issue after another in detail in the following chapters to show how Africa can turn things around for the better future of its people based on taking on the current corrupt and despot regimes that have used armies to bulldoze, exploit and terrorise citizens in many countries. Importantly, Africa still has the wherewithal to do away with unnecessary dependency and dearth be they enhanced by aid or military muscles. For, Africa sits on immense resources the whole world needs to be able to develop economically. It only asks for the resolve for Africa to turn things around by managing its resources well.

Another important thing for Africa to do is avoid heavy dependence on aid be it internal or external. Although in this section I have alluded to aid and its effectiveness or ineffectiveness, I have not touched on internal aid that some dubious businesses, especially those managed by either investors or foreign businesspeople that many irresponsible African government receive. They influence the laws of the countries they invest in so as to favour them; and thereby sabotage the economies of these countries simply because they are able to dine and wine with corrupt rulers. Ironically, when it comes to investing in Western countries, all laws are made by the host countries to favour their interests but not as it is for African countries whereby investors want the laws to favour their thuggery shamelessly.

In Tanzania where I was born, it is known that Indian businesspeople, their companies, communities and whatnots are the ones that are famed for helping African communities, organisations even their home government by way of generous donations. In East and South African regions Indians control a large chunk of the economies of the countries in the regions. Lebanese and others do the same in West Africa. You wonder why one community if there is nothing fishy. Again, when you look at who is behind tax evasion, capital flight and mega corruption, you get the same people. This tells you how their generosity has an ugly face behind it. So, too, Gupta family in South Africa provides an ideal example. This family is alleged to have hijacked the office of the president simply because it does business with one of his sons. This is a story everybody South African has heard many times. Ironically, to show how donors, especially internal corrupt ones our offices, they cross the divide and corrupt even the opposition. Who would believe that the former chair of Democratic Alliance, the main opposition in South Africa, Helen Zille, would be bought by the same family the opposition was supposed to take on for littering the office of the president? *iol.co.za* (29 January, 2013) quoted Zille admitting that she and her colleague, Ian Davidson, duly went to the Guptas' home where they were dined and wined to end up receiving the cheque for R200 000 from the individual. You can see how some of the so-called internal donors fry fish with its oil. Lodge (n.d year) notes that the Gupta were instrumental sponsors in the launching of ANC's loyal daily *New Age* in 2011) something that shows how such bogus donors and criminals use whatever means to get close to the upper echelons of power in Africa in order to use them to do their dirty laundry as it is in the case in point. They failed to trap Mandela to end up trapping

Zuma. Again, how many leaders in Africa fall prey to such economic predators; and how much money has Africa lost in such shoddy investments or deals?

Additionally, the *City Press* (10 June, 2016) adds more evidence. It quotes former ANC MP, Vytjie Mentor saying that as early as 1994, the Gupta tried to bribe even Nelson Mandela to no avail. She says that the Guptas wanted to specifically meet [the then] President Mandela, [the then] deputy [president] Mbeki and [the then minister] Essop Pahad willing to donate R50 000 towards the ANC's election [campaign]. Interestingly, Mandela and Mbeki did not allow the Gupta to exploit their fame for their personal gains as it later happened when they succeeded in netting Jacob Zuma whose repute they badly tarnished.

After noticing how corrupt and irresponsible some African rulers are, some Indian groups and community raise funds for bribing them either by using a ruse of donations, gifts and the likes. I have decided to wind up this chapter by briefly introducing a new type of donor that many scholars tend to ignore so that Africa can clinically and suspiciously deal with all those who approach African governments "generously" while they have a lot of skeletons in their closets. Many have made a killing through such hogwash; and unfortunately, many African rulers have never underscored the shame of being used so as to abuse their powers their people entrusted them. In the Gupta's archaic and childish hoax, Mandela and Thabo Mbeki were smart enough so as to avoid falling in the trap which, however, caught Zuma whose presidency will always be remembered as a hijacked one. How many out there whose dirty linens have never put on the agora? If anything, this is another avenue Africa loses a lot of revenues that it needs to deal with and watch carefully. Africa needs to know whoever that approaches their leaders. For, many countries such as Kenya, South Africa and many more ended up in troubles simply because they allowed their leaders to be easily accessed and corrupted.

You can see how donors care about their interests in the DRC after the fall of Mobutu. Joseph Kabila has been in power since 2001 after taking over after the death of his father Laurent Desire Kabila. His power can be defined as the failed due to presiding over the regime that fell short on many aspects such as security, freedom of the speech, democratisation principles and other human rights (Dizolele 2010) economy and rule of law. Kabila Jr. has since been doing just the same as what Mobutu did in selling his country. O'er, as long as the supply of needed resources is not cut off, whoever ascends to power does not matter provided takes orders. This is why Kabila Jr. has never been forced to introduce true democracy in the DRC. What he does also do not matter as long he does not endanger the interests of his maters. This is the way Western countries have conspired in exploiting and ruining Africa. Theirs has always been the rip off of poor countries provided that there are guarantees that such countries will pay in the future. Africa needs to change this situation so as to see to it that competent and credible leaders are taking the reins of power. Africa cannot develop with self-serving rulers in the office of the president. Instead of serving and developing their countries, such corrupt rulers ruin their countries by suffocating important sectors such as agriculture, trade, and social services. For example, Reno (1997 cited in Wright 2008) points out that:

> Social service spending during Mobutu's regime in the former Zaire fell from 17.5% of government spending in 1972 to 2% in 1990, and agricultural spending (mostly subsidies) fell from over 40% of the budget to 11% in 1990. Meanwhile, during that time, the president's share of the budget increased from 30% to 95% (p. 974).

If anything, this is the trend almost in many African countries where the budget of the office of the president is unquestionable just like that of the ministry of defence. For Africa to turn things around for the better, it needs to alleviate this anomaly that allows despots and ex-colonial powers to keep on exploit it. I will address this when I tackle how money is burned in many African countries on keeping big governments and do-nothing governments. Africa needs to invest in its people and economies instead of investing in armies and state houses.

Another area where aid money is burned is on the whole practices of maintaining presidency either through elections or keeping armies. The two institutions currently know that they mutually depend on each other like yin yang. They perfect each other in ruining Africa. After the African Union (AU) delegitimised coups in Africa, the armies know too well that backing corrupt and despotic rulers provides an opportunity for them to have an upper hand in running the country, particularly where the army is unquestionable in its corrupt deals. This is why in many African countries the budgets of the ministry of defence and the office of the president are neither disclosed nor deliberated up. Instead, they are given a *carte blanche* which adds up to poverty in Africa. Despots too know that there is no way they can survive without the backing of the army. So, the two are mutually using each other even if sometimes they can be strange bedfellows. Again, their inexorable mutualism is more important than doing the opposite for the peril of both. Therefore, when it comes to keeping private armies, it is done on public monies as it is for shoddy elections. This being said, Africa is now caught between the devil and the deep blue sea so to speak. For, if you look at how democracy is manipulatively abused, misused and the way armies are fleecing their countries, you find no reprieve in the two. In Cameroon, Fombad (2004) observes that:

In 1997, as part of the preparations for elections of that year in which, magistrates, judges and other judicial personnel were to play a key role in various provincial, divisional, and sub-divisional vote-counting commissions, a presidential decree was signed awarding them 'hush money" in the form of hefty salary increases and exorbitant allowances (p. 367).

There is no doubt about the above quote that the elections in Cameroon in 1997 were not free and fair due to the inducements players were given. It was publicly rigged even before being conducted. Basically, what voters did was to go to polling stations to justify this theft done on the expenses of their hard-earned tax money or loans secured to be paid by the same victims in the future. Why increasing salary during electioneering season? Interestingly, you find that the money that was used to sabotage democracy in Cameroon had a big chunk of money from donors. If this money did not come from donors, where did it come from? So, too, this money misused this way seems to come from somewhere if at all it was not set aside in the budget. This means the budget that was tabled in parliament deliberated on and passed in this year in Cameroon was not divulged to the Members of Parliament (MPs). Demonstrably, if it were divulged–thanks to the fact that many parliamentarians are from the ruling party–they just passed it knowingly that such money would be misused to sustain presidency for Paul Biya, Cameroonian president, who is famous for spending much time abroad as he extravagantly spends taxpayers' money and overstaying in power. Or maybe, the budget that the parliament passed was different from the actual one. So, too, it must be noted that when long-time ruling parties control all arms of the state, they usurp and retain the powers to abuse whatever laws without being held accountable. When it comes to squandering poor taxpayers' money in Cameroon–just like in any African country–Biya is not alone. The Cameroon *Concord* (22 October,

2015) reveals that Cameroon is among African countries whose many ageing cabinet ministers, and senior state officials shuttle between Europe and Cameroon for treatment at the expense of poor taxpayers. Such economic and political parasites do not travel abroad alone. They are accompanied by a coterie of aides, bodyguards, doctors, nurses and relatives, among others, who travel in business classes and stay in expensive hotels abroad. Actually, this is a chronic tendency of African big men and women in power that have turned their countries into a private estate.

In such an unreasonable and unaccounted for spending frenzy, nobody in the upper echelons of power has moral authority to question such mismanagement and embezzlement of public funds. Ironically, the country that spends such money on individuals still depends on aid to run its government! Donors who extend aid to such a government know all this! Yet, they do not care given that their interests are safeguarded. Arguably, such donors are accomplices to such criminal governments.

Furthermore, when the state or government keeps such aged, do-nothing and sick officials thanks to cronyism, nepotism, nihilism and mistrusts, among others–apart from spending much money and time on paying, remunerating and covering their medical bills–it denies young people jobs not to mention the general population that go without reliable and stable social services such as education, health, security and conducive environment for production. Interestingly, such aged and sick officials do not work; and if they do, it is not with efficacy.

Additionally, you will find that such officials are appointed based on technical know who but not based on probity or merit. Nonetheless, they are favourably and highly remunerated for doing nothing but adding a burden to the poor citizens. For, their house rents, oil their cars use, chauffeurs, guards, and other emoluments, among many, are paid by the government. Theirs is to extravagantly spend as pleased. This is the area that Africa needs to be quickly and seriously addressed by making sure that government officials are appointed based on merit and probity but not connections and loyalty to the president or head of the government. To put a stop on such abuses of power, Africa needs to scrap off presidential powers and prerogatives so as to have mechanisms that can control all public officers based on checks and balances. Africa needs to be serious in addressing this long time internalised malady. For, what has been going is like the game in which a constipated dog chases its tail as the way of dispelling unwanted energy. In serious business, dog chasing its tail is not a good game to emulate.

Thanks to internalised and normalised extravagance and embezzlement of public funds, Africa now has blessed another culture of begging on top of aid dependence. Before and short after independence, poverty and all degrading anomalies in the society, were among the enemies post-colonial governments sought to fight in order to reclaim Africa's dignity. This was then. Soon after colonial hangover kicked in everything was thrown under the bus. The dreams of having a dignified and prosperous Africa went out the window. Thanks to such toxicity and putrefaction, it has reached at the point where African leaders make begging their priority. They feel no guilty for begging. Days in days out, many African leaders are on the way to the West for begging missions. Their governments depend heavily on aid. Such an anomaly has created another problem. Many African governments, apart from embezzling public funds, do not collect tax sufficiently. This has motivated many foreign investors to go to Africa to take advantage of this weakness while Africans are dying from manmade abject poverty and acute lack of social services the post-independence government promised to their people when they were fighting for freedom. This is why many African countries endowed with various resources are becoming poorer and poorer while those plundering them are becoming richer and richer. You do not get it to find a country with huge resources begging or depending on aid instead of its resources.

In a nutshell, we now know who pays and who spends and why such contradictory state that those benefiting from it have maintained for the detriment of Africa and the Africans. We know that the so-called aid is not aid but instead it is an aid to death. So, too, we know that what we believe to be democracy is not democracy. Instead, it is the pretext Africa's former colonial masters use to dupe and exploit Africa. Aid has become a vicious circle that Africa needs to take head on. There is no way Africa can go on with such a culture and venture into the future safely and soundly. It is legally and clinically insane for Africa to keep on believing and hoping that the razzmatazz of aid will pull it out of poverty. Africa needs to get out of aid rollercoaster by planning for itself so that it can depend on itself instead of depending on aid.

That said, it is fair to draw a conclusion that aid has never worked for Africa. Therefore, the way forward is through the deconstruction and the demystification of the whole concept of aid which, naturally, is one of the engines of corruption, dependency and underdevelopment in Africa.

Africa Needs Homemade Strategies for Its Development

Apart from introducing true African democracy, Africa needs to plan for itself. This needs abler and visionary leadership that Africa has always lacked. There is no way one can successfully plan for another's family while he or she actually does not know the desires and needs of the said family. There will be no time when a lion will plan for an antelope. Doing so is madness and counterproductive in itself. Western countries preach market liberalism while they apply protectionism for their markets. Mansfield and Busch (1995) maintain that protectionism contributes to depressions that magnify political instability and protectionism so as to leads to war. Conversely, Mansfield and Busch go on exploring the genesis of the liberalisation of trade as it was championed by the United States in 1945 after the great depression saying that:

> Republican protectionists opposed the treaty because they felt it went too far in the direction of free trade, while free-trade groups failed to support it because it did not go far enough. President Harry Truman, knowing that it faced almost certain defeat, never submitted the Havana Charter to Congress for ratification (p. 299).

Why didn't Truman, the then president of US submitted the charter if it were good?

For Africa to benefit from the world market, it needs to retain its prerogatives over either to liberalise or protect its market all based on its needs and desire. I argue that the market does neither need protection or liberalisation. Anybody with any items that he or she wants to sell or buy must be left alone so that he or she can decide when and how to do so. Naturally, whoever has something of value and he or she needs to sell it does so geared by his desires, needs and want. Therefore, liberalisation of the market is immaterial here. Why should someone who does not own anything be given the power to decide how the market should be conducted while the natural law for trade is clear? If I have my eggs and I want to eat, sell or hatch them, it is nobody's business to decide what I must do with them. However, it is a challenge currently for Africa when it comes to exercise its prerogatives on the market. For, currently, many African countries are ruled by corrupt and dictatorial rulers who have created and presided over the system that they do not believe in so as to cling to power for fear of allowing somebody else to preside over the same and go after them due to having many skeletons in the closet. This reminds the author of the incident of a corrupt and stupid food vendor who used to order her lunch while she was selling food. When this happened, customers who witnessed it abandoned her. For Africa to turn things around for the better it needs to have competent and responsible leadership that the general population can hold accountable shall things go wrong. Africa does not deserve or need demigods who can abuse, misuse and mismanage their countries as deem fit. This is where abler and competent opposition comes in as far as African dictatorial regimes are concerned. You can easily see how many African long-time rulers are adamant to exit power. Fear of their own past, the unknown and system are the only factors that keep them on the helms. Given that a human being is subject to expiring, how long will they go on deceiving themselves? Some rules such as that of, *inter alia*, Paul Kagame Robert Mugabe, Denis Sassou-Nguesso, Theodoro Obiang, Yoweri Museveni, Paul Kagame and Joseph Kabila can speak to this well. Many of those mentioned above have always tampered with the constitutions of their countries to cling to power.

Apart from planning for its economies and revisiting its traditional institutions, Africa needs to heavily and hugely invest in its people. Currently, Africa leads the world when it comes to unemployment. As of the year 2011, Africa swanked of having a whopping 20% of youth unemployment (Anyanwu 2014) which was comparably the highest percentage in the world at the time. All this can be attributed to poverty, sluggish economies and bad planning, toxic investments, corruption, and above all big and do-nothing governments as we will see later. To do away with this, Africa needs to create jobs by seeing to it that African economies are growing correspondingly with its population. There is no way Africa can create jobs without embarking on industrialisation whereby light and heavy factories must be established in order to generate jobs and add values to African products. Africa will not be the first to travel this road. Page (2012) asks a good question: Can African industrialise? Page goes on to answer the same question citing an example of China and India that turned things around for the better through industrialisation by changing their structures. Africa needs to change its structures and systems as well. For example, soon after gaining independence, many African countries set the goal of industrialising. However, they put this task in the hands of the governments which ended up losing this opportunity due to inexperience, corruption, nepotism, and above all, politicisation of almost everything. Minus South Africa which was under Apartheid then, no African country became an industrialised nation. Tanzania under its founder, Mwalimu Julius Nyerere created many factories almost for every of its needs. Again, due to the above mentions maladies and the politics of the cold war, it did not succeed. This being said, Africa needs to create a very conducive environment for private sector to create factories. As it is in many rich countries, the duty of the government should be making sure that such factories or businesses pay tax. As we will show later, one of the holes that down Africa's revenues is, *inter alia*, tax evasion done by investors and local businesspeople.

Traditional economies based on exporting raw materials have not worked in the favour of Africa. Instead, they have kept Africa at bay instead of propelling it to prosperity and instrumentality in international affairs. This needs to change dramatically to see to it that Africa is playing an important role in exporting processed goods after adding value to them. By doing so, Africa, thanks to its bigger market, will not only create jobs but it will also enjoy this leapfrog by playing a vital role in the international market; and thereby cut reliance on imported goods which create jobs for the countries from which Africa imports such goods. Industrialisation should go hand in hand with investing heavily and hugely in education in order to produce educated and skilled people who will manage and work in various economic sectors. Bloom, Canning and Chan (2006) argue that much emphasis should be put on producing well trained teachers whose expertise will enable primary and secondary schools to produce graduates who will seize the opportunities industries present for economic achievement. Again, if we ask if African youth are well educated and well prepared, we find that something needs to be done. Circumstantially, due to keeping big and do nothing armies and government, chances are that much money is spent on maintaining the governments so as to leave other sectors out and unfinanced. This is obvious in many African countries where military upkeep is given higher priority than other sectors such as social services. Mhango (2015) claims that in many African countries armies and police forces have ultramodern gadgets for quashing riots while at the same time schools and hospitals have merely nothing. I think this is because African countries due to being ruled by corrupt and predatory regimes invest heavily in military in order to illegally remain in power while ignoring other sectors. Mauro (1998 cited in Gupta, Dawoodi and Tiongson 2000) argues that research shows that corruption does have impact on government spending in which corrupt countries spend less on education and health while they spend heavily on maintaining armies which in many countries are more of private property of the ruling class. This is clear, especially in the countries that do not appreciate or like academics. Tanzania founder, Julius Nyerere used to say that uneducated society is easier to rule than an educated one due to the fact that illiteracy makes people become unaware of their fundamental rights. In Africa, this is the order of the day. Many poor people do not see government as their institution. Instead, they think the government, as an institution, owns them. Also, uneducated people just complain and fight among themselves to make ends meet instead of taking on their corrupt and venal regimes. This is why many corrupt and thievish African governments have survived the wrath of the people despite increasing crimes, hardships and poverty. On their side, many inept rulers know this too well so as to sabotage and suffocate social services in order to create confusion and hardships that end up producing unquestioningly sheepish and docile society that they can rule easily under their discretion as it has been in many African countries.

Additionally, when governments spend less on social services, they create high demand of social services not to mention the increase of poverty. This has very negative knock-on impacts on running the state. Public employees use their offices to make money instead of serving the people they are supposedly duty-bound to serve. This adds more hardships to the people due to the scarcity and the rampancy of corruption. Swahili sage has it that a hungry man has neither choice nor ethics. Whatever that comes his way, whether it is illegal or otherwise, is okay. Whenever a society or a country is pushed to such limits, chances of internalising corruption and criminality are high. This is what Hung (2008) refers to as "the normalised collective corruption" which makes it a very chronic cancer (Alford 2012) that helps corrupt elements to become richer and richer while the majority becomes poorer and poorer. In such a country or society, justice becomes a subject of business whereby any bidder can purchase it at the detriment and expenses of the majority; also see Aidt 2003; Cosgel *et al.*, (2011); and Rothstein (2011).

For Africa to effectively combat internalised or normalised corruption needs to amend its laws or enact new ones that will enable it to take on corruption in the high place of power which negatively affects the economies of many African countries. Many pieces of laws operating in Africa are colonial and corrupt in themselves. For example, in Tanzania, section 286 of the Penal Code stipulates that "any person who commits the felony of robbery is liable to imprisonment for twenty years" (CAP. 16, 87). To the contrary, Section 304 of the same stipulates that:

> Any person who by means of any fraudulent trick or device obtains from any other person anything capable of being stolen or induces any other person to deliver to any person anything capable of being stolen or to pay or deliver to any person any money or goods or any greater sum of money or greater quantity of goods than he would have paid or delivered but for such trick or device, is guilty of a misdemeanour, and is liable to imprisonment for three years.

You can see how the law treats crimes categorised as white-collar crimes more leniently than other blue-collar crimes. Since, colonial times, colonial governments did not want to impose heavy punishment on their officials. Therefore, they enacted the laws that lightly punished them compared to lumpenproletariat citizenry who would at any time rot in the prison It is unfortunate that even after Africa became independent; such laws were retained so as to serve the new black colonial masters in public offices. Mamdani (2005) observes that "colonialism was not just about the identity of governors, that they were white or European; it was even more so about the institutions they created to enable a minority to rule over a majority" (p. 16) which is exactly what went on soon after many African countries acquired their political independence. The government as a concept and an institution—which in, essence, is a colonial creature—remained the same. The state houses remained the same. The spirit and the *modus operandi* of administration remained the same. Since, then, almost everything has remained the same. There is no way Africa can forge ahead with such colonial carryovers entrenched in its all systems. To do away with such detrimental and self-defeating systemic colonialism, Africa needs to deconstruct and overhaul everything pertaining with power and administration in order to address the problems of its people. For example, one wonders why many courts of law in Africa still have all dregs colonials system introduced. Alike, even the parliaments are still swimming in the same mess. What, for example, is the logic for the court of law to mete out just three year imprisonment term to a thug who has robbed the public billions while at the same time the same court of law metes out twenty years and above imprisonment term on a thug who just robbed an individual. It does not make sense or deliver justice however the court says it delivers justice. Again, who makes such laws? It is parliament obviously. Are such laws fair and good for the continent suffering from all sorts of mega grafts? For, if you look at two crimes, the latter is arguably an offshoot of the former that falls under the white collar crime category. I think this is the same in many African countries where laws are enacted to protect the high and the mighty while to the contrary, it heavily punishes the poor or the less powerful. You can see this colonialism almost in every sphere of life from salaries, emoluments and other services to almost everything.

To make matters worse, the same Penal Code bestows powers on the president to pardon person found guilty of any offence ex nihilo except colonial legacy that has its roots in enabling colonial agents to easily lord it over their subjects during colonial times. Ever since, in the countries where presidents are above the law, the president retains discretionary prerogatives to exonerate anybody he or she deems fit without either offering any explanation or breaking any law. Isn't this president a colonial governor by deeds and implications? Many African presidents employ such leeway and loopholes to pardon their friends, relatives and partners whenever they are convicted of crimes. I have always been the crusade of abolishing the colonial tendency of putting presidents above the laws of their countries which is a colonial backbone that enabled colonialism to thrive in Africa for many years even after it was partly abolished.

For Africa to turn things around and move forward it needs to seriously combat corruption at all levels by amending and re-enacting its laws. Governments that do not deliver should be removed from power. And all pieces of law that motivate the *hoity toity* to rob the *hoi polloi* must be expunged. In their place, laws that impose heavy penalty on mega theft and corruption should be enacted.

Africa Must Invest in Technology

We are now in the twenty first century of scientific and technological advancement. Africa, just like any society, needs to embark on the journey to heavily investing in technology in order to boost its output not to mention adding value to its products. Despite this reality, many African countries are still abaft as far as technology is concerned. This being the situation, one of the areas Africa needs to invest in is science and technology, especially making sure that no section of the society left behind. All produces be formal, informal, farmers or mine workers need to have some knowhow of how to make use of technology in their activities. Again, how will Africa invest in technology? China, India and South Korea, among others, provide an ideal example. As we will later argue, Africa needs to firstly use its already produced scientists and technologists that are now scattered all over the world. As well Africa needs to coax and entice them to go back to Africa for its services which are their services too. Lall (2001 cited in Lall and Pietrobelli 2005) argues that world trade has shifted from resource-based to medium and high technology-based products whereby Africa is left behind with the exception of Mauritius which is an exception to the general rule *vis-à-vis* tapping into technology to produce added value products for exports. They maintain that during colonial era and thereafter, there was little attempt to develop science and technology in Africa which is a challenge that Africa needs to take up and turn the situation around.

I understand that currently Africa depends on agriculture more than anything. Agriculture apart from feeding Africa's population generates produces for export; and thereby enables Africa to get foreign currencies. Therefore, agriculture is the backbone of many African countries. However, if you look at what has been going on in Africa, you find that this backbone is either sick or broken. FAOSTAT (2011 cited in Rakotoarisoa, Iafrate, and Paschali 2011) discloses that in 2007 Africa's agricultural imports exceeded agricultural exports by about US$ 22 billion. This is not an attractive picture. Africa does not need to minimise importing food but to stopping it by exporting instead of importing. It shameful for a continent that boasts of having the most fertile soil and vast agricultural potential to import, instead of, exporting food. It is puzzling and risky for African economies (Hallam 2009; and Hallam 2011). David Hallam, the Director Trade and Markets Division of United Nations Food and Agriculture Organization (FAO), is in a good position to tell how dependency on imported food is starving Africa economically and socially.

Nonetheless, despite being a backbone of many countries, agriculture has remained rudimentary and underdeveloped in many Africa countries due to various reasons from changes in weather patterns, global warming, lack of incentives and subsidies and poor planning among others. This needs to change to see to it that Africa is heavily investing in agro technology, *inter alia*, in order to boost its economies by increasing its outputs. An old hoe is no longer a viable way of doing farming. It consumes a lot of energy and time to end up producing a little that in the near future will never be able to feed a booming population in Africa. Therefore, Africa needs to address this impending demand to see to it that it forges ahead independently. For example, Africa needs to provide subsidies

46

to its farmers just the same way the West does to its farmers. Špička, Boudný, and Janotová (2009) maintain that subsidies complement the risks farmers may face and reduce farmers' and farm income unpredictability. They go on arguing that farmers need to be insured in case anything happens to their farms or products. This is why farmers in the West have always thrived while their counterparts in Africa have always become poorer and poorer due to the lack of subsidies. I know many may argue that Africa does not have funds with which to subsidise its agricultural sector. There is a lot of money, mainly if we consider the millions and billions Africa loses annually to crimes such as tax evasion, mismanagement, capital flight, under and mispricing, invoice falsification, huge government, extravagance, embezzlement, corruption and above all low prices Africa receives from its raw materials. When it comes to argument that Africa has the wherewithal to subsidise its farmers, the above argument will recur now and then in many examples. Subsidies provide motivation for farmers to farm more and work hard apart from providing them with a backup shall anything go wrong *vis-à-vis* weather changes, calamities, market falling and the likes. So, investing in technology should go hand in hand with subsidising African farmers.

When it comes to investing in technology, Africa can start with using tractors to top up to the hand hoe and animals where they are in use in order to expand its agriculture production. This is not enough however.

Furthermore, investing in machinery is not enough. Therefore, Africa needs to conduct its own research in various areas in order to identify various types of diseases that attack its crops so as to discover its own chemicals or whatever remedies needed in this area. Depending on foreign pharmaceutical companies to supply it chemicals is one of the rip off that Africa has suffered from that it needs to seriously and urgently address. Masha (2011) argues that technology should be transferred to end users who in this case are in the rural areas where many African produces come from. For Africa to robustly change and turn things around for its development, it does not only need to invest in technology but also to see to it that this technology investment does not end up becoming an academic domain. There are simple technologies that farmers are able to use freely. For example, if solar panels are made available at reasonable prices, they are likely to bring about major changes in production in rural Africa. Currently, we have the cell phones that have proved to be a force to reckon with as far as development is concerned. I postulate that Africa should start with providing means for rural areas to access power especially solar panels. Apart from enhancing production, solar panels are good at conserving environment which is a bonus to increasing production.

With solar panels, rural farmers are able to access information either from the media, and other means of communication. With solar panels, it becomes even much easier to educate farmers, particularly those who do not know how to write and read. The governments can come with the night programmes whereby some volunteers would be sent to rural areas to teach literacy to farmers so that they easily access information. Once farmers acquire knowledge, they will use it in their farming. So, too, it is easy to expand the knowledge basically acquired in order to know many things such as the fertility of the land they farm. Giller *et al.,* (2011) argue that technology development must particularly aim at labour-saving methodologies in order to help farmers save time and energy. The farmer who uses machineries is likely to have more time to relax and learn about her or his field than the hoe farmer who apart from producing a little after spending much time and energy. When it comes to the investing and using technology, Juma (2015) goes some steps further proposing that African countries should not aim at mere technologies but cutting edge ones in order to compete with other countries not to mention increasing their outputs. Currently, many African countries are importing obsolete and old technology thinking they can turn things around. This is not the way to go into the bright future for Africa. It discourages to find that African countries have allowed themselves to become modern technological dumpsite. Orisakwe and Frazzoli (2010) pose a very important question as to why do African importers pay for electronic junk they can't sell. Even if importers are able to sell their junk products, they surely will negatively affect Africa's economies due to the fact that such products do not function at the tune of cutting edge technology does. Africa needs to heavily invest in cutting edge technologies in order to turn things around. Consider a person who buys an old-fashioned used car. He or she gets nothing except a headache due to the fact that the said car performs bellow required performance. So, too, such a car demands a lot of fixing and servicing not to mention how hazardous it is for environment and security. Importing old and obsolete technology is as bad as for the farmer to buy a sick ox hoping to double her or his outputs. Instead of doubling outputs, this farmer will triple problems so as to become bankrupt. For Africa to turn things around for the better, it needs to embark on technological revolution along green revolution. It only asks for determination and good planning to achieve this.

It is very true that to continue with importing obsolete technology will push Africa even far back in development. Practically speaking, investing in cutting edge technologies guarantees those doing so of returns. Juma (*Ibid.*) cites Brazil as an ideal example arguing that between 1985 and 2006, Brazil's total agricultural production grew 77% because of public investment in science and technology. This is a good and ideal precedent for Africa. Many will agree with me that Brazil was a poor country a few years ago. Currently, Brazil is among the 20 big economies of the world. Africa has only one country, South

Africa in this group known as G-20. Therefore, Africa needs to raise money to see to it that invests in agro science and agro technology. Again, how much Africa does needs to realise such a dream. Fan and Rosegrant (2016) argue that Sub-Saharan Africa needs to invest at least US$ 5.8 per year which is small compared to the amount Africa loses to capital flight, corruption, mispricing, tax evasion, invoice falsification, extravagance and the likes. Africa however started a long time to invest in agriculture save that this was not done with required seriousness. Maputo Declaration (Union, 2006; Fan *et al.,* 2008; and Fan, Omilola and Lambert 2009) required African countries to spend 10% of their national budget in agriculture (Badiane 2008: and Fan, Nestorova and; and Olaofinbiyi 2010: and Benin and Yu 2012, viii) which many African countries did not meet.

Solar panel provision must go hand in hand with electrification of the rural area, especially those situated near power sources that in many African countries have for a long time been excluded from benefiting from power originating from their areas that is exported to urban areas or mines. You find a community surrounding say a mine being favoured by the mining company by building a school or a hospital instead of paying tax to the government. There are no policies that enable communities in which minerals are found to benefit from their minerals. After providing solar panel, governments should add internet in order to enable farmers to learn how their counterparts produce in developed world. With solar panel or electricity, farmers will be able to use videos and online programs to educate themselves about farming and the way it can be done scientifically. For example, a chicken farmer who has solar or electricity will be able to double her or his outputs by using hatchers and other technological gadgets in farming. Msoffe *et al.,* (2002 cited in Masha 2011) claims that if local chicken farmers enhanced so as to get supplementation, their performance is likely to be enhanced. This can cover all ranges of production of various types of products. Therefore, investing in technology to boost Africa's agriculture and economies should target spatiotemporal needs of the continent.

My experience in rural Canada tells me that there is no miracle about boosting farming outputs. Farmers in Canada and other Western countries have access to science and technology such as GPS, many ultramodern types of machinery and other sophisticated techs. When farmers have access to electricity and internet, they are able to even know what is going with regards to markets at home and abroad. Such knowledge helps them to know when to sell and when to not to. Once farmers are provided with essentials and incentives, chances of turning things around are high. I am trying to imagine farmers in my home district who are famous for producing fruits of all kinds without having a stable market simply because there is no value added. It they can be provided with power and knowledge, I am sure my district can become leading in processing fruits ready for export which, apart from adding value, would add incomes for them and for the country as well. Paarlberg (2009) argues that "fruits and vegetables are now a more important part of the diet than historically" [Sic] (p. 41). Paarlberg goes on arguing that the growing appetite and numbers have led to the expansion of farming land and pasture that can be attributed to the Green Revolution and other technological advances. However, the said green revolution does not involve or include Africa. Otsuka and Kijima (2010) concur with Paarlberg saying that many scholars have doubted if Africa can learn from Green Revolution that was carried out in Asia in the 1960s and 1970s. They argue that Africa needs to know the policies that were used in realising green revolution. I may argue that Africa does not need to copy everything but instead it needs to have its own green revolution based on its own polices, interests, and environment. Furthermore, Otsuka and Kijima (2010) conclude that green revolution is not only good for improving food security but also in stimulating African economies also see Scoones and Thompson (2011); and Khan *et al.,* (2011).

Considering how currently people in rich countries are shying away from genetically manipulated products and other junk foods, for Africa that produces organic food which are exorbitantly expensive in rich countries chances of increasing its income resulting from exported processed fruits and other produces are high. If Africa could plan well to make sure that competitive and quality crops and products are produced, it can access the international market to see to it that it benefits from it the same Western countries benefit from its market. However, quality is not the only impetus Africa needs to access Western market. It needs to renegotiate the reformation of current international trade system that is not only exploitative to Africa but also preferential to the West. With education and knowledge African farmers will be able to access weather information not to mention the general knowledge on farming. This is only possible if and when Africa invests heavily in education, its people, science, and technology so as to become independent and stronger so as to have a say in international affairs be they economic or political ones.

Apart from agro science and technology, Africa needs science and technology almost in everything. Information Technology, medicine, mining, gas and oil exploration and many, many more areas need to be covered all depending on the interests and needs of Africa. Although Africa has recorded a surge in telephonic communication by using cell phones, it still lags behind in IT and the use of its product. Hellström and Tröften (2010) disclose that 40% East Africa's population own cell phones. This is not a small number if it is taught about how to effectively and nicely use the gadgets. Africa needs to build in the already achieved pace and speed to make sure that its population is doubling the use of technological gadgets such as cell phones. How is the situation currently? Porter*, et al.,* (2012) maintain that by 2006 Africa had an estimated 192.5 million mobile phone users, compared with just 25.3 million in 2001 (UN International Telecommunications Union), and it had increased further to 280 million by 2008; also see Masinge (2011); and Bornman (2012).

In a nutshell, Africa needs to embark on multifaceted undertakings. It must send people abroad to study various areas such as petroleum and gas that are now available in some African countries, minerals of all sorts and the likes. This should go hand in hand with importing cutting edge technologies topped up with education the general population to use the said technologies. The genesis of cellular phones can be used as a good example on how the general population can make use of technology to better their lives, their economies and compete with others.

Good Land Use and Reforms

No doubt; Africa has the most fertile land on earth surrounded by rivers, lakes and water catchments not to mention fertile valleys. This puts Africa on the advantageous position shall it invest in modern agriculture. The fertility such valleys are endowed with, if maximally and nicely used, can transform Africa from being a basket case to the breadbasket. Again, what is done to exploit such resources? What is it done to conserve such resources mainly currently when Africa is facing acute soil erosion (Reij, Scoones and Toulmin 2013) due to old faming, overpopulation, tree cutting and overgrazing in some areas? We propose technological revolution in which Africa must confront this phenomenon in order to be able to produce for its consumption and export. There is no way Africa can sustain itself without producing massively. It needs fertile land to do so. Therefore, one of the challenges Africa faces is to stop soil erosion. Ester Boserup (1965 cited in Reij, Scoones and Toulmin *Ibid*; and Beddington 2010) argues that population density has major effect of agriculture which as well has a lot to do with soil erosion that is now rampant in Sub-Saharan Africa. To do away with this, Africa needs to control its population growth. The situation become even worse when the said population is underutilised as it is the case for Africa currently where illiteracy, diseases and unemployment is higher than other continents. Africa needs an educated, health and sizeable population that it can sufficiently feed. It is an antithesis for Africa to suffer while it sits on humungous resources as mentioned above.

However, despite Africa having such resources are not used well. Jung-a *et al.*, (2008 cited in Cotula 2009) maintains that "Africa has most of the underutilised fertile land in the world" (p. 59) which is very true. For, in many countries such as Kenya, Namibia, South Africa and Zimbabwe big chunks of land are still in the hands of a select few either politicians, their friends or settlers who in many cases use it to secure loans from banks without necessarily using it. Many investors of this time are still streaming in Africa seeking land they can use to secure loans. And the land is still plenty. Fischer *et al.*, (2002 cited in Cotula *Ibid.*) disclosed that based on satellite imagery, provides the most comprehensive survey of global agricultural potential. It suggests that 80% of the world's reserve agricultural land is in Africa and South America. This being the case you wonder why some African countries still have landless indigenous people while its land is underutilised and used by foreign investors to mint and print money? Here comes corruption, myopia and bad land policies in Africa. Greedy, corrupt and selfish rulers and government officials take advantage of such evils to allocate big parcels of land to themselves or their friends. This brings us to another challenge that Africa is faced with. Africa needs to redistribute such lands so that landless people may have land that they can put on use for the development of Africa. The *New Zimbabwe* (16 March, 2012) quoted the late Andy Brown, former Zimbabwean music as when he was explaining why supported land reform in Zimbabwe as saying "I took a stand on the land reform programme. You cannot have 4,000 people owning 80 percent of the land that is arable, and then have 13 million people scrapping around that... That is a serious injustice." This being the real situation in many countries, African countries need to amend and enact laws to see to it that land is available for all its population. Therefore, many African countries need to seriously address this anomaly before the situation becomes worse than it currently is. For Cotula (*op.cit.*) concludes his book noting that "decisions taken today will have major repercussions for the livelihoods and food security of many, for decades to come" (p. 110). There is no way landless people can produce adequately. Cotula goes on arguing that Africa needs to invest in science and technology that is able to allow it to improve its food outputs instead of allowing foreign countries to invest in Africa for the purposes of producing food for their citizens while many Africans are starving. He cites examples of companies such as Jenat from Saudi Arabia in Ethiopia and Sudan, Lonrho in Angola and others from China and elsewhere that are now negotiating deals of grabbing land in Africa so as to produce for their home consumption. Although such investment is called investment, it is but a bad one. Africa needs to use its land the same way oil producing countries use their oil and land to prevent foreigners to grab it. By allowing their land to produce food for foreign countries, African countries are creating more poverty not to mention endangering their security (Bräutigam and Zhang 2013). Notably, when I suggest that Africa must reform its land policies, I incorporate all aspects such as legal and practical facets. For example, distributing land evenly without taking on soil degradation, population growth, and food production will never add up in the efforts to turn things around.

Also, Africa needs to force investors who sit on land without using it to return it the authorities or use failure to which it must be reclaimed. For, if it keeps on allowing such investors to go to Africa and take advantage of corrupt and inept system, it will find itself in a limbo due to the fact that such investors will need a lot of money to resell the land back to the same gullible governments that sold it to them. Many African countries are like to suffer. Vermeulen and Cotula (2010) cite an example in Madagascar where "'rights' holders can grant free consent to incoming commercial claims'" (p. 24). Thanks to such clauses, many foreign investors are like to take advantage of them so as to exchange property and property rights without paying any coin. Furthermore, Africa must reconsider its law governing land leasing. Vermeulen and Cotula (*Ibid.*) note that land deals for biofuel production is raising macro prospects in Africa which is a bonus for recipient countries as opposed to the detriment for the local poor who directly depend on the said land. How does a continent whose big chunk of the population goes on empty stomachs offer its land for the production of fuel instead of food and still be safe? If anything, this is the major question Africa needs to ask; and provide the right answer to. There is no logic in fuel production investment in Africa. Africa needs to invest heavily in food production for its consumption before contemplating about leasing its land to biofuel production. There is no way you can call such actions investment but land grab. Franco (2012) notes that "'land grab' has become a catch-all phrase to refer to the current explosion of (trans)national commercial land transactions mainly revolving around the production and export of food, animal feed, biofuels, timber and minerals" (p. 34); also see Wily 2011; Cotula 2011; and German, Schoneveld, and Mwangi (2011). How does Africa lease land to companies that want to produce animal feed while its people are dying of hunger and malnutrition? If anything, for Africa to turn things around, it must put a stop on such dangerous investments. There are some measures that can be taken to stop land grab in Africa. For example, Bruce (2014) notes that in 1961 after acquiring its independence, Tanzania commuted land freehold to state-owned land with 99 year leaseholds for whoever wants a title deed to operate on the land. This is revolutionary as far as land policies are concerned.

Chapter 2

What Africa Needs Socially?

If there is a feeling that Africans in their totality need to experience is nothing but the feeling of being guilty of Africa's pointless dependency on donors, aid and handouts it has for a long time received without thinking about how to reciprocate. Many scholars accuse the West of lacking morality due to their tendency of perpetually exploiting Africa. This is the right thing to do however, even those who allow such exploitation lacks some moral grounds if not qualities. I therefore argue that Africa too needs to be blamed when it comes to the lack of morality. Being at home with dependency on handouts and aid is immoral even if those doing so are in dire needs. So, the first thing I can propose for both is to invoke rules of morality. Those exploiting others should feel guilty the same way those exploited must feel, particularly when they make such a crime-cum-sin a natural thing.

Africa needs to embark on social change by allowing its population to think and behave the way they deem fit. As we have seen above, many African countries are under corrupt, undemocratic and despotic rules. It takes immorality of the high amplitude for one person to bulldoze and exploit others. This is why to me internal and external colonisation is equally evil regardless who is behind it be he black or white. This being said, there are some evils Africa needs to fight from within before accusing others of the same. For example, Africa is facing greed and selfishness of a high degree. While Africa accuses its colonisers of immoralities that dehumanised Africans as they were perpetuated under slavery and colonialism (Viriri and Mungwini 2010), it turns a blind eye on its own modern time slave masters and colonisers. For Africa to rightly and deservedly blame the West, it must turn things around by creating equity and justice among its own people. We know that all those who invented and created the above evils did so geared by greed which is now rampant in Africa. Some accuse these vices to colonialism. Garvey cited in M'Baye (2006) wonders how humans could be hunted like deer not to mention robbery, plundering and killings that ensued in this heinous encounter. This is true; however, after Africa became independent, one would argue that if such evils were geared by colonialism, they would have come to an end as a sign of independence. If you compare what transpired, and what still goes on, under many dictatorships in Africa, you see no difference[s]. Logically, the leader or ruler who causes poverty to her or his people while he extravagates the hard-earn taxes is immoral no matter what. The ruler or her or his consigliore or partner in crime who amass wealth while citizens are becoming poor because of her or his criminality is immoral. Consider countries with many landless populations ruled by land grabbers. Such a person is modern time coloniser Africa needs to fight and change. How many does Africa currently have? These are very important issues Africa needs to arrest first before pointing fingers at others.

My moral consciousness tells me that whoever exploited or exploits Africa is not only immoral but also causes others to question their consciousness *vis-à-vis* morality. I have never ceased to feel guilty whenever I see rich countries degrade Africa in the name of aid which I have discussed in detail above. I feel pity, particularly when I see the pictures of Africans in the mall, universities and bus stands. Those *immoral* Samaritans who pretend to solicit monies to help Africa display such degrading photos everywhere. They make a killing by the help of blind and greedy African rulers who allow them to take photos of our destitute people and advertise them the way they deem fit for their interests. It needs hypocrisy, ruthlessness and selfishness of its own type. Harper (2006) queries this tendency asking if those advertising destitute people aim at raising money or raise awareness of poverty rich countries have created. These are no different from the rulers of poor countries who go cap in hand begging pretending they are doing so for poor people while they are the ones who partly or totally made such people poor. Nathanson (2013) gives an example in which he maintains that Canadian perception of poor countries is often dominated by the images of hunger, hopelessness and calamities and whatnots. This perception might be right if such a country would like to know how they were created; and how they can be practically addressed and resolved. Brei and Böhm (2013) emphasise the importance of charity donation, especially if it is directed to those in need. This is very true, chiefly for Africans living in Canada. I remember how I feel when many people in my street ask me if I ran away from wars or poverty. I feel sometimes bad to be an African whenever I am out of Africa thanks to such wrong assumptions that some immoral charities have created in order to make money on the expenses of poor Africans. Provocative as it is, has a lesson in it that Africans need to collective feel guilty of their destitution the same way those who created must feel.

More on what is needed to be done; citizens too cannot escape the blameworthiness. When you look at what has been going in Africa, you find that the general population has always been aware save that it decided to keep quiet while it seeks an alternative[s] to make do with such abhorring situation. Instead of taking on the vices, many Africans decided to internalise them while a few decided to take on them as it happened in Burkina Faso in 2013 when the mass booted down their long-time dictator Blaise Compaore. Why Burkinabe were able to topple their brutal and corrupt regime while Sudanese or Ugandans were not able to do the same?

Arguably, when colonisers arrived in Africa, they found that many African societies were naturally collectivistic. To weaken them, they destroyed this virtue. In its place, they planted individualism which saw Africans start hating and sabotaging each other as they sold their secrets to the colonisers who used these secrets to destroy and thereby occupy Africa. Africans used to share success, burdens and belonged together, (Seriki, Hoegl, and Parboteeah 2010; and Roesen and Rozendaal 2010) something that was their source of strength and wellbeing as a people and a society. Therefore, before being colonised, just like any other society had its plans for its development. Sadly however, when colonialism was introduced to Africa such plans were felled. African economy, politics and other antics were badly destroyed after being forced into the monetised economy. Muponde (2015 cited in Magosvongwe 2017) observes that forcing Africa into the money economy forced Africans to start from point zero while their conquerors used it as an advantage ahead of them. Therefore, Africa is bound to and continues to borrow while the occupying forces take a lead so as assumes special significance in the light of the fact that profit-making is the basis and the decisive factor for the continued existence of the prevailing money economy that needs to be overhauled if not deconstructed in order to benefit Africa.

As argued, once Western cultures touted as modernity kicked in, slowly and systematically, Africans started to act individually. This is where the corruption we evidence today emanated so as to gnash the whole Africa society. Romanticising aside, up until now, Africa still has some elements of collectivism. Shall Africa reinvent itself so as to embark on transformation and revolution based on its collective institutions; it is likely to turn things around. For Africa to turn things around positively, it needs to revisit the institution of collectivism. By so doing, Africa will be reducing the negative effects resulting from individualism which essentially seems to fit in rich societies but not poor ones. I may argue that this is why Africans did not colonise any country due to their belief that all humans were interconnected and equal something the Western society learned later after accumulating capital made by the way of slavery and colonialism. As well, Africans did not discriminate against whites due to the fact that they thought all humans are equal. For, discriminating against one another starts with individual inner feelings of superiority. One must think about her or his race and everything as opposed to our humanity or similarity and the likes. Up until now, whites still resist the idea of racial equality despite the fact that the world is in the post-civil-rights era (Tarman and Sears 2005). However, we cannot paint all white with the same brush. Not all whites subscribe to this tendency individually. However, collectively, one may argue that whites still harbour the feeling of being superior to others. Mhango (2015) questions the rationale of referring to Barack Obama, US outgoing president as an Afro-American but not George Bush Anglo-American president. This is one of the evidence that systemic racism still goes on either consciously or otherwise. Again, if we look at Western society that is composed of white majority, it is this virtue that convinces them to keep on becoming rich on the expenses of poor countries they have always colonised either under old colonialism or neo-colonialism entrenched in the international systems today.

For Africa to socially turn things around for the better, it needs to re-institutionalise collectivism. If the West was able to institutionalise individualism, what is wrong for Africa to revisit its natural collectivism in order to counter the evils individualism has created and caused? We have touched on Chinese *guanxi* or personal relationship, networks prior which sponsor Chinese to secure jobs abroad. However criminally these networks may seem to their victims, for those who belong to them is a force to reckon with. This shows typically how collectivism can help its members as opposed to individualism.

We maintain that individualism created many evils such as egoism, selfishness, and above all, corruption that are now destroying Africa. For Africa to be able to pragmatically turn things around for the better it needs to seriously and fight corruption at all levels on top of invigorating its collectivistic institutions as its main social capital. Ironically, despite priding themselves of being and advocating individualism, "most developing economies tend to have a collectivistic orientation" (Ralston 2008: 33) which they ironically deny others when it comes to economic activities aimed at liberating them from colonially created poverty. This is why Western countries have always forced Africa to embrace their political democracy but not economic one. Due to this hypocritical double standard, in some following chapters, we are going to use two case studies to show how divide and rule gave birth to ethno conflicts and terrorism in order to link the international community in working hand in hand with Africa so that it can keep on warrying while those who divided it rob it easily in conjunction with homemade thieves in power. If this can be addressed decisively, chances of turning things around for the better future of Africa and that of the world at large are possible. These two facets of Africa's colonial legacies, *inter alia*, consume much money and time as far as Africa is concerned. The former is used by both local and foreign elites to rob Africa immensely and immeasurably. For apart from denying Africans the opportunity to plan and produce, conflicts burn and gulp a lot of money by the ways of purchasing weapons, fighting and above all destroying people's livelihood and wellbeing. When it comes to terrorism, the truth is the same. It denies the society peace, harmony and security. This is why I have decided to use the two facets as case studies in order to show where the dent is for Africa to deal with shall it aspire to turn things around and move forward.

Africa Needs To Have Peace but Not Conflicts

One of the components that any country needs to develop is production. So, too, production needs very conducive environment enhanced by the abundance of peace and harmony. For many years, Africa has faced all sorts of conflicts, especially ethno conflicts resulting from the division that colonial regimes created. Since the inception of Western administrational structures and systems, Africa has evidenced many violent conflicts resulting from power struggles pitched on the desire to control resources across the continent. Historically, soon after acquiring independence, many African countries found themselves facing *coup d'états* which however have been banned and many other types of squabbling among elites that were largely aimed at controlling the reins of power as the automatic means of controlling resources that Africa is richly endowed with. Arguably, African politics in the post-colonial era evidenced many underdevelopments resulting from the anti-developmental nature of power struggles in many countries, especially countries that were under military juntas or corrupt dictators who divided their people along ethnic and ideological lines in order to exploit and rule them easily. These regimes fought each other in order to control resources that ended up becoming a curse in lieu of a blessing (Frankel (2010); Van de Ploeg and Poelhekke 2010; Haber and Menaldo (2011); and Van de Ploeg (2011). In tackling the important issues regarding violence, power, politics and anti-development that have pervaded post-colonial Africa, this chapter explores, *inter alia*, divide-and-rule strategy that colonial masters employed viciously and perpetually to arrest African development; and the that post-colonial African leaders have adopted to heinously entrench and sustain themselves in power. Added to this, Rodney (1972) observes that the whole plot of crafting of colonial African politics and governing powers based on violence was and still is one of the major causes of Africa's underdevelopment by

Europe. The same project of serving West's colonial interests has been continued through neo-colonialism after the colonial masters exited Africa temporarily under the ploy of independence that is wanting since.

Since African countries got independence and thereafter, their politics have been dominated by European way of doing things thanks to aping almost everything colonial powers left behind after handing over independence. African governments, parliaments and other national institutions are but Europe's typical replicas. Africa currently have almost all political and institutional settings mainly based on European models as opposed to the ones African had for many centuries before the coming of European colonisers in the late eighteenth century when they "officially" put their stamp on African politics. To underscore how Africa fared before the introduction of colonialism emanating from the 1884 Berlin Conference mentioned above, one needs to ask a question: Were there any political and institutional structures and systems in Africa before? The answer is obvious and simple. There were a lot of them on the African soil, some of which were arguably even at par or above if not better than European ones. Dahomey provides an ideal example to show and prove how some African societies were ahead of European ones as Claessen (1987: 210 cited in Mhango 2016b) maintain that the Dahomean governmental system that was used in the ancient Kingdom of Dahomey in modern West Africa was large and complex in which several categories of officials and functionaries can be distinguished. Essentially, the art of administration is nothing new to Africa just like any society given that even some animals and insects run their groups through certain types and settings of administration. If animals and insects can achieve this, how and why could this be impossible for Africans? Nonetheless, what makes the current administrational structures and systems new is the fact that Africa adopted European structures and systems of administration as its colonial relics and carryovers if not hangovers. Doing so divorced African original structures and systems of administration almost in all aspects of life. Dahomey's example provides a window into how African societies ran their affairs and organised themselves before the coming of colonialists from Europe who destroyed these structures and systems by replacing them with theirs. As such, the question would be: what, more evidence do we need to prove such a claim about pre-colonial administrative structures and systems? There is much evidence subscribing to the fact that Africa was not as redundant and underdeveloped society as many bigots alleged and others still maintain up until now. Many European thinkers such as Darwin, Hegel and Darwin, among others, dubiously viewed Africa as an uncivilised continent; and therefore colonising it was not immoral or illegal. Such arguments were made purposely in order to justify colonialism which is a crime by all standards.

It defies logic for a person or people who portray themselves as civilised to openly argue that Africa was redundant and primitive as far as governing structures and systems are concerned. They were a lot of such structures and systems that saw Africa trade with other continents such as Asia and Far East before Europeans were even aware of the existence of Africa and other continents. What does "complex and distinguishable categories" that Claessen notes above mean if we face it? When it comes to how advanced and developed Africa was, this chapter does not want to touch on Egypt, one of the giants of civilisations of the world. So, too, it must be underscored that Dahomey was one of many African advanced empires from Zimbabwe, Maravi or Malawi, Luba Lunda, Buganda, Karagwe, Mali, Songhai, Ghana not to mention the Coastal Swahili City States. I, therefore, address myself to what brought Africa to a desperate situation that it is in today. I use only one facet of colonial lies and plots namely divide-and-rule, among others, as a strategy colonial masters used to explore the major concepts this chapter uses in tackling the problems resulting from divide and rule strategy. I will try as much as I can not to venture outside due to the fact that there are many ploys that European colonial monsters employed to deceive themselves and the world that Africa was devoid of anything to do with civilisation. However, for matters of clarity I may venture out a little bit, my focal point will be divide-and- rule as the harbinger of violence, power struggles, divisive politics and anti-development practices as evidence in Africa from the colonial era. I must categorically state from the outset that violence, power, politics, and anti-development are the sour fruits of colonialism and its machinations that have perpetually been maintained by those with colonial mentality and malice against Africa as means of subduing and exploiting Africa perpetually. I will base, as argued prior on divide-and-rule strategy based on ethno political dimensions of African societies, countries, and the continent at large.

Although most of ethnic and ethno political conflicts that Africa is currently encountering may be blamed on parties to conflict, mainly the victims due to the fact that they are killing each other, they have all hallmarks of colonial strategy famously known as divide and rule. European colonial monsters I like to use instead of masters given that they were nobody's masters except monsters who devoured our continent (Mhango 2015), introduced, and used this strategy aimed at easily weakening, sabotaging and exploiting their former colonies which indirectly went on becoming neo-colonies although they still refer to themselves as independent states today. However, in many cases, the divide-and-rule strategy which colonisers used to create and fuel negative ethnicity and ethno political conflicts in many places they colonised went unnoticed. And if it were noticed, those that perpetrated it have never been brought to book.

In this chapter, I seek to show; and thereby explore, how the divide-and-rule strategy created many ethnic and ethno conflicts that Africa is witnessing today. For example, through segregating, pitting Africans against each other, and favouring one ethnic group against another, European colonial monsters created identity conflicts in Africa which have haunted the victims even after colonisers physically left the continent. Mawere (2014) makes the same claim *vis-à-vis* how the victims of colonialism suffer identity crisis. Carter *et al.,* (2009) identify two major causes of ethno political conflicts; *inter alia*, namely 1) identity and 2) politics. Carter *et al.,* argue that "neither identity nor values are negotiable" (p. 302), chiefly when they have the baggage resulting from artificiality and negativity attached to them as it has always been the case in many African countries and societies. Undeniably, under divide and rule, colonial monsters [re]invented their victims. They based their rationale on pseudo physiological and historical features of the groups so as to create new and artificial, as well as antagonistic, entities and identities that ended up turning each against another as it was envisioned by the inventors and the perpetrators of this heinous systemic crime against humanity. This crime has hanged on up until now. Burundi's and Rwanda's ethnic conflicts that have been going on intermittently since the introduction of colonialism provide an ideal examples whereby German, Belgian and French colonial monsters used historical and physiological features such as the height, the length of feet and the nose of Tutsis to indicate that Tutsis were superior to Hutus which they did maliciously knowing how it was a sheer lie that went on up until 1994 culminating in the genocide that shocked the indifferent world. Thanks to this inferiority and superiority at an international level, when genocide was prepared and committed for a long time, the same international community did not act up until thousands of innocent people died. Why did the international community behave this way? The simple answer is because such carnage was committed in Africa. I have argued many times that if Rwandan genocide were committed in America, Asia or Europe, the international community would not let it go on as it occurred in Rwanda.

Interestingly, even when the international community was warned that genocide would take place in Rwanda its response was tantalisingly negative (Adelman and Suhrke 1996). Again, the then regime in Rwanda and the international community did not put any measures in place to avoid it despite all warnings. This proves how divide and rule has always been maintained by those who enacted it. One can argue that, at the moment genocide was committed in Rwanda; the international community was divided between West and Africa. Essentially, after divide and rule was introduced in Burundi and Rwanda, the two countries in which the two communities used to live harmoniously and cooperatively before, the natural identities of the two communities were completely altered so as to give rise to artificial and fake ones that the victims used to disparage, discriminate against, and exterminate each other wantonly. Unfortunately, given that the victims blindly and gullibly accepted their artificial new identities, they did not venture outside the box by trying to assuage or terminate such artificiality of their identities. For, even when German and Belgian colonial monsters lost these two colonies after losing in their wars in Europe, French colonial monsters who took over expanded on this poisonous system thereafter.

As if it was not enough, post-colonial governments in these two countries–that took over after French colonial monsters handed over the two colonies–internalised and reinforced this identity artificiality and toxicity that, as argued above, culminated to genocide in Rwanda in 1994. French colonial monsters used the same elements of hatred and deception to fuel divisions among Hutus and Tutsis in two countries even after acquiring independence. However, this does not mean that the two communities did not have conflict between themselves before. The thing is that their then conflicts did not amount to what happened after the colonial masters maliciously divided them. McNulty (2000: 105 cited in Mhango 2016) maintains that:

France, uniquely in Europe, prides itself on having a global humanitarian mission, and evidence that this "homeland of human rights" was implicated in genocide through its military support until 1994 for the extremist regime in Rwanda shocked many who had applauded the declared pro-democracy, pro-humanitarian stance of President Mitterrand since 1981 (p. 121).

Apart from Burundi and Rwanda, the West once did the same in the DRC after some neighbouring countries invaded and plundered it. Instead of forcing the invaders to get out of the DRC and face international laws, the West became the destination for many resources that were plundered from the DRC, including coltan especially after the fall of Mobutu, former Zaire's (then the DRC) dictator who ruined the country for over thirty years. Coltan has always featured high as one of the resources that rich countries get from the DRC. According to the *CBC* (10 December, 2010), coltan–a heat-resistant material that can hold a strong electrical charge–is used to make capacitors used in a wide variety of electronic devices, from cell phones, avionics to nuclear reactors. Coltan is also used in high-heat-resistant steel alloys for applications such as aircraft engines. Due to the role coltan plays in the economies of rich countries and its high demand, many beneficiaries turn a blind eye to the conflict or just offer lip services to it as it has been since the conflict started in the DRC. Nathan and Sarkar (2011) refer to cell phones as "bloody mobile phones"; and they want the international community to declare mobile phones illegal just like it did with the blood diamond which used to fuel wars in Liberia and Sierra Leone. Once, the diamond was illegalised and declared blood diamond, the conflicts in the two countries were resolved and thereby, the suffering these countries faced subsided or came to an end.

Due to the international divide and rule, the West has failed to illegalise coltan as means of putting a stop on the conflict in the DRC. The failure to declare coltan illegal and bloody and cell phones bloody cell phones shows how the whole world can be blamed on fuelling, and benefiting from the conflict in the DRC. I, therefore, advance that, in a sense, or by implication, whoever uses cell phones, he or she voluntarily or otherwise fuels and funds the war in the DRC.

Proxy and Homemade Colonialists as the Extension of Divide and Rule

Due to the fact that colonial monsters changed the shape and manners of colonising their former colonies by re-colonising through homemade-black colonialists or call them stooges who stodgily perfected the art of division, even after theatrically relinquished their colonies, colonial monsters kept on interfering in the business of these countries. They did so by taking sides or reinforcing and perpetrating divisive politics based on power struggles among various artificial communities they created in many African countries facing ethnic conflicts. Under such politics, there evolved divisions along *hoi polloi* and *hoity toity* not to new acquired state identities such as citizenships of various African countries which have become the obstacles of the reunification of Africa. Despite this being contrary to the law and the meaning of independence, these colonial monsters were not reprimanded or made to redress their victims under the international law that seems to favour them as opposed to their victims. Again, due to the archaic and anarchical and unfair nature of the international system, for example Belgium, German and France have never been sued for the genocide they authored and fuelled in Rwanda. Such international political

72

racism brings us to the fact that all types of powers be they political, social or economical in Africa, are still artificial and much more, are still controlled by the West which authored colonialism based on divide and rule as we will see later. Arguably, before this knife that–to borrow from Chinua Achebe–slit their cord of harmonious coexistence and interdependence so as to fall apart, two societies in the two countries used to live peacefully cooperating in happiness and griefs before the introduction of colonialism that left them perpetually divided and antagonised wantonly. When it comes to ethno political conflicts that colonials created and fostered, current elites in many African countries egoistically and blindly use and fuel them in order to easily and heinously reach their artificial and short-time evil goals. Wimmer *et al.,* (2009) refer to such tendency as a pretext of protecting or advocating the rights and the wellbeing of "their peoples," which provides incentives to align political loyalties along ethnic divides," as opposed to their natural harmonious and coexistent relationship based on interdependence and cooperation. Such toxic politics of "our people" versus "their peoples" does not dwell on issues as far as seeking and using socio-political and economic power are concerned. Ironically, they are used even in the so-called democratic politics.

Worse enough, most of, if not all political parties in countries facing toxic and negative ethnicity or ethno conflicts are formed along ethnic lines which many scholars such as Marx and Durkheim among others thought would disappear as societies modernised. Newman (1991) argues that from the early 1970s scholars argued that ethnic conflict would subside with the emergence of the so-called 'modern' societies. Again, they got it wrong given that most of such scholars were Europeans who wrongly thought that Africa would follow the same trend and trajectory that Europe went through to reach what they wrongly refer to as modernity. Due to such biased and misguided assumptions propounded by Western and pro-Western thinkers, there arises the need for African thinkers to revisit the root causes of ethnic conflicts and troubles and their links with colonialism instead of wasting time erroneously thinking that 'modernity' would solve Africa's problems that colonial monsters created. As has been established above in Newman (*Ibid.*), the so-called modernity has exacerbated the conflicts by allowing exploitative laws and systems to become what is referred to as international institutions. As long as colonial systems that regulate African economic, political and social power remain the same, the problems that ethnicity and conflict pose will grow even bigger. For, if we examine the polities and policies under which our elections are convened and governments formed, we find that they largely revolve along ethnicity almost in all countries facing antagonistic ethnicity, such as Burundi, Rwanda, Nigeria, Kenya and the Central Africa Republic (CAR), among others that provide an ideal example.

When it comes to deliberating upon how to form political parties that are used as representative vehicles in forming governments, instead of dwelling on human needs based on justice, equality and parity, groups dwell on personalities especially "who is ours" and "who is not ours" all based on their fake and superimposed ethnicity and loyalty to the group as it was the case in Rwanda during the genocide of 1994. In so doing, those who subscribe to such hallucinations and machinations, create artificial enemies due to their artificiality or blindness in seeing things during the conflict or stalemate. Given that the protagonists were maliciously and artificially invented and created, they, too, fall into, and follow the same diabolic and misleading pattern by creating obnoxious and artificial enemies among those naturally and practically deemed to be their brothers and sisters as it is in the case of the two Hutus and Tutsis communities in Rwanda above among others in Africa. Instead of looking at their tool box as far as their future is

74

concerned, the protagonists found themselves entrapped in the impasse so as to fail to underscore the fact that "the future lies in mustering all our energy to design imaginative but viable alternatives" (Max-Neef *et al.,* 1992: 197). Instead of creatively and cooperatively looking for strategies to overcome the impasse, the groups ferociously and blindly find themselves in, the parties to the conflict reinforce and internalise everything for their self-destruction based on their acceptance of artificial animosity and negativity based on artificial reasons. The politics of "our-turn-to-eat" (Burgess *et al.,* 2010) in Kenya provides an ideal example of how ethnicity can blind and hijack people even if such people are viewed as educated as it is the case in Kenya. Instead of doing justice, such politics revolves around ethnical favouritism, romanticism, vote rigging, and sometimes, results into persecution and violence. Merits become nothing at such a juncture. Arguably, co-ethnicity becomes a merit. The situation becomes even worse given that most of those running the show are the ones we presume to be elites or enlightened ones. Once such allegiance–based on tunnel and destructive view is maliciously, blindly and artificially created based on bastardised and misrepresented ethnicity–causes fear and stonewalling which complicates and exacerbates the conflict even more so that all parties to the conflict become completely blindly unaware of the human rights and human needs of others. To survive, such groups create shared memories glorifying their illusive golden past. Olick and Robbins (1998: 106 cited in Armstrong and Crage 2006) argue that "collective memories are "images of the past" that social groups select, reproduce, and commemorate through "particular sets of practices" (p. 725) that are obviously destructive to the protagonists and productive to their inventors however temporally they may be.

While toxic ethnicity resulted to genocide in Rwanda, in Kenya, it resulted to what came to famously be known as the 2007 Post-Election Violence (PEV), (Roberts 2009). Under such ethnical rationale based on the allegiance and alliance to ethnic groups, it becomes difficult to avoid the politics that author anti-development for the society. When such politics of fear and hatred kicks in, we experience what happened during the elections in Kenya in 2007-08 whereby over a thousand innocent people were killed simply because they were not the members of the community that killed them. Instead of thinking and behaving like Kenyans, people altered and chose the identities they thought would protect them and their interests however wrong and deceptive this was. Such colonial carryovers have affected even our much touted Western democracy which totally failed to address this problem as we have seen in Kenya among others. For, when it comes to the needs of the societies and people, the electorate or the constituency–in such ethno politics–does not address issues; but, instead, it revolves around what Cikara, Bruneau and Saxe (2011) refers to as "us" versus "them" binary which elites use to strengthen the in-group solidarity and in-fighting as well; all aimed at getting away, literally with the murder by taking the members for a ride. Under such ethno politics, elites preach fear and hatred in order to make those they deem to be "their people" to conceive and see the danger their farfetched 'enemies' pose. Africa needs to put an end to the politics of the tummy that depends on artificial ethno enmity resulting from ethnocentricity.

What happened in Rwanda before the 1994 genocide when media was used to preach hared speaks volumes. Essentially, when it comes to toxic and negative ethnicity, politics always produces the "politics of fear" (Wodak 2015; Martin 2013; Smith 2012; and Altheide 2006). In such pointlessly antagonistic politics, it is easy to see how divide and rule plays its role of reinventing and [re]creating ideologues that churn out the propagandas of the hate of the ethnic other. For, the victims of divide and rule do not see things the way they actually are; but, instead, they look at them based the lenses of fear and suspicion resulting from hatred caused by divisions ensued after the malicious creation of such artificial entities entangled in an artificial conflict whose effects may lead to endemic and chronic negative effects to the protagonists on both sides of the divide. For them treating others unfairly is a fair thing to do. You can see how blind such ethno politics are in Rwanda where the minority Twas, a minority society made of pigmies were not considered in the preparations of genocide. For Hutu extremists, Twas did not exist and if they did not matter or they were not Rwandans. When the killings between Hutus and Tutsis started, Twas, just like anybody else, had to flee their country simply because two powerful communities were at each other's throat. Swahili sage has it that war is always blind.

Africa Needs True Resolve to Resolve Conflicts

Principally, we need to carefully, rigorously, open-mindedly examine and explore divide and rule and the way various colonial monsters maliciously created and employed it in various African countries as a vehicle of reaching their heinous goals of colonising, exploiting and running colonies easily and cheaply. Arguably, in doing so we seek to adduce some examples from Africa, and if need be, Asia and Europe, to support the arguments made and solutions prescribed. Therefore, I have tried to be as carefully and honestly as possible in exploring the strategy of divide and rule from when it was invented–at colonial time–to the aftermath of colonialism in various places in Africa. By so doing, I seek to substantiate and show the legacy and the consequences of the strategy even at the modern times when Africa is pointlessly accused of not doing its homework timely and rightly to get rid itself of the consequences of such chicanery as it was maliciously enacted by colonial monsters. Ironically, when things become worse we tend to invite and entrust with the role[s] of resolving the conflict hoping that they can solve our problems and resolve the conflicts we face while they want to reinforce and advance them to their advantage which is our peril.

It makes more sense to survey, explore, criticise and, in the end, offer some recommendations of whatever nature and undertakings to be taken as means of addressing the conflicts all aimed at transforming or resolving them if not positively managing them. I therefore offer my recommendations based on the deconstructionist view which aims at unveiling all flaws and malice behind divide and rule the colonial monsters enacted and reinforced in the minds and psyches of their victims. Such recipes are offered as the means of avoiding or dealing with ethnic and ethno political conflicts in constructive and innovative ways all aimed at helping those entrapped in them out of them productively. The deconstruction of the strategy of divide and rule is a good measure aimed at stopping the repetition of the mistakes and flaws by maintaining superimposed divisions, fake identities and difference among victims among other things.

So, too, I sincerely and strongly propose reparations of the victims by their oppressors aimed at helping the former to deal with the effects of imperialism that followed after colonial masters left their former colonies. Importantly, I strongly urge parties to the conflict to seek what unite them; instead of clinging to what divide them. Here history provides a good prospect of resolving the conflict productively based on the opportunities the conflict offers. I firstly argue that members of such artificially created ethnicities must revisit their past, for example, for Burundi and Rwanda, they must cautiously and judiciously explore how they lived and fared before the introduction of colonialism. Mhango (2015) proposes the deconstruction of the strategy of divide and rule by urging its victims to turn it upside down to mean to unite and rule themselves where they were divided and ruled. This discourse, critical as is, calls such attempts to resolve such ethnic conflicts the reversed nature of the problem whereby the solution is obtained by reversing everything.

Second, instead of looking forward to getting the solution, the victims must look backward in order to move to the forward. The parties to conflict must revisit their past in order to salvage what used to unite them. This is logical; given that what transpired amidst them in the past is easy to trace compared to predicting the future that ignores the past of the victims. As argued above, in so doing, the parties to the conflict must seek all nuggets that used to unite them as they put aside or divorce anything and everything that fosters or fuels divisions and animosity among them although this is not a cookie-cutter methods.

Third, it is important for the victims to seek their own ways of delivering justices be they restorative, distributive even collective ones. Despite their shortfalls, Gacaca Courts in Rwanda (Brounéus (2008) provide an ideal example of how victims can deal with their own conflict conditionally that they do it in a transparent, constructive and goodwill all aimed at getting out of the impasse and move forward. Rwandan experience in seeking justice based on traditional justice is an exception the general rule whereby many African countries wait for the West spearheaded by the international community to resolve their conflicts. I would suggest that the AU must have the mechanism and plans to look into many African traditional mechanisms of conflict resolution instead of waiting for the West to come and muddle in its conflicts. I would argue other African countries facing identity and other sorts of conflicts to embark on their own journeys of using their own local mechanisms to resolve the conflicts instead of depending on foreigners who do not their ways of life well apart some being the cloners of the same conflicts as we have shown in divide and rule. There is no need for Africa to be dependent on everything. Rwandan cases shows how rich Africa can be if it revisits its past and ways of life. However, it is unfortunate that many ethnic conflicts in Africa are left to the same people who created and fuelled them to resolve them based on their own type of justice which does not fit and help the victims. The current ethno conflict in the CAR provides an ideal example. France that ridiculously created the division in the CAR (Giroux, Lanz, and Sguaitamatti 2009) is now messing even more by investing and banking on militaristic means instead of rebuilding relationship among the protagonists. In many cases, foreign intervention in conflicts in Africa seeks to synchronously help the victims while at the same time protecting the interests of those interfering as opposed to the interests of the victims. France will never resolve the conflict there shall doing so endangers its interests. What matters in such circumstances is nothing but the interests of the France but not those of the CAR. So, too, France is using this opportunity to avoid its liability in creating and fuelling the said conflict. I would argue other African countries to learn from Rwanda that openly implicated France for abetting the commission of genocide in Rwanda in 1994.

Others interfere in the conflict so as to seek leverage or show off internationally as any hegemonic state would like to do. For example, Clark (1998) maintains that "France has managed to preserve its rank as first regional security provider, although by default, mainly in crisis situations (including in the Ivory Coast, Mali, and the CAR)" (p. 5). Ironically, despite the farce of interfering in African issues to be all over the place as far as foreign interventions are concerned, many African countries still pin their hopes on them while they actually know that their intervention is geared by self-interests and self-promoting goals at the expenses of those of the victims. France would like to always interfering in Rwanda in order to seal its tracks as far as the commission of genocide is concerned. On their part, African thinkers and politicians need to underscore this travesty; and thereby make sure that they empower their own people instead of depending on foreigners to maintain their power. Such foreign interventions, given that involve the people who do not know the history of the victims or if they know they misrepresent it for their interests; and thereby alter the true history of the victims, do not help anything except reinforcing divide and rule strategy based on conditionality such interveners set for the victims the pretend to help. The Democratic Republic of Congo (DRC) provides another ideal example. When Burundi, Rwanda and Uganda supported Laurent Kabila to topple Zaire's (then the DRC) long-time dictator, Joseph Desire Mobutu, later Mobutu Seseseko, the Congolese thought that the trio was helping them to rid them of the parasite while they actually wanted to plunder their resources which attracted opportunists from within and without the society or country facing the conflict. All this was done to take advantage of shaky government after Mobutu fell. As argued above, Burundi, Rwanda, and Uganda helped Kabila; and later invaded the DRC in order to plunder the resources. This too shows the intra-division among African countries. Instead of pulling together to repel colonialists, the same Africans were used to ruin another African country. Griggs (1996: 76 cited in Mhango 2016) argues that "the geostrategic interests of Zairean Tutsis Rwanda Burundi and Uganda were laid bare in October 1996 with the creation of pro-Tutsi controlled 300km strip of eastern Zaire from Uvira to south Goma in North" (p. 128). At this juncture, local Congolese Tutsis invited their colleagues from neighbouring countries renowned for having exploding population and scarce land and resources. You can see how the card of ethnicity played a great role in this ethnic conflict that ended up becoming an international conflict so as to negatively affect the cohesion and security of the region at large.

Essentially, the above Tutsi strip is the result of the demarcation of the country the colonial monsters did in 1884 during the scramble for and partition of Africa whose internal effects is the division of some societies in more than one country. Here we can see how divided and rule does not only end up on people but also on their land. This is geo-division and partition. Again, if we consider the relationship between Tutsis and non-Tutsis in the region, chances are that ethnicity has a great role to play in this setting. Jackson (2006) argues that "Secret Council" (p. 109) of Tutsi elders obsessed with the "purity of their race" which in Conflict Resolution Field is called "the chosen ones mentality." Given that colonial monsters invented negative and toxic ethnicity to perpetuate exploitation based on superiority (for the exploiters) and inferiority (for exploited) complexes, one can see how toxic such ethnicity can be. Vlassenroot and Higgins (2005) argue that the DRC makes a good target for local opportunists due to the fact that "there are natural resources of much greater value, and much more 'lootable' character, than agricultural or pastoral land" (p. 119) which gears such power struggles. This is in itself provides motivation for warlords from both sides of the divide to put their hands on whatever brings money quickly. Precious stones such diamond, coltan, gold and others are easy to conceal and transport. Africa needs to address such artificiality, artificial identities and enmities that have always been good sources of conflicts. It is important to comprehend that whenever Africans fight against themselves, they are the ones who suffer but not the outsiders who fuel of fund their conflicts or supply weapons to them so that they can finish each other. By allowing themselves to be used by foreign powers that seek to perpetually exploit them, Africans are becoming their own enemy number one on top of the foreign ones.

Horowitz (1985 cited in Byrne and Irvin (2000) observes that ethnic conflict features high in the politics of divided societies. The conflict in the DRC also has all hallmarks of divide and rule whereby Tutsis famously known as Banyamulenge have been playing a destructively important role supported by

Rwanda and Uganda based on sharing ethnic ties. Also important is the fact that after Kabila toppled Mobutu easily, there was created an assumption-cum-precedent that anybody with a good backing and guns can topple the government; and thereof controls the reins of power which directly accords him/her control over resources. In such a greedy and cutthroat situation, whoever that has numbers from "his people" can come to power and serve himself/herself with his people as it happened to Kabila after taking over after his forced ousted former dictator Mobutu whose army did not have enough numbers to defeat Kabila's force. Africa needs to fight negative ethnicity tooth and nail in order to turn things around for the better. For, without taking on negative ethnicity and its offshoots, ethno conflicts, apart from losing a lot of money that would be channelled to other important areas, Africa will never have peace as the most conducive element of production, creativity and planning for its future. Peace is the pillar of everything under the sun.

Africa Must Address Ethno-conflicts and Resource Curse

Another area that Africa needs to address is the whole concept of resources tied onto what is known as resource curse. The West has always benefitted from the conflicts mainly in African countries endowed with resources such as Angola, the DRC, Liberia, and many more. Due to benefitting from the plundering of the Africa, the international community cares much about its interests even if doing so means trampling on the rights of victims in the Africa. As Montague (2002) argues, after the international community distance itself, the invaders, and the warlords seize the opportunity of militarizing even the economy of Africa by transforming it into a combat economy. Ballentine and Nitzschke (2005) argue that in the military or combat economy the security apparatus of the state (military, paramilitary groups, police) and rebel groups not to mention domestic and foreign play double roles as conflict entrepreneurs to fuel and support and fuel the conflict in order to benefit from it as it has always been since the conflict broke out in many parts of Africa. To do away with this, Africa needs to step in conflicts such as the one going on in the DRC, the CAR, Nigeria and Somalia instead of letting foreign powers to come and mess even more. The longer the conflicts take, the heavier the price the continents pays, especially if we consider that such delay enables big quantities of minerals and other resources to be illegally siphoned out of Africa not to mention the lives and property Africa loses thereof.

If we consider the fact that such institutions mentioned above, are run by men as it has been in a patriarchal society, gender exploitation becomes higher, largely when rape and sexual exploitation are committed with impunity and as weapons of war (Maedl 2012; Kirby 2012; Bourke 2014; and Burke 2014) due to the fact that the international community after distancing itself from the conflict, has always turned the blind eye. Again, toxic ethnicity gives birth to another calamity namely gender violence which becomes a resource curse based on the Gender Based Violence (GBV). Once such indifference becomes the order of the day, chances of the GBV to be committed are high as Defeis (2008) notes that the continuation of sexual abuse discredits the UN, especially when peacekeeping soldiers are involved in the same crime as it was evidenced in the East DRC recently. The international community needs to do justice equally and equitably; otherwise such indifference and complicity can be misconstrued as international racism against Africa where the society is gendered and divided along sex and gender lines.

Currently, the legacy and effects of divide and rule can be seen in politics in many affected countries in Africa whereby loyalty to whatever political party or group, as indicated above, is misleadingly based on artificial and all-time-destructive ethnicity. There is "us versus them" (Cikara, Botvinik and Fiske 2011) divide socially, politically and economically as Carter *et al.*, (2009) argue that access to ; and thereby access to other natural resources, notably oil and water is used as a tool of oppression based on ethnicity in many countries mentioned above, *inter alia.* In other words, you do not exist if you do not belong to "us"; and if you do, you are our enemy or a second class citizen in our country in which *you* are automatically an obstacle to *our* wellbeing and development which cannot be achieved without your underdevelopment. In such a situation and rationale, protagonists do not consciously become aware of; and whenever they become aware of, do not accommodate the needs and humanity of those they deemed to be their enemies. They think it is the right thing for them to eliminate or maltreat their artificial enemies. So, in such lethargic way of doing things, *you* deserve to be gotten rid of by all means so that *we* can thrive and survive.

When clear and sane mind views the conflict, those calling each other enemies are brothers and sisters who used to live like friends and partners in everything before the introduction of such obnoxious and poisonous system in place given that there is no recorded animosities among African communities that amounted to an apocalypse. Such animosity helps ethnic and parasitic ruling parties to divide the citizens even more. Facing such a catch-22, ethnic ruling parties or groups tend to turn their enemies into second class citizens or inferior ones as de Paor (1971; and Lijphart 1975 cited in Mhango 2016c: 131) offers the example of Northern Ireland where Catholics are referred to as the Blacks who happen to have white skin who are not Africans denoting how blackness is viewed as an anathema before *white* humans who are now pontificating human equality based on human rights. This shows how artificial categorisations under divide and rule work. So, too, it shows the ruthlessness of those who created, especially against black people. For, due to its toxicity, they tend to rebrand and reinvent even those thought to be theirs. Despite, getting out in order to clearly substantiating our claims, as prior promised, this categorisation shows how dynamic divide and rule can be. Lijphart wonders how Catholics can be perceived as blacks while they are not on tropic, and do not have non-white population. Lijphart goes on saying that the closest parallel Northern Ireland and other fragmented societies is South Africa during Apartheid under which blacks were the third or fourth class citizens however the situation has since changed in the two countries.

Furthermore, ethnic and ethno political conflicts resulting from divide and rule have since caused many mistrusts and misunderstandings among societies that used to live together harmoniously before the coming of colonialists when conflicts were solved without causing losses of great magnitude as it happened after colonialism in some countries. Identity-based conflicts occurred and were experienced in many different places divide and rule was introduced to. Divide and rule–as a strategy of domination– as indicated above, changed names according to where and who used it. Again, the effects and aims of division were and remained the same to all colonised people almost in all places. It, among others resulted in the creation of animosities, artificial identities and differences.

Moreover, the effects of divide and rule and power struggles in Africa can be observed by applying social cubism theory to show how deeper and wider divide and rule strategy affected the colonised people in various countries and communities as far as ethno political conflicts are concerned. To gauge how much deeper and wider divide and rule as a colonial strategy affected the countries or people to whom or to which it was introduced, social cubism theory that I introduced above applies well. Under social cubism, Byrne, *et al.,* (1996 in Matyok and Mendoza 2014) analyse six facets of the conflict namely demographics, economics, history, political factors, psycho-cultural factors and religion. Social cubism covers six facets of the society and shows how divide and rule use them to antagonises, divides and exploits the victims.

Social cubism theory argues that demographics were used almost in all cases whereby the minority was favoured while the majority was side-lined, exploited and belittled not to mention being shunned in the administration of the colony. This situation forced them to capitulate and live with anger and hatred against the favoured ones. When I claim that side-lined locals were excluded in the administration I do not mean that their counterparts did. I mean not to be involved at the grassroots level where chiefs that the colonial rules appointed would customary some aspects of administration. Colonial monster preferred those they favoured to those they demonised and victimised. Also, discriminating against the majority covered all areas such as provision of social services such as education and medication. In Rwanda, for example, Tutsis were favoured in the provision of education as it was for Kikuyu in Kenya.

Along demographics, social cubism addresses economics which was used whereby the minority was enhanced to exploit the majority through ethnic favouritism that colonial monsters extended to them through small favours which were aimed at being used as ruses to make them accomplices to the crime. Jobs in the colonial governments and other privileges went to the favoured groups something that caused hatred and vengeance as was witnessed in Burundi and Rwanda after the two countries got their independence whereby in Rwanda the majority started persecuting the minority while in Burundi the minority clung to power through *coup d'états*. In a sense, the victims became perpetrators and vice versa. Essentially, the system revolves around the hinge of ethnicity whereby any members of the same community are left out economically, and politically.

Another aspect social cubism explores is history. The history of the colonised people was used to pity one against another.

For instance, as argued above, in Rwanda, Tutsis were made to believe that they were intruders or invaders who settled in Rwanda 900 A.D compared to Hutus who appeared in Rwanda 2000 B.C (Byrne and Carter 2009: 130-131). Before the coming in of colonisers, Africans, for example the two communities in Rwanda generally lived peacefully despite having small-scale conflicts (which are normal in any human society) that did not tear them apart as it happened after the coming of colonialism with its divide and rule strategy that left Africa divided and weakened. Lonsdale (1981 cited in Zartman (1994) shows how solidified and peaceful Africans were before the introduction of divide and rule which lead to many ethnic and ethno political conflicts as argued above in that conflict among African societies did not record any conflict of great magnitude comparably.

In trying to weaken, and cheaply run colonies, colonisers, especially, Britain, invented the divide-and-rule strategy which affected the colonies negatively as Carter *et al.,* (2009) note that "…both communities have been deeply influenced by the strategy of "divide and rule", promoted during European colonialization" (p. 159). Carter *et al.,* refer to Hutus and Tutsis who during the 1994 genocide killed each other while they had lived harmoniously together for many generations before. Divide and rule was not only introduced to Rwanda. Other African countries suffered or are still suffering from the same vice save at different magnitudes. Therefore, the first thing divide and rule did was to create antagonism between or among groups based on what they perceived to be their slight and immaterial differences be they real or mindboggling. In so doing, colonisers created artificial identities and differences based on physical or biological guises or historical realities of the groups. Such artificial reinvention of the groups added new identities to the groups which took them to be real while they actually were not. For example, Tutsis in Rwanda were made to believe that they were superior to the Hutus based on the length and shape of their noses. Likewise, in the then Sudan, Northerners who are predominantly Muslims were made to believe that they were superior to the Southerners who are mainly Christians and traditionalists. So, too, the Southerners were deemed inferior based on slight pigments of their skin because Northerners are a bit brown. All these groups took this to be a true part of their identity thereafter. North Sudanese were duped to think they were Arabs while they actually are Africans. Arguably, they acquired a new and fake identity.

However, sometimes, there comes time when such duped people realise the trap they are in. for example, it is only recently after the 1994 genocide in Rwanda that both groups saw themselves differently so as to start to deconstruct such artificial identity German, Belgium and French colonisers created under divide and rule. Currently, in Rwanda, nobody is referred to his or her ethnicity. Instead, they are all referred to as Rwandans which is good and the first step of deconstructing toxic ethnicity. However, this approach may work temporarily if we consider what happened in the former Federation of Yugoslavia after the death of Marshal Josip Broz Tito, former president, who abolished ethnicity which surfaced soon after his death. Whether the de-ethnicisation will work or not in Rwanda, it is too early to tell. As for Sudan, the reward of caging in artificial identities culminated to the separation of the two in 2011.

Another important fact is that it takes a long time for groups to realise how artificial some of what they perceive to be their identity is not to mention the danger such fake identification has caused to them. Sometimes, such awakening happens after miseries strike as it is for the case of Rwandan genocide or the division of Sudan which became detrimental to both sides, especially if we underscore the fact that colonisers wanted people divide so that they can become weak; thus easier to control and exploit. Other African countries and communities facing the same but have never got to the abyss like Rwanda.

Such countries need to learn from what happened in Rwanda. Africa in general needs to re-educate its people to see to it that they know who they actually are. They also need to know that whatever creatures and identities those that cloned them imposed on them did not serve their interests; but instead, they served the interests of their tormentors.

Moreover, in applying divide and rule, European-colonial monsters played one community against another while favouring the minority as opposed to the majority. Such a strategy worked well where there were some differences or historical animosities such as in the case of what British colonial masters called 'warrior community e.g. Zulu in South Africa and Ndebele in Zimbabwe. The duo were favoured, thus; they had more rights than other communities that were excluded. Wolff (2006) refers to as a "second-class status" those whom coloniser excluded. To make exploitation easy to their advantage, colonisers favoured the minority against the majority due to the fact that they wanted to run their colonies at a low cost. By dividing their colonised people, colonisers were able to get some secrets on what brought cohesion among Africans; and they used these secrets to divide the groups so as to easily tame both groups. Through the antagonism created, groups were ready to betray one another as a strategy of winning colonial favours at the expenses of their enemy groups. This is how colonialism was easily introduced in many places in Africa and elsewhere.

Africa Must Restore Its True Identity

As I have indicated above that Africans gained new fake identities so as to fight even kill each other, colonialism is credited for creating this problem through its divide and rule strategy. However, colonial governments were not alone in this criminality. Religious groups that paved a way for colonialism also did the same through baptism or converting Africans into certain religions by changing their identities names and the way of thinking and doing things. Sometimes, divide and rule was called indirect rule whereby the favoured community was appointed and supported to vicariously rule the communities that were not favoured as it was in Rwanda. Scholz (2015) maintains that Germans used ideology about race as it was reinforced the biblical lineage. And this became the foundation of indirect rule in Burundi and Rwanda. In so doing, Germans started what is known as Tutsificatication which means favouring and supporting Tutsis to occupy all important positions in the country which culminated in the 1994 Rwandan genocide. Mamdani (2001: 271 cited in Bangerezako 2013) argues that "the Tutsification of state institutions" has gone on even after genocide under which he calls victor's justice. Interestingly, Rwandan genocide was only blamed on Hutus but not Germans who enacted this system, or Tutsis whom Germans used to rule and exploit the majority Hutus or Tutsi who used victor's justice to re-enact the same system that sent the country to its bloodbath. Essentially, animosities and hatred between Hutus and Tutsis were created to enable Germany, and those who followed after them to smoothly run the colony. Under divide and rule, colonial monsters created "artificial races with artificial identities" which segregated and hated one another for colonisers' easy preying. After Germany was defeated in the Second World War; Rwanda was handed over to Belgian colonial rule. Essentially, Belgium went on with the same policy of division the Germans had created. Hayman (2010) maintains that the Belgians went on with the same policy of favouring the minority Tutsis which triggered hatred for the majority Hutus who were left out in this equation. This policy created enmity that became the root cause of the 1994 genocide. Tutsis were made to believe that they were superior to Hutus and vice versa. Such dichotomy created mistrust, vengeance and fierce division among the people who used to live together peacefully before the arrival of colonisers.

Arguably, as noted above, racism was introduced based on things such as the length of the nose, history, wealth (Burundi and Rwanda), history, religion and region (Nigeria) among others. Carter, *et al.,* (2009) note that "regardless of which ethnic groups arrived first, both communities have been deeply influenced by the strategy of "divide and rule" promoted during European colonisation" (p. 159). Such artificial and mind-boggling reasons were applied almost in all countries that have faced ethno conflicts for example Kenya that has suffered hugely from tribalism. After the colonisers left, they made sure that they left division so that they could use it to weaken and keep on exploiting their former colonies. Ironically, even after colonisers left, Kenyan elites who took over from them, replicated the same strategy in order to remain in power and plunder the country. This is why the 2007 PEV is blamed on the two governments under Jomo Kenyatta, and Daniel arap Moi, the first and the second presidents respectively that perfected it after attaining independence, (TJRC Report 2013) and built on it to stay in power for a long time.

Furthermore, Nigeria provides another ideal example of divide countries that colonial masters left abaft. The division between North and South Nigeria which was before divided around religious lines was reinforced whereby colonisers so as to present a challenge even on the day the country attained its independence (Uzodike and Maiangwa 2012). To seal Africa's fate, such perpetual exploitation was enhanced by dividing African into small and weak states during the scramble for, and partition of Africa of 1884 which itself was a geographical and political divide and rule strategy towards the whole continent. Many ethnic groups found themselves divided between two or more countries as it was for some African ethnic groups such as Masai (between Kenya and Tanzania), Makonde (among Malawi, Mozambique and Tanzania), Nyasa (between Malawi and Tanzania) and many more (Mhango 2015). Post-colonial African leaders did not escape the curse of divide and rule. Some of them used it to entrench themselves in power unconstitutionally.

If anything, this is the tool European colonisers used during and after occupying and colonising Africa that they left after handing over the colonies to black colonialists who perpetuated the same based on religion, region, clans and whatnots. Thanks to divide and rule and the role it played, Africa has, since independence suffered greatly under black colonialists who used and still use the same strategy of divide and rule to remain in power. What African black colonialists did was to turn divide and rule upside down so as to become *rule and divide* in that the one dividing the people so as to rule them, comes to power first; then uses it to divide his people while the colonial powers, used their agents divided first then came to power thereafter. However, what is obvious is the fact that all strategies beget the same things namely weakness, enmity, disunity and inability to take on whoever applies them. And above all, divide and rule or rule and divide culminate into chaos, conflicts and underdevelopment.

So, too, geographical and political divide and rule affected the reunification of Africa which has become impossible to attain due to the fact that many post-colonial African leaders championed it and failed because African countries were, and still are divided even after the colonial monsters left over five decades ago. Divide and rule which later became rule and divide has always been a stumbling block against the total unification of Africa. Colonial puppets and cronies such as Mobutu Seseseko (the then Zaire currently the Democratic Republic of Congo (DRC) Dr. Hastings Kamuzu Banda (Malawi), Jomo Kenyatta (Kenya), Omar Bongo (Gabon), Denis Sassou Nguesso (Congo) and many more made sure that Africa remained divided so that they could safely remain in power provided that their colonial masters supported and protected their corrupt and predatory regimes that revolved around ethnicity, cronyism, nepotism, nihilism, regionalism and the likes (Mhango *Ibid.,*). Power to such puppets was the means and the end that could be safeguarded by dividing their people without being cognisant of the future of the whole continent; particularly when rich countries keep on exploit it even more.

Differently from the colonial monsters, when African rulers got in power then started dividing their people which helped them to remain in power for long periods. Zimbabwe's president Robert Mugabe is a recent example of rule and divide perpetrated by African rulers. He used divisive tactics to rule Zimbabwe for over three centuries. First, he divided Zimbabweans between freedom fighters and collaborators. Once this ploy started to lose its mojo, he furnished the ploy by dividing Zimbabweans along pro-revolution and anti-revolution. By exploiting ideological and colour divides, Mugabe took farms from white farmers and gave them to his cronies while leaving out all those he perceived to his political enemies out be they real or imaginary. However, land redistribution in Zimbabwe has its backers especially those who benefitted from it and those who think that Mugabe's move aimed at redressing Africans after suffering from landlessness for many decades. So it depends on how you look at it arguably. His ploy worked. For, soon after taking land from white, some Zimbabweans even some African leaders supported him after viewing him as a true Africanist who stood to assuage colonial evils. Voters in Zimbabwe, too, supported his policy so as to survive in the elections that followed the seizure of land from whites.

Chapter 3

World's Duty-Bound Responsibility to Africa

Although the world is now grappling with terrorism, Africa suffers more due to its poverty and having nothing to do with the phenomenon. In this part I shall try to show how terrorism in Africa originated outside; and the burden that it created must be internationally shared. The history of modern-time terrorism in Africa started in Lamb (1982) argues that if Africa remains sick, the whole world will suffer, especially their economies due to their dependency on Africa for supply of resources and materials not to mention their stability. You can see it today on how terrorists are starting to use Africa as a breeding ground for recruits. Howard and Hoffman (2012) argue that "failed state hold a number of attractions for terrorist organizations" (p. 80) by providing opportunities for acquiring territories it is currently is in Mali, Nigeria, and Somalia not to mention new recruits who are made to believe that if the groups win their miserable lives would be changed. Chaliand and Blin (2007) argue that "jihadist influence became evident most rapidly in the Horn of Africa" (p. 343) were there are poor countries such as Eritrea, Somalia and now South Sudan. For the international community to be safer from terror threats, it needs to help poor countries as the way of reducing or eradicating recruiting grounds. For, when it comes to such threats, it is not Africa alone that bears the brunt. According to *Al Jazeera* (August 1, 2015), Kenyan government's clampdown has forced over 3,000 youth to cross the border and thereby join al Shabaab in Somali; and 1,500 Kenyans have been shot dead by the police since 2009. This is a reported number. What of those who join and remain undetected and go unreported? If one country like Kenya that is relatively wealthy compared to others in the Horn of Africa can supply such a bigger number, how bigger is the number of the recruits that al Shabaab gets from such poor and failed countries?

Primarily, the major aim of any terrorist group is to make a political statement by attacking soft targets in order to coerce its opponents to comply or negotiate or act repressively Chaliand and Blin, 2007; and Martin, 2015). This is exactly what happened in East Africa which represents the whole Africa when in 1998 Al Qaeda, an international Islamic terrorist group, simultaneously attacked two United States (US) embassies in Dar es Salaam and Nairobi capitals of Tanzania and Kenya respectively claiming many lives. Al Qaeda terrorist attacks on the said embassies in East Africa captured many headlines internationally; and it created panic and precedent worldwide. The *New York Times* (August 8, 1998) reports that two massive bombs exploded minutes apart killing at least 80 people, eight of them Americans, in what U.S. officials said were coordinated terrorist attacks." The *New York Times* (ibid) quoted Otieno Osur, the Director of Police Operations (DPO) in Nairobi as saying, "This is a real national disaster and we highly suspect it is a terrorist attack." However, the number of those who were actually killed is controversial. The *CNN* (August 7, 1998) reports that almost simultaneously, bombs explode at U.S. embassies in Nairobi, Kenya and Dar es Salaam, Tanzania, killing 224 people. More than 5,000 were wounded. Twelve of those killed in Kenya were U.S. citizens. The number of casualties and fatalities is very high comparably.

The Kenyan *Daily Nation* (February 26, 2015) linked former Al Qaeda leader Osama bin Laden reporting that a New York jury on Thursday convicted Osama bin Laden aide, Saudi exile Khalid al-Fawwaz, over the 1998 Al-Qaeda bombings of US embassies in East Africa which killed 224 people. Although the number of who actually was killed is controversial, it is clear that many of the victims came from the region that had nothing to do with terrorism. Lyman and Morrison (2004) link Al-Qaeda with terrorist attacks on US embassies in East Africa noting that "on August 7, 1998, two massive bombs exploded outside of the U.S. embassies in Dar es Salaam, Tanzania, and Nairobi, Kenya, killing 224 people-including 12 Americans-and injuring 5,000. Responsibility was quickly traced to al Qaeda" (p. 75) which claimed to be behind these terrorist attacks that opened up the war on terror thereafter.

Federal Bureau of Investigation (FBI) (November 18,1998) noted that "the bombings were carried out by members and associates of Usama Bin Ladin's organisation, known by the Arabic word "al-Qaeda", literally, "the base")," [Sic]. After the East African bombing, Osama bin Laden became an international celebrity after the international media picked his name up. While bin Laden gained, Africa lost heavily. For, thereafter, the West shifted its attention to Afghanistan and Pakistan that were thought to be Laden's hideouts. As we will see, much money was poured to these two countries to fight terrorism. All economic and social effects the East Africa suffered from the attacks were not addressed up until now. In simple parlance, Africa was used by both terrorists and the West to launch wars against each other.

Importantly, it must be noted that traditionally and historically, Africans have never participated or, been associated with terrorism prior to 1998 bombings. No existing history or literature whatsoever, oral and written that traces terrorism in Africa before the attacks in case and point. Recorded incidents of terrorism that occurred in African soil were not typically terrorism but political which had a lot to do with liberation struggles in Algeria and South Africa. Even their branding as terrorist groups resulted from the cold war politics of the time. Even if such liberation movements–that were treated as terrorist groups–did not threaten African identity as the current ones do. Instead, they were fighting to safeguard and protect it by means of achieving independence which is opposite from the current

97

type of radical Islamic terrorism. The movements mentioned above that fought for independence had clear goals and missions that aimed at liberating the populations of their countries. Their activities were conducted under pure nationalism but not religion as it currently with radical Islamic terrorist groups. What tantalises now is the fact that terrorism has affected African identity and solidarity. Again, Kaufman (2006) maintains that "status, and security of the group depends on the status of group symbols, which is why people are willing to fight and die for them—and why they are willing to follow leaders who manipulate those symbols for selfish goals" (p. 205) which for Africa currently is an antithesis due to the fact that some Africans are now are willing to fight and die for artificial identities foreign ideologies pushed on them. Kaufman is dead right save that such people who are willing to fight and die for their identity must first of all be aware of who they truly are. This is where Africa needs to put its house in order. It is only for people who are truly conditioned and taught who they truly are that can qualify for Kaufman claim. Africa needs to truly condition and educate its people to truly know who they truly are. This can only be achieved through education at a national level. This is where the importance of the right kind of education for Africa lies. Africa, thanks to its assumption and conception of all human equality, did not teach its people to put themselves first just like others that used their dictate to dupe and manipulate Africans who ended up forgetting who they truly are so as to kill each other serving foreign ideologies and personalities. A society that does not truly know what it truly is sounds like the society of automata if not parodies. I do not intend or want to be judgmental. If you ask why Africa was not baptised and colonised, the answer lies on this tendency of being unaware of what its people truly are. Aughey & Morrow (1996; Bloomfield, 1996; Fitzduff, 1996 cited in Byrne 2001) argue that there is a need of embarking on "education for mutual understanding, and prejudice reduction" (p. 339).

Before the coming of colonial faiths and governments, Africans used to know who they are. However, things seem to have changed dramatically.

Africa Must Fight Sectarian Proxy Wars

It is no longer a taboo for Africans to kill one another after acquiring foreign identity based on their faiths. Since the attacks on the U.S embassies in East Africa, some Africans have already been pulled into this conflict to end up killing each other because of foreign beliefs and interests as opposed to African traditions. The *BBC* (September 30, 2015) discloses the clashes between Muslims and Christians that left over thirty people dead in the CAR. The *BBC* reports that "the capital of the Central African Republic is under a night-time curfew after days of intense fighting between Christian and Muslim groups." Remember, these are the people who lived together for many years without necessarily turning against each other. But once those who robbed them of their true identity came in and ordered them to kill their tribesmen, things changed abruptly.

Furthermore, East African countries are now experiencing a cold war in which they are involved in as proxy players. Kenyan president, Uhuru Kenyatta, was quoted in 2014 on YouTube as saying that the war in Somalia is a proxy one (see https://www.youtube.com/watch?v=hKkhma83zcg).
Additionally, you can call such war a Third World War resulting from religious ideology which is now fought in Somalia where Kenya is leading other African states to take on Al- Shabaab, another Al-Qaeda affiliate radical Islamic terrorist group operating in Somalia. Al-shabaab, just like the Islamic State in Iraq and Levant (ISIL), a fundamentalist Islamic terrorist group, has a clear agenda of declaring an Islamic caliphate in Somalia. To prove even more that the African identity is attacked, Al-

Shabaab has already pledged allegiance with ISIL instead of the African Union (AU).

Essentially, Africa is no longer out of reach for radical Islamic terrorist groups. Lyman and Morrison (2004) note that:

> South Africa has seen the emergence of a violent Islamist group. And in West and Central Africa, criminal networks launder cash from illicit trade in diamonds, joining forces with corrupt local leaders to form lawless bazaars that are increasingly exploited by al Qaeda to shelter its assets (p. 76).

Arguably, weak and corrupt governments, among others, can be singled out as the reasons that attract terrorist groups to operate in Africa. And given that many African governments are currently weak suffering from economic and social underdevelopment, chances for more operations for terrorist groups are very high. Abadie (2004) maintains that "poverty creates terrorism" (p. 1) due to the fact that many youths are disgruntled and unemployed and poor. However, De Mesquita 2008 disputes it arguing that terrorism is a policy if we critically examine how the number of people that terrorists kill is low compared to other types of political violence. Therefore, Africa needs to start the journey to its development based on its own mission and vision all gyrating around policies put in place. When it comes to why poverty causes terrorism, it is easy to underscore. For poor people it is easy to be duped to join terrorist groups due to the fact that they are promised solutions to their problems even if such promises end up to be ruses to get them. Therefore, whoever come to them promise heavens will get them easily even if such a promise a lie or ruse to entrap them as it has proved to be recently. Many terrorist groups cash into the prevalence of poverty either in their communities or countries to make victims believe that they can turn things around for them for the better where their countries or governments failed. What happened recently in Mali speaks volume. A less known radical Islamic terrorist group, Ansar Dine held over 170 hostages in the Radisson Blu Hotel in downtown Bamako. The *BBC* (November 20, 2015) quoted an anonymous witness saying that "the gunmen stormed it shooting and shouting "God is great!" in Arabic. The hotel says 138 people remain inside." Mali is now in the verge of collapsing due to oft-attacks that have cause insecurity and instability. Muslims in the North want to break away from Mali so as to form their new country Azawad. In this case one can concur with De Mesquita. Nonetheless, poverty helps terrorist groups to easily get recruits. Krueger 2007 cited in De Mesquita *Ibid.,)* maintains that "there is not much question that poverty has little to do with terrorism" (p. 2) provided that terrorism is more of a political issue than anything. Again, if we consider the policies we end up recoiling to the same conclusion that wherever politics and policies can cause insecurity for a group in which one of the characteristics is the lack of access to resources and some freedoms, poverty becomes a very good cause of terrorism. I think here terrorism becomes a perception issue depending on how one looks at it.

Of all East African countries, Kenya has borne the brunt as far as terrorist attacks are concerned. Due to proximity, and oft attacks on its territory, Kenya found itself being drawn into the conflict. In trying to safeguard its borders and economic interests, particular tourism, Kenya invaded Somalia in October 2011 to smoke out Al Shabaab which was formed after the disintegration of Somalia in 1991 (Kapteijns 2001; and Marchal 2007). Such a decision was reached at after Al Shabaab operatives oft-sneaked into Kenya kidnapped, abducted and killed some citizens and some tourists something that started to negatively impact on Kenya's economy. According to the *Guardian* (October 19, 2011), Kenya decided to invade Somalia after Al Shabaab operatives on 1st October, 2011 kidnapped, and later killed a French woman Marie Dedieu, 66, in Kiwayu, in the Coastal Province.

However, Kenya's decision has one major lesson in that Kenya went to Somalia hoping to finish the war quickly. For, as it was for the U.S in Iraq, the war on terror in Somalia seems to drag on so as to cost Kenya heavily. The *Guardian* went on reporting that "the initial justification for the operation–Kenya's first significant cross-border military campaign since independence–was that the army was hunting down the kidnappers" (page not provided). Thereafter, Kenya found itself fighting two wars at home and in Somalia. For, some Kenyans suspected to be terrorists are now targeted by their own government in its dragnets. Some Kenyans of Somali origin are apprehended, and later, summarily killed. The people who used to be united as one Kenyans with only one identity are now divided into Kenyans of Somali origin and other Kenyans, Muslims and non-Muslims and infidels. Kenya is now trapped in Somalia making it harder for it to make a choice of either to stay or leave. Either way it goes, Kenya is paying dearly in Somalia and at home. Ironically, the West that cloned former Somalia despot, Mohamed Siad Barre who destroyed the country has never came in to help Kenya which is now trapped in Somalia making it harder for it to make a choice of either to stay or leave. At home, Kenyans society is now divided along ethnic lines whereby those with Somali origin who are mainly Muslims are regarded to be terrorists or supporters if not sympathisers active and silent simply because they share the same pedigree or they are Muslims.

According to *Al Jazeera* Television documentary (August 1, 2015), People and Power: Killing in Kenya, the government is accused of introducing shoot-to-kill policy whenever its agents come across those it deems to be terrorists. *Al Jazeera* interviewed Mombasa Police County Commissioner, Nelson Marwa who was quoted as saying "those are the people that…

those are not the kind of people who you catch with a 'smoking gun'. You just finish him on the spot. You are taking them to court? To do what? He has killed six people. Let me be clear here. We must be fair here. When we see him, we will kill him instantly on the spot," [Sic]. This shows how this proxy war resulting from religious ideology is affecting Africans' brotherhood and cooperation altogether. For Africans who used to share the same identity, such remarks were not heard of before the rising of terrorism in Africa. In other words, when Kenyan authorities are killing their people suspected to be terrorists they do so assuming that they are either killing terrorists or Muslims which is bad and dangerous for African identity. It is sad that this has become an assumption of both sides namely the authorities and the victims as headline in the *Globe and Mail* (July 2, 2015) reports that "anti-terror tactics targeting Muslim leaders are provoking tensions in Kenya." Once the same people start "othering" each other between "us" and 'them" chances are that they will treat each other more of enemies than human beings with common needs and rights. Such othering, apart from erasing their original identity, creates new identities such as Muslims, terrorists, infidels and many more depending on the context of the conflict.

Furthermore, *Al Jazeera (Ibid.)* interviewed Kenya's Information Minister, Fred Matiangi who denied the allegations that the government has the policy of shoot to kill saying that the government does not maintain hit squads because they are maintained by criminal regime.

Also, *Al Jazeera (op.cit.)* interviewed, Paul Wanjama Central Nairobi Chief after two youth were shot and killed on spot. Wanjama said that police arrived on the crime scene and managed "to gun down two," Wanjama said that the victims were criminals, however, a salon worker who witnessed the killing tells a different story alleging that even after the youth were gunned down, the police officers came and shot their dead bodies to make sure they are dead; and planted near the dead bodies. This shows how this two-front war is becoming problematic.

The war on terror in Kenya reached a turning point after Al Shabaab separately attacked Westgate Mall and Garissa University which forced the government to start randomly apprehending and killing some people living on her border with Somali suspected to be terrorists. Evidence has surfaced unearthing shallow-mass graves connected to the way authorities in Kenya deal with suspects. According to the Kenyan Human Rights Commission (KHRC), in Garissa area, 50 people were reported missing in a three-month period prior the documentary was aired. According to the Al Jazeera anchor, Kenyan government's clampdown has forced over 3,000 youth to cross the border and thereby join Al Shabaab in Somali; and 1,500 Kenyans have been shot dead by the police since 2009. *Al Jazeera* cites the reports by the panel of leading pathologists saying that Kenyans are more five times more likely to be shot by the police than the criminals. In the capital Nairobi 127 people were killed by police in 2014 according to *Al Jazeera*. This translates into one fatality every three days. Furthermore, according to Al Jazeera, Kenyan army is implicated in the torture and disappearance. Such revelations have their negative impacts on the country. Kenya depends on tourism. Due to insecurity, tourism is no longer flowing as it used to be before going into Somalia.

On the one hand, considering three elements of terrorism namely making a political statement, using violence aimed at creating terror and attacking soft target, what the Kenyan government has been doing arguably amounts to terrorism too. This is known as state terrorism that causes bigger harm than that terrorist groups cause. On the other hand, the difference is that this type of terrorism is committed by the state against its people. Again, can Kenya stand by and watch as its innocent citizenry are killed? Such a situation makes it harder to solely blame or exonerate Kenya altogether. So, too, looking at the number of victims, the government has already killed many more people than the terrorists. The *Guardian* (30 April, 2015) discloses that Kenya lost 148 people during the assault on Garissa University College in North-East Kenya on 2 April, 2014. And according to the *Daily Nation* (September 21, 2014), 67 people were killed when Al Shabaab attacked Westgate Mall in Nairobi. These are two major attacks in which many people were killed. However, there have been other incidents, especially kidnappings and attempts to kill or kidnap. Again, looking at the reported figures, it is obvious that the state has killed many more people than al Shabaab. This is in line with Martin (2005) who argues that state terrorism kills many more people than terrorist groups. Although Al Shabaab is a threat in the Horn of Africa, the international community needs to know that currently, the ISIL is attracting jihadists from all over the world. So, too, if al Shabaab and Boko Haram succeed, chances of other likeminded groups to be created are high anytime, especially in Mali where some groups have already carried out terrorist acts. Libya is now pregnant with the ISIL and other Middle East terrorist organisations.

The situation is surreal so as to need the international community to help Africa in fighting terrorism. The *Daily Nation* (October 10, 2015) reports that the 14-year-old unknown to his family and teachers, the boy was recruited by Al-Shabaab agents operating in one of Nairobi's most expensive suburbs where he was offered radical religious teachings and training on how to use guns. As if this was not enough, the government started the crackdown that left Kenyan society polarised along religious lines. The *Daily Nation* (September 24, 2014) quoted the Kenyan Director of Criminal Investigations (DCI) as saying Kenyan authorities had already ordered a madrasa in Machakos, one of Kenya's towns, to be closed, and we are monitoring others around the country. By targeting Islamic schools in the entire country, the government is hardening Muslims to the extent that some of them end up sympathising with Al Shabaab which has already tricked it by killing non-Muslims and sparing Muslims in some attacks; also see Aghedo and Osumah (2015).

Essentially, many young people who join terror groups are the ones that are either unemployed or those disgruntled after their governments failed to realise their dreams of living good lives. Apart from that, Africa, as of recently, recorded a high number of immigrants seeking green pastures in Europe. As usual, countries in the Horn of Africa such as Eritrea and Somalia featured high as far as these numbers are concerned. The *BBC* (15 September, 2014) discloses that "migrants crossing in the central Mediterranean–from Libya and Tunisia–have up until recently come mostly from Eritrea and Somalia, although increasing numbers of Syrians fleeing the country's civil war are also making the journey." Therefore, when we say that the international community is duty bound to support Africa in its efforts to move forward, we are not speculating or just crying foul.

Practically, evidence shows that the West has paid much attention to Asia and Middle East while turning a blind eye to Africa. Basically, terror attacks started in Africa in Tanzania and Kenya in 1998 when two embassies in Dar es Salaam and Nairobi respectively were simultaneously attacked. Despite this, the West has been burning and pumping billions and trillions of dollars to Asia and the Middle East while nothing goes to Africa to combat terrorism. Cohen and Chollet (2007) note that "during the past five years, the United States has given Pakistan more than $10 billion in assistance, channelled primarily through the Pakistani military" (p. 9) not to mention the fact that up to March 2009, the US had already authorised the expenditure of $ 1.08 trillion including $ 709 billion for Iraq; and $ 300 Billion for Afghanistan (Belasco, 2009) which is a wastage of money and resources that would have been used to bring about some change had this money been spent on peacebuilding in the affected countries. Instead, such humungous amount of money was spending on killing and pauperising the affected countries. Thereafter, the US pulled out of these countries so as to leave inexplicable destruction abaft.

Lederach (1997) argues that, instead of using military muscles, efforts must be addressed to fostering a deeper understanding of the broader evolution of the conflict. Looking at how the international community–led by the US–is fighting terrorism, you find that much more efforts are exerted to bombing, catching, degrading terrorist networks; and killing terrorist leaders without taking on underlying causes such as basic human needs (Maslow 1943; Staub 2003; and McLeod 2007) in affected areas, geopolitics of the regions, power play in fighting terrorism and the peaceful future of the affected regions and the world at large. Why has Africa been excluded and ignored while it still bears the brunt? Are swathes of land in the Middle East and Afghanistan better than countries like Somalia, parts of Nigeria and Mali which are bigger in size comparably? How do you call this if at all those whose acts and policies created terrorism are ignoring the victims? If you look at the history of terrorism in Nigeria, there is no way you can exempt the West from liability for this phenomenon thanks to colonialism and neo-colonialism. Many scholars blame ethnicity on Nigeria without underscoring the fact that it was purposely created by British colonial rule.

The blame game has gone on almost in all African countries facing ethnic conflicts. In Nigeria for example, when Biafra sought to secede from Nigeria, it was blamed for being used by communists. Those who created the mess in Nigeria were the first to either blame or jump in to the bandwagon to resolve the conflict they created without assuming any responsibility. Such mentality of blaming those in ethno conflicts can be seen in the words of Post (1968) who maintains that "Nigeria has joined the Congo (Kinshasa) as the sick man of Africa. The high hopes of 1960-62 became the forebodings of 1964-65; now there seems little to feel but sickness of heart at the death of one's friends and despair at the end of a dream" (p. 26). Post accuses Nigeria of its ethno conflicts without mentioning or underscoring the fact that it is the British that created them. This has been the take of the world; blaming victims alone without including those who invented divide and rule which caused all these conflicts.

Differently however, Post goes on showing how British created all ethno conflicts Nigeria has ever experienced observing that "when Britain carved out Nigeria for itself it created, in the words of one of the more enlightened colonial experts, 'perhaps the most artificial of the many administrative units created in the course of the European occupation of Africa" (p. 27). Post shows the contradiction ethno conflicts draw even for those who analyse them. He started by blaming Nigeria for its failure that borders it with another failed state of the time, DRC (then Congo Kinshasa before it was renamed Zaire then DRC). Post realises his mistake of hurling insults at, and blames on Nigeria so as to admit that Britain is the one to blame for creating such an artificial political entity so as to foster her interests even after attaining independence as it has ever been for many African countries.

Apart from ethno conflicts, currently, Africa is facing terrorism in modern times whereby radical Islamic terrorist groups have exploited poverty, ignorance and insecurity to penetrate so as to operate in Africa. Howard and Hoffman (2012) argue that "terrorists are more likely to find weak but functioning states, such as Pakistan or Kenya, congenial bases of operations" (p. 94). This is especially true due to the fact that many African countries have weak security systems. Also, poor countries do not fulfil basic human needs which failure helps terrorist groups to get recruits to carry their acts of violence. Staub (2003) argues that:

> Frequently, groups that engage in ethnic/political violence, as well as terrorist groups, start with grievances, often some form of injustice, and political action to bring about change. People who are dissatisfied or want to justify their actions may claim injustice, even where there is none (p. 7).

If anything, this is what is going on in some African countries where poor people become good targets for recruitment. After their governments failed to meet their basic human needs, they end up being targeted by terrorist groups that promise them better life that their countries failed to realise even after becoming independent. This ruse helps terrorist groups to get easy recruits who join them believing their lives would change for the better even if, in the end, they become entombed in the crime without necessarily getting what they were promised. Howard and Hoffman (2012) argue that "failed state hold a number of attractions for terrorist organisations" (p. 80) by providing opportunity to acquire territories it is currently is in Mali, Nigeria, and Somalia. Chaliand and Blin (2007) argue that "Jihadist influence became evident most rapidly in the Horn of Africa due to the assistance provided in the early 1990s by Hassan al Turabi to ten or so radical groups in Eritrea, Uganda and, Somalia" (p. 343). Many people in the affected countries are now more identifying themselves as Muslims than citizens. Even when radical Islamic terrorist groups attack those they presume to be their enemies, the non-Muslims, they view them as Christians or infidels but not their conational who are their brothers and sisters. This is purely an attack on African identity that aims at precariously dividing Africans even more along sectarian lines as mentioned above. Modern-time terrorism has since been expanding to almost cover a large part of Africa due to the reasons mentioned above.

The only way for Africa to defeat terrorism, apart from international support, is by strengthening its political institutions so as to become competent to serve Africans. With competently accountable and responsible governments, Africa will be able to provide social services to its people; and thereby get rid itself of breeding grounds for terrorist recruitment geared by poverty and ignorance. Well educated people cannot be easily and pointlessly brainwashed. Well taken care of people will have no need to join such groups. As it has mentioned in the section of big and do-nothing armies and governments, Africa needs to keep the armies of educated, employed and healthy people instead of military. Africa needs big army of middle class but not big governments. Time for Africa to invest in politics must come to an end shall it aspire to turn things around for the better.

Africa Must Rethink Beefing up Its Security

Apart from feeding big and do-nothing armies, Africa also feeds the big armies of politicians who spend much time bickering and fighting for power so as to forget the common citizens whom they terrorise so as to end up forcing youth to join terrorist groups seeking better life the groups promise them. Also, bickering politicians do not eat alone. They have their relatives, friends and praise singers. If you sum them up, you discover why Africa has always been poor. To turn things around for the better Africa needs to put this type of corruption to an end.

To avert being a breeding ground for terrorist recruitments, there are a couple things that Africa must do. I recommend the following to be done in this regard:

First, poor African countries need to embark on programs that will cut down poverty rates so that they can save many young people from being recruited by terrorist groups. Along poor African countries, the international community has the role to play in helping African countries either financially or by reducing exploiting them under current trade terms so that the can become economically sufficient so as to cater for their people, especially youths that terrorist groups dupe and recruit.

Secondly, African countries need to strengthen their security institutions to see to it that those getting into their territories are thoroughly checked. This will help them to detect terrorist elements before they commit their acts of terror. For, currently, in many African countries any person can get in and out without being noticed. This has become much easier due to the rampancy of corruption and rent-seeking practices. This needs to change to see to it that whoever cross their borders must be accounted for.

Thirdly, Africa needs to curb the proliferation of small arms that terrorists can use to commit their acts of violence. Due to many ongoing conflicts in the C.A.R, the DRC and Somalia among others, Africa is littered with small and medium-size arms.

Fourthly, it is important for Africa to be addressed is the whole issue surrounding purchases. In the 1998 terrorist attacks in Dar es Salaam and Nairobi, it came to light that the terrorists involved were able to easily buy fertilizers such as TNT they used to make bombs that were used to blow buildings. When such dangerous materials are available and easily sold locally, it makes it easier for terrorists to commit their acts easily and quickly due to avoiding ferrying them to the targeted countries. It also came to light that terrorists were able to buy TNT locally without security agencies being aware. The FBI Website, November 18, 1998 notes that "the FBI is of the opinion that the bombs used in Nairobi and Dar es Salaam both employed TNT as a principle explosive component." African countries need to review their laws pertaining to such sensitive materials.

Sixthly, in the same breath, African countries need to monitor financial institutions such as banks and money transfer agents that terrorists use to send and receive money. George W. Bush cited in Gunaratna (2002) says that "financial sanctions may be appropriate for those foreign persons that support or otherwise with those foreign terrorists" (p. 66). Such measures should also apply to all businesses suspected to have links with terrorist groups in these countries. Gunaratna (*Ibid.*) notes that Al Qaeda used international banks such as Citibank in New York and Sun Trust Bank (p. 106) and "Barclay's bank in London" (p. 62) among other international banks. The international community needs to keep an eye on such banks instead of just trusting them simply because they are Western ones.

Seventh, charity organisations aligned with Islamic charity services must be thoroughly investigated. Gunaratna (*supra*) notes that "posing as an Islamic preacher, Khalifa, the above mentioned suspect, established both the International Islamic Relief Organization (IIRO) and Mercy International" (p. 182). Ironically, some of these organisations are still operative under charity pretext in many poor African countries. In Tanzania–for example–the IIRO is available at this address, PO Box 70450, Dar Es Salaam, Tanzania. If Al Qaeda and its affiliate organisations were able to penetrate some international banks; and they are still operative as it is in the case above, what of unprotected and unscrutinised local banks in various African countries? Arguably, banking and investments need to be oft-scrutinised. Haynes (2005) argues that "sources in banking industry in Dar es Salaam said the accounts belonged to several banks on initial post-9/11list issued by the US government of 20 globally sought international companies said to be al-Qaeda owned and run businesses" (p. 1324). Gunaratna (*op.cit.*) goes on arguing that Osama was able to disguise as an investor in Sudan while he actually was doing two things, business and terrorism. How many investors can exploit such loopholes and carry out terrorist attacks in African countries? It must be clear understood that terrorism is there to stay. Therefore, the stint some countries have enjoyed without any terrorist activities should not deceive them so as to become lax.

Eighth, African countries need to take is making sure that all organisations, especially religious and ideological ones operating in their territories must comply with the laws of those countries. For example, nobody or organisation should be allowed to preach any ideology that goes against their cultures and traditions. Remarkably, the type of education offered in many African countries needs to be decolonised so that those receiving it must be taught about the importance of their identity, culture and ways of life.

Ninth, African countries need to cooperate militarily in gathering and disseminating and sharing intelligence information about terrorist activities in the territories or regions in order to see to it all loopholes terrorists can exploit are sealed.

So, too, Islamic madrasas must be regulated by the government instead of allowing them to operate free. This will help them in curbing all breeding grounds for future recruits. Above all, the type of education provided should make citizens to be citizens first before being believers or followers of certain ideologies or faiths. Whatever faith that opposes or contrasts the natural identity of African citizens or harmony should be banned right away. Why does the same apply in the so-called Islamic or Arab states but not to other states? All schools should be under inspection time after time to see to it that the type of education and skills provided comply with the national goals. Teaching the culture of the country must be mandatory in all schools at all levels.

Tenth, educational curricula and systems must allow those receiving education to freely comment on the type of education they are given in order to enable the authorities to keep on improving the syllabi to meet the demands of the time and society.

Eleventh, African countries must make sure that they constitutionally stipulate that any institution[s] be it political or religious that teaches radical ideology will be legally banned and possibly those behind it being punished. This move should also go in tandem with confiscate whatever property such organisations own. African countries should openly declare that there is no culture or belief is superior to others.

Twelfth, African countries need to declare openly that religious rights and freedoms are subject to the laws, freedom and the rights of the host country.

Thirteenth, African countries must openly declare that nobody has the right whatsoever to alter in any way the natural identity of the citizens by superimposing or propagating faiths which aim at altering their identity. Those which have already altered the identity of the citizens must be legally forced to recant their new identities and teachings and, if possible, apologise for that.

In sum, what is regarded as war on terror is but a proxy war that has directly attacked African identity and solidarity. As indicated above, some Africans have become more Muslims or Christians or whatever than Africans so as to kill their African brothers and sisters in the name of ideologies that are counterproductive and foreign to Africa. So, too, looking at how the war on terror started in Kenya after Al Qaeda attacked U.S embassies in Dar es Salaam, the chances of ending it soon are slim given that the number of players has been increasing. Al Shabaab, Boko Haram and other terrorists operating currently in Africa seem to be hell bent to go on with their campaigns as they recently created links with other terrorist groups; thus making war on terror a possible WW III. Once, again, African identity and solidarity are at risk due to the fact that soon many outside forces–either directly or indirectly–will join the war as

114

we have seen above whereby Al Shabaab and Boko Haram have already pledged alliance to the ISIL. Importantly, African countries, need to be careful to avoid wasting time and endangering their identity, economies and solidarity fighting a proxy WW III resulting from ideological and cultural animosity between the West and the Middle East.

Again, the history of terrorism in Africa indicates that Africa has nothing to do with it. Therefore, the burden such a crime has imposed on African countries is huge and unbearable. The international community needs to help Africa to fight this scourge not for the security or survival of Africa but for the survival of humankind in general. I will develop this topic on another coming volume on terrorism to show how it is used to scramble for and reoccupy Africa this time militarily.

There is nothing on earth that turns human beings into zombies or killing machines such as religion. Refer to how terrorists are killing innocent people simply because they are carrying the orders of their God; or how Indians Hindus for many years have exploited and discriminated others simply because their God decided so? I do not think if the untouchables are happy with such a ridiculously obnoxious God who disadvantaged them. I would argue that the forces and resources the international community is spending fighting against violent terrorism should also be directed to this endemic nonviolent terrorism hidden in the name of religion and the orders or commandments of God. Racist or violent God cannot be a true God. Africa is now losing a lot of money due to this madness as it was imported through cultural colonialism. Recently, Kenya lost an opportunity to host the oil pipeline from Uganda simply because Al Shabaab, a Somali-based fundamental terrorist group, oft-attacks the area where the pipeline would pass. This is not a run-off-the-mill matter. Since Uganda–because of security concerns–preferred Tanzania to Kenya, chances that the East African Community is likely to be shaken. Then you wonder. If all members of the EAC are striving to achieve full cooperation aimed at unification, why then should Kenya worry or feel it has been robbed of its morsel it had already assured itself of getting?

Generally speaking, terrorism is no one person business. Africa and the international community need to work hand in hand to stamp out this scourge. So, too, the West must stop its double standard in dealing with non-Western countries.

Apart from needing international community support to fight terrorism, Africa needs the same to return back the money many African despots stole and stashed abroad. This too is terrorism if we consider the millions of people it kills; however it has not been categorised so.

Chapter 4

The New Scramble for Africa

Although the scramble for and partition of Africa remains to be in historical books, it seems to have resurged recently when raising power along the old powers decided to revisit the two historical occasions. However, what seems to be the new scramble for Africa is going alone without necessarily partitioning the already partitioned Africa. Currently, the rise of China and India has forced rich countries to go back to the drawing board to see to it that everybody either gets a chunk for those who had none while those who already had retains or doubles their chunk. Goldstein (2006) observes that "Africa is endowed with extractive industries such as oil, mining, and timber that are very capital-intensive" not to mention other natural capitals such as fertile soil, minerals and the people. To the contrary, Africa has never benefited from such precious resources. This needs to change drastically. I postulate that Africa has the chance of using its resources such as minerals to forge ahead shall it renegotiate its corrupt and exploitative contracts corrupt governments entered with rich countries due to the ruse of the cold war. There is no way Africa can benefit from its vast minerals without renegotiating the terms of the contracts operating currently. This is inevitable for both Africa and foreign mining companies. The *Economist* (11 February, 2012) offers the example of Zimbabwe repressive regime noting that "regardless of Zimbabwe's heavy-handed treatment, mining companies do not necessarily object in principle to giving locals a larger stake in their operations." This observation is dead true. The duo in this equation inevitably needs each other. There is no way Africa can benefit from its resources without technology to bring them to the surface of the ground. Likewise, there is not technologically advanced countries such as the West, China and Japan can benefit from their technology without having a supplier of raw materials their industry needs to produce. It takes two to tango.

As it was in the partition of and scramble for Africa at the Berlin Conference 1884, currently Africa is subject to the same though with a difference face, strategies and players. There is no more underground and secretive movement or activities of the partition of Africa as it was at the said conference that resulted to the partition of Africa. Nevertheless, looking at how those scrambling for Africa are partitioning if not repartitioning themselves based on the agenda, Africa is facing a modern-time scramble or new scramble or whatever of such nature (Dzingirai 2003; Lee 2006; Frynas and Paulo 2007; Habiyaremye 2011; and Moyo, Yeros and Jha 2012). The Berlin conference was about scrambling for Africa as it was aimed at occupying and thereafter colonising it as it happened. The current scramble is about leverage and extraction of resources whereby those scrambling for Africa do not necessarily need to occupy it directly. Instead, they want to use Africans themselves to do the show. Henceforth, we can say from the outset that the attraction Africa is causing to the new comers in the game is not geared by love of Africa or the intention to help it out but to exploit it just like those who did so did before. While Africa was not aware of the scramble for itself during the pre-colonial era, it now is now well aware of the modern-time scramble. This offers an opportunity for Africa to not repeat the same mistakes it committed during the first scramble. Hence, Africa cannot offer any excuse as it has been for the first scramble. This being said, Africa has what it take to avoid becoming the subject of scramble if it plays its cards smartly based on the experience of its past history of colonialism.

While the first scramble for Africa was enhanced by manipulations, and con spearheaded by explorers, merchants, and missionaries as the camouflaged agents of colonialism, the current scramble is spearheaded by academics, diplomats, investors, politicians and scientists, among others. Of recently, there have been many annual conferences, meetings or summits between Africa and other rich and upcoming countries either convened on African soil as it was for the recent Sino-Africa in Johannesburg or Afro-Japanese one in Nairobi or in the capitals of courting countries. All such conferences and the likes are aimed at either enticing Africa, or make it keep toeing the line if not to establishing new ties where they are not or strengthening old ties. The game has remained the same. However, the strategies have changed due to the competition new entrants posed. Britain used to use commonwealth while France used francophone. Now we have new kids on the blocs such as China, India, Japan and Turkey, among others, that have adopted this system. The *Daily Nation* (August 29, 2016) quoted Zhang Ming, China's Vice-Minister for Foreign Affairs recently saying that "there is a never shortage of conferences and promises for Africa, and yet action and implementation have not always followed" and even when they followed, there was no gains for Africa. This is a true statement that is supposed to make Africa think deeply and twice. The *Daily Nation* went on noting that "China questions Japan's ability to fulfil Ticad promises" soon after Japan convened its Tokyo International Conference on African Development (Ticad VI) in Nairobi on 27th–28th August, 2016. All these conferences were aimed at gaining leverage from Africa. Once again, Africa was in the centre of the world; and promises were many. Again, was Africa well prepared to take advantage of this new demand for its cooperation? Is there anything substantial that was achieved for Africa or it was business as usual as it has been since colonial times?

As noted above, before the Ticad VI, there was China African conference famously known as Forum on China-Africa Cooperation (FOCAC) which was held in Johannesburg, South

Africa from 3rd to 5th December, 2015 at which China promised heavens. Before then, there were others between Britain, France and Africa not to forget even a weak bidder such as Turkey. Other courters such as Iran, Oman and Qatar have been sending silent emissary to meet some African leaders of the countries that have resources these courters need. Due to this new scramble, Africa is in between like a beautiful virgin who should watch if she wants to avoid ending up in the hands of a quack or bloodsucker if not a misogynist.

After the Johannesburg FOCAC, *Xinhua* (8 February, 2016) quoted Chinese President Xi Jinping as saying that "China is greatly concerned about the poor harvest caused by El Nino in many African countries and will provide one billion yuan (156 million dollars) of emergency food aid to the affected countries." Does Africa really need to be fed by China that has a big burden and many mouths to feed due to having such a big population? The *China Daily* (4 December, 2015) added that "Happy Life" projects and special programmes focusing on women and children and cancel outstanding debts in the form of bilateral governmental zero-interest loans borrowed by the relevant least developed African countries that mature at the end of 2015. The Paper went on quoting Xi as saying "let's join hands ... and open a new era of China-Africa win-win cooperation and common development." Is there any win-win cooperation between Africa which is poor technologically with China one of current technology giants? How will Africa benefit from and enjoy this *win-win* relationship while it has less to export to China compared to what it imports? To see how the so-called win-win trade is a sham. Haugen (2011) maintains that whereas Chinese exports and imports from Africa have followed each other closely over time, their spatial patterns are highly disparate. Out of the 53 African countries for which trade data is reported, only 13 have a trade surplus with China, while the remaining 40 countries run a trade deficit. Is this real win-win or lose-win? Nevertheless,

Xi's assertion is very attractive to make and hear. To the contrary, when you ask yourself how win-win Afro-Sino cooperation is going to be realised, you do not get an answer. Even Xi himself did not bother to explain how. Instead, he offered a wholesale promise with many ambiguities without showing how such a win-win equation will be realised. Again, for how long will rich countries vilipend Africa so as to be summoned to be given some handouts while it sits on immense resources? This is the question many African leaders and activists need to ask and provide the right answers to. This is where Africa needs to do its homework carefully shall it want to turn things around for the better future of its people. I would argue that African countries, instead of putting high premiums on exports, they should negotiate resource-technology exchange whereby China has to top up Africa's exports with offering many opportunities for Africans to go to China to acquire technology they will take back to Africa and jumpstart it.

Moreover, we used to see British ex-colonies congregating either in London or any host commonwealth country to deliberate on their postcolonial affiliations or francophone congregating in Paris to rekindle their vows to their colonial masters. Due to the nature of this new scramble, as argued above, Africa has no excuse whatsoever to offer. In the first scramble Africa as the excuse of being caught off guard. In this new one, Africa needs to avoid offering any pretexts due to the fact that everything is strategically very obvious. For, once bitten, twice say the axiom has it. To prove that Africa is not a crying baby asking for help or a stranded person waiting for a saviour, it needs to turn this new scramble to an opportunity by making sure that those seeking to court it (Peters 2003; Tull 2006; and Stolte 2012) are doing so based on its terms but not their terms. My African experience tells me that when a man courts a girl, it is the girl whose terms are followed but not those of the man. Again, whose terms are now used in this engagement-cum-courtship? The answer is obvious that by being summoned–or put it in a soft language–invited to the bi-summits, it seems; Africa does not have any terms in the arrangement. What I know is that in African culture, whenever a man wants to court, he presented himself or his agent to the home of the girl but not vice versa as it is in this courtship in question. If Africa wants to turn things around, it must not wait for being invited. Instead, it must plan; and thereafter invite those inviting it to their summit that they sugar-coat by calling them afro-so-and-so summit. There is nothing African in such summits. If there is anything African is nothing but its resources.

Those who summon Africa prepare themselves based on their interests, strategies and timing while Africa just fits in without any pre-prep arrangement. Sometimes back in 2000, I was appointed by an NGO in Tanzania to review and translate the ACP-EU Development Cooperation after the expiration of the Lome Convention, a trade and aid agreement between the European Economic Community (EEC) and 71 African, Caribbean, and Pacific (ACP) countries. Apart from being enormously voluminous, I found that the document that EU has presented to the ACP, the ACP had a few days to read and ratify the same. How do you do that? Africa did not ask the EU how long it took to write the document and why the EU wrote it alone to end up just present it for the ratification? Even the time I was given to review and translate was so short. I, therefore, had to hire other assistants and work days and night to make sure that I review, translate and present it to the NGOs which would then write their recommendations to the government of Tanzania. Knowing how African politicians do not have time to read between lines, I recommended that the NGO that had hired me should recommend that the government ask for more time in order to have enough time to read the document and if possible comment on it before ratifying it.

Interestingly, one of the members of the NGO told me that African leaders do not torture their heads to read such volumes. Instead, their concentration is on how much money is offered in per diems. I was baffled. To be sure, I asked the officer who made such allegations to substantiate her claim. She summarily replied by asking a simple question: if time given is short for a professional like you, how will it be enough for politicians who are not professionals in the area? If they were interested in what you are proposing, why didn't they ask for more time to read the document? From there I got what I wanted. To cut a long story, I would suggest that African leaders should not attend such summits or ratify such agreements before getting enough time for themselves and their experts to go through the documents those courting them prepare for them to ratify and end up signing their own rip offs. They should write the documents together so that African countries become well versed with what they ratify instead of following per diems those countries offer in plenty knowing how they are a good ruse for such greedy and myopic leaders.

Before the first scramble for Africa, African chiefs signed many contracts without knowing what were stipulated in these colonial and criminal treaties. They did so unwillingly because they did not know how to read and write. They used their thumbs to append their signatures. Mhango (2015); and Clemm (2009) cite an example of Chief Mangungo of Msovero Tanzania who on 25 November, 1884 along with other chiefs in his area sold his country to Germans after signing a bogus treaty with their agent Karl Peters. How many Mangungos do we have today who know how to read and write but do not employ them to avoid selling Africa? Differently from Mangungo, Mhango questions the intensions and motives of Mangungo so as to exonerate him. For, when he signed the treaty, his intention was clear and good in that he was entering an equal and equitable treaty for trade benefits of his people. To the contrary, modern

African modern Mangungos are driven by greed, myopia and selfishness to sign such treaties. You can ties this with the type of education that Africa needs to provide to its people. Africa needs to provide right education to its people if it wants to turn things around for the better.

Looking at how African chiefs sold their empires to colonial monsters one can underscore the fact that those who came after them, did the same. For example, North Sudan has been recently to Qatar using its soil to produce foods for their population (Cotula 2009); also see Cotula and Vermuelen (2009); and Telesetsky (2011). Equatorial Guinea is now used in the hands of Americans extracting oil (McSherry 2006) while Congo and the Gabon have always been in the hands of their former colonial master, France (Alves 2008); also see Terheggen 2011; Appel 2012; and Campbell 2013). Arguably therefore, the current scramble is the second and the third for some countries. If African countries were smart, they would turn the scramble for African resources to their advantage given that they are now many suitors, especially after the rise of China and India. Africa needs to know the fact that there is no goodwill or love in business, especially when it is dealing with hegemonic powers that seek to take advantage of their economic and financial muscles not to mention their technological advancement. Instead of targeting money gotten by the way of such investment, Africa should strive to exchange its resources with technology so that it can use it to create factories it will use to add value to its raw materials that Africa has always exported to end up importing processed goods from the same.

When Resources Become a Jinx

Africa has immense resources that many rich countries need. But Africa has never benefited from its humungous resources. Thanks to colonial and the archaic and exploitative nature of international trade, Africa's resources have become a curse of its own. This resource curse (Robinson, Torvik, and Verdier 2006; Mideksa 2013; Ploeg 2011; and Haber, and Menaldo 2011) has turned Africa into a witness of its robbery. If there is anything that Africa needs to do is turning things around to see to it that those courting it must now also change their approach. Africa needs to turn resource curse into blessing, (Arezki, and Van der Ploeg 2007).

In his infamous book, *The Bottom Billion,* Collier (2007) as with others like (Bannon and Collier 2003), argues that if Africa should address the root causes of conflict resulting from resources, chances of attaining sustainable peace and development are high. Essentially, Collier used an economic lens to view the conflict. If we buy into his view and attempt to view peace based on economic view in that we can invest in peace as opposed to investing in wars, we surely can turn resource curse into blessings. For Collier, the root causes of conflict in Africa are: civil wars resulting from the struggle for controlling resources, costs of war, lack of rule of law, bad governance that results to mismanagement of resources and corruption among others. As could be underscored, Collier's view is that: if Africa could address the above mentioned root causes, chances of developing, and thus have peace are viably high. Hoeffler (2008) maintains that a few studies can quantify the overall cost of war. He cites a briefing paper by The International Action Network on Small Arms, Oxfam International and Safer World (2007) which focuses on conflict in Africa since 1990 which found that wars cost $284 billion in lost GDP. This is roughly the amount of foreign aid these countries received over the period (page not provided).

The amount above is not small money. It is humungous, especially for poor African countries. How much improvement would that money have brought to this poor continent? Hoeffler (*Ibid.*) goes on observing that the average GDP of conflict-affected low income countries just prior to war is $19.7 billion.

Therefore, the cost of a single war is around $49 billion. To this we must add $5 billion of health costs, giving a total cost of $54 billion for a single low-income country. Here we are talking of the money that pays to finance the conflict. How much does Africa lose resulting from the robbery of resources and manpower that occur during the wars resulting from conflicts? To the contrary, Bannon and Collier *(Ibid.)* maintain that private capital inflows in countries facing armed conflict "have assumed greater importance than foreign aid" (p. 218). Again, what does private capital inflow contribute to the country facing war compared to public capital inflows? I would argue that such private capital inflows benefit only warlords be they those in power or in the opposition. For the common citizen in the street facing war, such inflows add more problems. For such a person African resources are but a curse but not a blessing.

Basing on the economic lens in addressing conflicts resulting from resource curse, other theories such as dependency, relative deprivation and archaic nature of the world system were propounded. By turning these theories on their head, Africa can successfully turn the resource curse into blessings.

In fact, basing on the failures and weaknesses of the world system that has always fuelled resource-based conflicts, the disengagement theories call for a total disengagement of the "developing world" with the world capitalist system. Proponent theorists in this school of thought such as Frank (1967), Josue de Castro (1970); and Vincent (1995), thus, that large rent from natural resources can weaken state structure and make government less accountable (Bannon and Collier *op.cit.:* ix), especially if such a government operates under clientele relationship with capitalists as it was in the former Zaire then the Democratic Republic of Congo (DRC) under Mobutu Seseseko, former DRC's kleptocrat who ruined the country for over 30 years in conjunction with the United States (US) and other Western countries.

However, Mhango (2015) criticises disengagement theories as he concurs with integration theory maintaining that "Africa Reunite or Perish"; suggesting that the only way to turn the resource curse into blessings is only through reunifying Africa so as to have a say in international affairs just like the US or Canada have whereby the money and resources that fund war and the war economies will be channelled and invested in economic and social beneficial uses. Differently from Collier, Mhango addresses colonial legacies as the major causes of Africa's underdevelopment. He avers that the division of Africa did not only weaken Africa but it also created artificial identities, dependency, perpetual exploitation through neo-colonialism and enmity among Africa countries. If anything, these are among the things Africa needs to turn around so as to develop. So, Mhango opposes disengagement theory and fully concurs with integration theory. Despite their appeal, both integration theories of development and disengagement theories have not worked well for Africa. This being said, Africa still faces a stalemate as far as turning resource curse into blessings as far as peace and development are concerned. Underscoring this dichotomy, I am convinced that investing in peace as the means of reducing or eradicating violent conflict resulting from struggle for controlling natural resources will enable Africa to turn its resource curse into a blessing especially at this time many rich countries are courting Africa. doing so, will not only contributes hugely to doing things in a different way hoping to get different results where other theories have failed but will also make Africa peaceful therefore good for investments. Try to imagine. How much the money, time and resources spent on conflict can do for Africa economically and socially? Africa needs to tackle conflict, especially through having good governance and true democracy. I am trying to imagine, the manpower, resources and finance that conflict-prone countries have already burnt in the conflicts and how much such humungous money would usher *vis-à-vis* development, welfare and wellbeing for African population. Without meritoriously tackling conflict, the situation will become a lot worse for Africa due to the fact that conflicts resulting from struggle for controlling resources rich countries, in the West and elsewhere, are scrambling for will increase. It is better to turn this new scramble for Africa to a win-win equation based on securing good deals based on African terms and interests. Sometimes, these countries may support warlords and criminal regime in order to get a supply for resources it happened in North Sudan after the International Criminal Court (ICC) interdicted its dictator, Omar Bashir. China did not help Bashir financially old. It went ahead by providing even military support. Pati (2008) maintains that is not new to longstanding criticism for its human rights record; and it had no interest in highlighting its close relationship with Sudan, especially since the BBC accused it of "fuelling war in Darfur" by providing weapons to the Sudanese government and by training fighter pilots in Darfur, in violation of the UN arms embargo.

Such behaviour shows how china's win-win relationship with Africa is more of a verbal thing but not pragmatic one. For China, just like any other rich countries, what matters is to get what it wants. The rest only rest on the supplier to negotiate good or bad deal. Again, dealing with criminal states is a very lucrative business due to the fact that some are facing shunning from the international community while other are under pressure from dissent voices at home and abroad as it currently is in Congo, the DRC, Equatorial Guinea, Gabon, and Uganda among others. In such circumstances, rich countries are like to fuel conflicts in order to get cheap resources and supply weaponry sold at hiked prices.

However, avoiding this very trap needs a very careful and skilful bargaining power which is only possible for Africa through pulling together but not severally as it currently is whereby some countries are called individually to enter into some trade agreements that are particularly detriment for such countries and Africa in general.

To benefit more from its resources, Africa must encourage internal investments whereby rich Africans should be given priority in investment. Currently for example, the richest man in Africa Aliko Dangote from Nigeria has invested heavily in Tanzania. The *Africa Global Fund* (6 October, 2014) maintains that Dangote was planning to invest significantly in the Mbinga coal mine in Tanzania's southwestern region in order to use the coal to produce energy for use at his cement plant in Mtwara which was then under construction. When completed, the Dangote Cement plant will produce three million tonnes of cement per year, almost half of the country's net production. This means, Dangote will create jobs that will be taken by Africans. This is different from any foreign investors who prefer to create jobs for their home citizens. China is a leading type of such investors. Whenever it extends loans to any African countries, it forces them to use its people and almost everything that the projects if funds. Bräutigam and Xiaoyang (2011) maintain that the impact of China's economic engagement in Africa is debatable whereby some argue that it is neo-colonial in nature: almost exclusively about getting access to natural resources not to mention the influx of competitive Chinese products, small-scale Chinese traders, and Chinese labour in infrastructure projects is seen as a serious threat to African manufacturers, market vendors, and workers.

Chinese style of investment and economic cooperation is no different from Western colonial and exploitative one. This has led to some scholars to reach a conclusion that what China is doing in Africa currently is nothing but neo-colonialism (Robertson and Pinstrup-Andersen 2010; and Lumumba-Kasongo 2011). In essence, for Africa to benefit from such investments and relationships, it needs to think in terms of today based on its interests, needs and terms failure to which, truly,

China is going to be another colonial hegemony looking for making a killing at the detriment and expense of Africa as the West has always done. Africa needs to be preparedly watchful and scrupulously alert.

Bad Investment, Capital Flight, Corruption, Embezzlement...

Since attaining their independence, African countries have been doing bad business based on poor investment that has cost them their prosperity and development. Despite becoming poorer and poorer from this type of investment, African countries seemed to have become satisfied with it. They have never changed. Now they need to change. For example, African countries have since independence invested heavily in the crops that neither benefits them nor they cannot eat. Such crops were introduced by colonial powers during colonial era. And the only consumers of such crops are Western countries something that make them unmarketable out of their traditional market. Through neoliberal policies based on one side open market and closed market for the other enhances such exploitation. Such regime of exploitative and unfair trade becomes stronger due to the fact that African countries strive either to entice the donors in order to get aid or doing business with rich countries. Almost everything gyrates around such unfair axis of cooperation so as to include even aid. Bourguignon and Sundbeg (2007) argue that the IFIs impose aid conditionality on receiving countries in order to control the implementation of their policies tailored to exploit them which African corrupt and myopic rulers accept in order to get the money for running their corrupt regimes at the detriment of their people.

Bourguignon and Sundberg hit the aid in the crux as far as conditions are concerned as they have always aimed at robbing Africa by using a few of its rulers that have always myopically and selfishly offered themselves to be used in betraying Africa.

The *Daily Nation* (28 August, 2016) quotes Dr Akiwumi Adesina, the President of the African Development Bank (AfDB) as saying "African agriculture cannot get water out of a rock. Aligning Africa's markets will unleash the potential of Africa's agriculture. There is no need to produce 70 per cent of cocoa, but only get two per cent of the chocolates (made from cocoa)." Cocoa is not alone. Coffee, sisal, pyrethrum, flowers and others that Africans cannot eat are experiencing the same apart from the fact that their market is only in the West and now China. To turn things for the better, Africa needs to investigate heavily in food production first. I do not say that Africa should shun those colonial crops. Instead, Africa should produce them as secondary income generating crops.

Another area that Africa needs to vigorously address is capital flight. Since the introduction of capitalism, Africa has been bleeding to death economically. For, in just three decades, Africa has lost a lot of money that would have helped it to turn things around. When it comes to capital flight, how dire the situation is for Africa is known. Boyce and Ndikumana (2012 cited in Asongu 2014) note that up until the end of 2004 Africa had already lost at least 814 billion in capital flight. This money is huge, mainly for a poor continent. On his side, Ojo (2015) puts the amount Africa lost even higher arguing that over the last 50 years, Africa is estimated to have lost in excess of $1 trillion in illicit financial flows (IFFs) which he says that it is roughly equivalent to all of the official development assistance received by Africa during the same timeframe.

Again, when it comes to dealing with criminal activities, what is unearthed is the tip of the iceberg compared to what actually was committed. This may roughly show us how Africa is robbed big time and big money. For Africa to turn things around positively, it needs to create institutions and systems that will put such robbery to an end. Africa can; given that such criminality is an open secret that most of African rules partake of and know too well. This is embezzlement. As for corruption, Asongu (2013) argues that it is estimated that in 2004, the continent lost more than $148 billion to corruption; approximately 25% of its Gross Domestic Product (GDP) if you compare to the undisclosed amounts of money Africa loses in other areas annually, you find that Africa needs to tackle corruption so as to turn things around. Asongu goes on disclosing that 50% of tax revenue and US$30 billion in aid for Africa ends up in corrupt hands. This estimate is however small if we consider how the government of Ibrahim Babangida former Nigerian president is said to have lost US$12.4 billion in oil revenues only in the year 1991–1992, while his counterpart in Angola was accused of mislaying US$4.2 billion from 1997 to 2004 (Baker 2005: 51). If two countries could lose more than 15 billion in such a short time, how much does Africa lose under over 50 corrupt presidents? No one can precisely tell how much Africa loses to corruption annually. Alemazung (2011) maintains that in September 2002, corruption in Africa was said to cost the continent nearly US$150 billion. What is clear is that Africa loses billions annually. Ironically, while African rulers allow such criminality to cause losses to their countries, they shamelessly go out cap in hand begging. Without turning things around and put a stop on such loses Africa will always be poor pointlessly. However, if Africa decides to stop this theft it can, particular in this century where computers have simplified the work of controlling and tracing revenues. The so-called developed countries decided to computerise their systems in order to avoid such corrupt and negligent loses resulting from corruption, tax evasion and other financial crimes. On top of computerisation of their institutions, developed countries hand down heavy punishment on whoever found guilty of robbing the country regardless whether he or he is big or small.

Another area that Africa needs to reconsider and redefine is work. In Western countries, it does not matter what type of the job one does. What matter are two things; namely that one has a job and one earn income. In some African countries things are different. Whenever I used to go on leave, many people used to ask me the type of job I was doing. Many were interested in hearing whether I was an accountant, a lawyer, a taxman, a border officer and the likes because these jobs rank in big monies. For Africa to turn things around work should be valued and be given added value in that the essence of any work for whoever has it is nothing but to enable a person to work and earn an income despite how dirty or clean the said job is. Currently, thanks to corruption that divided works and its value across race (Bonilla-Silva 2001), many people do not work, and if they do, their jobs are not known. Yet, such people are becoming richer and richer without legally showing cause as to how they made their wealth. Because of loopholes for people to either earn illegally, especially through corruption and thuggery, work in Africa lost its value. Many laws in many countries do not require their citizens to declare how they accumulated and made their wealth. This has created a crisis whereby work is not taken seriously. You find a person whose job is not known becoming rich all of the sudden; and nobody doubts or questions her or him.

I see street sweepers and lawnmower drivers park their cars and go to work in Canada. I see dirty farmers in stores soon after finishing their jobs. They are always confident simply because they have a job to do and the income to make. And nobody looks down on them. It does not matter whether someone bathes cat, dogs or pig. What matter is the fact that one has job to do, contribute to the national cog and earn. While in many parts of Africa people are interested on what type of job one does, in the West a job is everything. Some commit suicide or divorce for lack of job. In many African countries, the situation is sadly different. One is respected not according to the work he or she does but according to the type of works he or she does.

All depends on if one does a white-collar job or blue or *black* job (Royster 2003). Colonial administration created job segregation in order to tear local African colonial workers apart from their people. During colonial times, those who worked in office were highly respected than those who did dirty jobs. They therefore thought that they were privileged so much that some decided not to fight for the independence of their countries. This tendency has gone on up until now so as to encompass where one lives. Those living in upper market regard themselves as being better than those who live in sharks and unofficial residents in many African cities. The car they drive and the food they eat do differ completely. This needs to change. What should matter is the contribution to the income of the person and nation and the role the job plays to an individual and the nation at large.

Chapter 5

How Did It Start and What Should Be Done?

Essentially, Africa took off poorly and wrongly; and it was running on empty from the outset. Nunn and Puga (2012) maintain that colonial powers left behind devastated and collapsing institutions and fragmented society which, so, too, was abhorrently illiterate and poor. What made ex-colonial powers is the fact that newly independent countries did not agitate to be redressed for the devastation the leaving colonial government left behind. There are no literatures that show that postcolonial African leaders took this problem seriously. Instead, they assured themselves that they would turn things around before later they realised too late that they could not do so. An ideal to substantiate this can be drawn from the newest countries on earth, South Sudan which is now entangled in civil wars. Instead of telling the world how devastated South Sudan (Maxwell, Gelsdorf and Santschi 2012) that North Sudan, it former colonial power handed to the new leadership without anything to begin with, they are busy fighting over power so that they can run such a crippled country. North Sudan that caused all this carnage is just laughing and praying that this issue should not be brought to the attention of the international community. Sadly enough, the same South Africa, despite ceding with nothing still has the burden to pay North Sudan some money to transport its oil (Themnér and Wellensteen 2013) using the same pipelines that were built by the money that came from the same oil. Instead of agitating to get a share of the pipelines, South Sudan spent much energy and time negotiating the construction new pipelines through Kenya (Shankleman 2011) which later became another problem after civil wars broke out on 15 December 2013 (Pinaud 2014) when former vice president Riek

Machar and his group boycotted the meeting of National Liberation Council; also see Bakke, Cunningham, and Seymour (2012).

How do you expect any newly independent country to perform well while it did not have skilled workers or experienced leaders? These were supposed to be important issues postcolonial governments were supposed to settle before accepting independence that ended up becoming nothing but dependency. Many African countries had many deficiencies at the time they attained their independence. Apart from having uneducated manpower, they also had the burden of keeping on serving colonial economy. How would African countries perform well while they did not have even the structures of running their countries? Conversely, starting from the scratch, many African countries created political institutions however weak they may seem. What do you expect of the country that started with three doctors as it was in the case of Tanzania? Nyerere (1967) observes that in Tanzania in 1961 at the time of attaining independence, Tanzania had only 11, 832 children in secondary schools of whom 176 only were in form IV. This means; Tanzania received its independence with illiterate population. And the situation was generally the same all over the continent. Some countries such as the DRC had a worse situation than this. Although no colonialism was civilised (Machel 1987), well-intended or good, some colonies were better off than others. Grier (1999) maintains that ex-British colonies performed better than French ones. Again, despite comparing two sick people, colonial education was isolating people from their society. It did not give those who got it the tools with which to function well in their societies. You can see this in ex-French colonies where almost all teachers were imported from France while the British trained a few locals to teach their colleagues; also see White 1996. Essentially, colonial education created zombies who would gulp all sort of colonial garbage in the name of education.

As for Tanzania, it was Nyerere and a handful of Tanzania who had a university degree at the time. With such deficiency, would any sane person expect Tanzania to compete with European countries that has millions and millions of elites in various specialisations? Doing so is not only indifference but also insanity. To add salt to injury, Africa suffered the second blow after educating its people. Due to the fact that a few semi-illiterates Africa had had entrepreneurial deficiency thanks to the colonial education they were provided with, ended up producing literature gurus but not economic ones. I think this is why post-independence Africa produced many literary gurus such as Okot p'Bitek, Chinua Achebe, Shaban Robert and many more. I do not mean to underrate the contribution of literary gurus whose contribution was to awaken Africans. However, not all were welcome at home. Some regimes such as that of Idi Amin in Uganda killed many scholars so as to add more pangs to Africa's predicament. Amin killed scholar openly. Other African rulers who did not want to be challenged either frustrated scholars or sent them packing so as to benefit Western countries. This has gone on up until now. Not many African governments like scholars. This is why you will see in the section of brain drain how Africa needs to turn this around so as to fully utilise its diaspora brains powers as a capital for development. Bloom, Canning and Chan (2006) note that as of 2005 the United Nations Conference on Trade and Development (UNCTAD) estimates that roughly 30 per cent of the region's university trained professionals live outside Africa. A recent estimate suggests that up to 50,000 African-trained Ph.Ds. are working outside Africa which is a big number for a poor continent like Africa that spent billions of dollars to educate them to end up losing them. This number is equivalent to almost 1, 000 PhD holders per country. Additionally, you find that such crème de crème were produced by using either donor or borrowed money that Africans are now paying or will pay at one time while those it produced did not serve them. Africa therefore, needs to turn this around to see to it that the investment that was put in such a people is regained in order to help Africa turn things around for the better. This can only be done by creating favourable environment that will motivate them to come back home on top of being welcomed and fully utilised. To bolster and jumpstart, and rekindle confidence for investment its economy, Africa needs to embark on the rule of law not just because the West wants it to do so. Instead, it must aim at fulfilling its commitment to its people. Good investment can give Africa a leg up.

Africa Must Create Networks of Infrastructure
Another area we need to be explored is infrastructure at the time African countries got their independence. No country can develop without having infrastructure which acts as artilleries and capillaries that transport blood in the body. Even if we consider the infrastructure such as railways and poor roads that colonial regime built, you find that they were strategically and purposely built to service colonial economy but not the colonies. Arguably, African countries had nothing to start with as far as capital, infrastructure, administrative structures and sound economies are concerned. Africa needs highways, superhighways telecommunication, telecommunication, roads, railways, waterways, airports, harbours and the like that can competently meet its current needs. There is no way a country or continent can develop without having these infrastructures. Currently, Africa has only one road that connects it from Cairo to Cape Town. The best investment a nation can ever make (Cox and Love 1998) is in infrastructure. They credit President Dwight Eisenhower for reaching this milestone that saw the US becoming a world economic powerhouse after the United States

in mid-fifties invested heavily in Bridges, roads, highways, superhighways and whatnot in order to connect the country. This super network of infrastructures became the catapult that saw the US to perform miraculously economically and politically due to the muscle it got from its investment. For, the network of infrastructure created fast and free movements of goods and people. This is what Africa can learn from the US and now China. Currently Africa has only one trans-Africa highway from Cairo to Cape Town (Gedecho 2014) which is not sufficient to link all African countries. Africa needs to construct roads, highways, superhighway, railways and waterways to see to it that it is solidly connected. When it comes to infrastructure, Africa needs to do more. Sometimes, apart from poverty and bad planning, you can blame apartness and disconnection among African countries to their political division as their former colonial masters dubiously created it. It becomes much easier for the person travelling from one African country to another through Europe than doing so within Africa. If anything, this is what neo-colonialism is all about. Create chronic dependency almost in everything.

America and now China had good visions and policies that saw them outdo others in the world. When it comes to Africa however, if there were anything colonial rules left behind, was nothing but ignorant, poor and desperate population. Currently, China is doing the same (Bai and Qian (2010); Holslag (2010); and Xu, Ye and Cao (2011) in order to fast-track its development after investing heaving in technology. I would argue that next must be Africa shall it want to turn things around for the better. Africa needs roads and high way from all directions namely east to west, north to south, west to south, north to east and centre to right and left to right.

We have touched on what colonial regime left behind as far as underdevelopment is concerned. Also, if there is anything new postcolonial governments inherited was only their raw materials to sell to the same criminals not to mention low prices they received from the bulks of the produces they exported. This is why we are saying that many Africa's problems lie in its history *vis-à-vis* colonialism and its legacies. No doubt; many postcolonial governments were not well prepared and experienced to run governments, especially when the said governments inherited bankrupt countries due to the fact that the role colonialism played in these countries was to not only exploit colonies but not to ruin them by creating antagonistic environment they would use in the future to ruin Africa even more as it later happened to be. Colonialism left no universities or advanced hospitals, roads and other amenities a country needs to develop in both facets of life.

Africa Needs To Take on Toxic Education....

Although colonial regimes educated some Africans to serve them, when they left it, they left behind crisis as far as education is concerned. Apart from leaving an illiterate continent, they left toxic education that sadly though has never been detoxified. Nyerere (1967) maintains that colonial governments provided education to their colonies not for the intention of enabling the people to build and develop their countries. Instead, colonial governments were motivated by the desire to inculcate their values and getting some locals who would be available to render their service of colonial state. This is why it was next to impossible for post-independence African governments to be put at par with their ex-colonial masters who had the advantages of exploiting them before and after independence. This is not a new knowledge for Africans who bother to study and research things. Therefore, for Africa to turn things around, it must make sure that it invests heavily on infrastructure, administrative infrastructure and structure.

Even if you consider the quality of the manpower colonial regime produced was poorly educated. Nyerere goes on arguing that colonial regime produced just local clerks and junior officials. How do you develop a country with such ill-equipped semi-illiterates? If anything, this was the predicament of Africa whose results are the sufferings and underdevelopment Africa suffers now. This is why we emphasise that Africa needs to use its history to make its case and turn things around based on its experience however bad and traumatising it is. One of the areas that Africa's past experience must address is the creation of the new regime of education made in Africa, for Africa and about Africa. The regime of education that Africa has been under was introduced by colonial regime in conjunction with missionaries whose goals and targets were different from those of Africa. Africa needs to ask itself what such education has delivered or failed to deliver; and how it can be deconstructed. Nyamnjoh (2012) discloses that colonial education emphasises mimicry over creativity which has turned African academics into the tools the West still use even after being independent for over fifty years. This needs to change dramatically whereby Africa ought to revisit and reinvent its own epistemology. African academics ought to lead in this crusade by authoring their own books and influence policymaking bodies in order to come up with a new form of education that is emancipatory. Nyamnjoh makes a great point. You can see how mimicry has affected some of African academics who are smart in cramming what Western biased scholars fabricated and called them philosophy. While some Western thinkers are now questioning their own gurus of education, philosophy and science such as Darwinism which Dennett (1995) calls dangerous, due to using science to justify racism (Dennis 1995) Africans are still gulping the same garbage while they actually negatively affected them more than any human society, particularly when we consider how racist they were. While many Western scholars are divided right between the middle as far as Darwinism is concerned, African ones are silent. Why while Africa is the most affected by the same

141

philosophy? Darwin is believed to be the father of the science of evolution that gave birth to racism that left Africans enslaved and colonies. Another dangerous scientist that African scholars have never taken on among many of this type is Klaatsch, a prominent German evolutionist cited in Bergman (1993) maintaining in that "the blacks came from the gorillas, the whites from the chimpanzees, and the Orientals from the orangutans, and it is for this reason that some races are superior" (p. 2). All this has its roots in Darwinism. For example, Bergman (2004) notes "this stereotype presented in texts is not true of many Negroid people groups, yet reinforces the image that has caused much of the prejudice and fuelled much of the racism in America and the rest of the world" (p. 69). How do African historians, for example, keep such insults in textbooks without questioning while they are harmful to them? Some Western academics compare Darwin to Hitler and find that the former was even worse than the former as Dr. Benjamin Wiker (cited in Ellis 2011) maintains that "many folks just don't like it when you trace a revered scientific icon to an icon of evil . . . . Darwinism is responsible for a lot more destruction than the eugenic fantasies of the Third Reich" (p. 176). What else does Africa need to strike Darwinism out of its textbooks? How much trauma and suffering such display of stereotypical materials have caused to Africans? Don't Africans deserve redress for such crime committed against the whole race? How will the world react today if an African thinker propounds a philosophy showing that whites are morally and physically inferior to Africa that is why they enslaved and colonised them due to the fact that they cannot perform heavy duties? These are the very thorny issues Africa needs to redefine and revisit altogether in order to show all those who have always taken it for a ride to understand the moral, psychological traumatic quagmire it has been in. Doing so aimed at reminding everyone that the issue of turning things around for the better for Africa is not a solely African responsibility. It is the responsibility of the whole world the same way it was in creating all messes Africa has been in for a long time.

Furthermore, Africa still calls criminals such as Livingstone, Vasco da Gama, Mungo Park, Henry Morton Stanley and many more missionaries and explores while they actually were criminals. Africa is still a member of colonial affiliations such as commonwealth, Francophone and others while they actually are traumatising it.

Here we are talking about illiteracy not to mention the rampancy of poverty that coupled with ignorance, costed Tanzania and other African countries greatly. It is obvious that whatever little post-independence African countries got from selling their raw materials went to social services such as education, and health something that forced them to not invest in economic sectors such as industry and the construction of infrastructure. How do you invest while your children are going with empty stomachs?

CPR-Like Administration

If one asks me why the West has always been "kind" to Africa so as to extend aid to it, I would not budge to say CPR namely, they look for Control, Profit and Resources (CPR) not love or morality or anything less than this. Therefore, when they offer aid to African countries that the pauperised, Western countries do it the same way someone performs Cardiopulmonary resuscitation (CPR) where the emphasis is the resuscitation of the person is paramount. Once such a person comes back to life, what follows is slow process of examining, and prescribing remedies which may take longer than expected. The difference however from this example is the fact that the West has always performed this economic CPR on an animal called Africa that they need for its meat, milk, manure, labour and everything. The administration of CPR is not out of love for an animal. It is geared by its products. Understanding the real situation colonial regime left behind, they came up with the aid project all aimed at enabling them to go on getting the supply of raw materials that their home factories needs and markets for their processed goods. With such tick-cow-like relationship, Western countries doubled their wealth. For, they bought raw materials from Africa at low prices. They processed them and sold them back to Africa at hiked prices. This has been going since the inception of slavery and colonialism and other parasitic isms. If anything, this is what Africa needs to turn around shall it want to forge ahead positively. Due to this criminality, I have been a staunch believer in redress of Africa. This is why, the international community is duty bound to help Africa out of its impasse.

I understand that many governments and scholars alike think aid was offered to African countries as goodwill. This was not the case. Colonial powers extended aid even loans with the intention of avoid the suffering for their economies. One can arguably call this bailout of their economies made through aid. It is like a person who partly feeds her or his cow so as to double the production of milk he or she needs to survive. Feeding the cow here is not about the cow but instead it is about self-sustenance if not survival. Unfortunately, up until now, former colonial powers still play the same card.

Apart from handing the reins of power to unexperienced governments, colonial powers, in many countries, left them in the hands of their stooges. You could see this in the DRC, Ivory Coast, Malawi, Kenya, and Zanzibar among others. Other countries that had stable leaders, either those leaders were overthrown, died or became inept so as to produce another crop of corrupt and inept leaders. You could see this in Cameroon, Ghana, Congo, Gabon, Togo, the CAR, Uganda and Burkina Faso among others.

Moyo (2009) notes that:

144

More than US$2 trillion of foreign aid has been transferred from countries to poor over the past fifty years Africa the biggest recipient, by far. Yet regardless of the motivation for aid-giving economic, political or moral- aid has failed to deliver the promise of sustainable economic growth and poverty reduction (p. 28).

However, if you look at how much money that was transferred to the rich countries through capital flight, hiked debt interests that African pay, bad policies, corruption and others, you find that what Moyo cites is a drop in the ocean as far as Africa is concerned. Moyo claim if compared to what Africa loses annually, you find that Africa has always been a loser. Christensen (2009) cites the Christian Aid (2008) claiming that Multinationals corporations (MNCs) cost developing world over USD 160bn annually through mispricing and falsified invoice. If you multiply this amount time over fifty years you get 8tn. Christensen goes on noting that corruption and tax evasion amount to between US$1 trillion and US$1.6 trillion a year: approximately half of this flow originates from developing and transitional economies. Acha, Akpanuko and Unuafe (2013) cite the *Global financial Integrity* (2010) which in its study covering 1970–2008 found that about US$ 1.8 trillion were illegally taken out of Africa. They cite Nigeria as the highest loser at the tune of US$129.6 billion in the period from 1970 to 1996; also see Asongu and Efobi (2016). If you look at who loses much more money than others, you find that it is Africa due to having immense resources and rampant corruption. Collier, Hoeffler and Pattillo (2001) observe that in 1990 Africa had the highest incidences of capital flight. What is 2tn compared to such huge amounts of money Africa loses? Here I am talking about mispricing, tax evasion, and falsification of invoice. Ndikumana (2015 cited in Frantz 2016) maintains that unrecorded capital flights in Africa have increased recently. This means; if all monies siphoned out Africa through tax evasion, capital flight, phoney consultancy and other vices can triple the amount we have calculated above. Frantz found that many African countries lose much money during the electioneering seasons than normal times. For Africa to turn things around, it must seal all holes that for a long time have allowed above discussed crimes. Capital flight, mispricing, falsification of invoice, tax evasion, tax exemption enhanced by corruption in the upper echelons of power, and underestimation of the value of imported property and machineries, *inter alia*, should be addressed ruthlessly shall Africa want to turn things around. Africa must recalibrate its economy by creating factories so as to add value to its raw materials it has always exported.

For Africa to turn things around for the better, it needs to avoid living on CPR that has never brought life to it. Instead, it has exacerbated its malaises pointlessly.

Create Cartels and Localise the Market

It is evident that Africa has been producing a variety of products it sells to the international markets. However, Africa does not have any control over the markets of its products. This makes it vulnerable due to the fact that the markets to which Africa supplies, instead, have an upper hand on prices and supply. For Africa to turn things around for the better, it needs to have an upper hand on its products. Therefore, one of the ways of realising this is for Africa to have its own cartel [s]. This can be done by either forming one African cartel or every country can create its own cartel for the purpose of managing and regulating the market for its products. Nonetheless, one cartel is important for Africa in order to have a powerful bargaining hand in international markets. Jensen and Gibbon, (2007) note that the policies of industrialised countries low international prices and the end product of such policies have always turned Africa, *inter alia*, into a dumpsite for their surplus. By lowering the price, it means industrialised countries are

146

purposely killing Africa economies and farmers altogether. While industrialised countries dump their surpluses; and thereby make money, Africans are losing their capital. This is immoral even though it is not criminal according to the definition of the term which means to commit an act that is prohibited by the law. While African farmers are struggling to feed their families, to take their kids to school, to pay their medical bills and, above all, spare some money for farming, Western farmers are dumping their produces to make more money after satisfying their home market in which much of their produces are used to feed animals. This is not the end of the chain of reaction as far as making profits by exploiting Africa is concerned. To make matters worse, industrialised countries introduce protectionism in doing business with Africa so as to enjoy both markets at home and abroad. Additionally, industrialised countries provide subsidies to their farmers while African farmers are not subsidised by their governments. And third, farmers in the industrialised countries get more profit from suffocating African farmers. Apart from facing surplus dumping in Africa, African farmers have to face other menaces such as drought, bad governance, not to mention competition in the world market which makes their production harder and harder due to the lack of access to the international markets, motivation and returns. This is why Africa has always starved and become poorer and poorer. Dale, *et al.,* (2010) argue that currently over 80 agricultural production in the United States is used to feed animals (page not provided) while humans in poor countries are dying of malnutrition and undernutrition. Ironically, such unfairness is normalised and reinforced under the neoliberal policies. Clover (2003) notes that, in 2003, about 38 million people in Africa faced acute food insecurity; thereby facing the outright risk of famine, with 24,000 dying from hunger daily. The US is the bigger market compare to Africa put together. This shows how, for example, farmers in the US access a reliable market. The situation is the same for all farmers in rich countries. Again, despite enjoying supplying stable markets, the same farmers supported by their countries through subsidies suffocate African markets by dumping their surpluses which is terrible. Africa needs to have the mechanisms and laws that must seriously address this inhumane business.

Looking at the nature of greed and selfishness involved in surplus dumping, Africa needs to protest against such inhumanity perpetrated under the pretext of free market. Also, Africa needs to enact laws that must purposely prevent such surplus dumping. This can only be achieved for African countries through refusing to sign trade agreements with rich countries which, in the main, favour them but not their poor counterparts. Here is where the importance of forming its own cartel[s] for it products becomes more imminent for Africa shall it aspire to turn things around for the better.

To do away with blatant exploitation that many African countries have always faced, they need to form their own cartels of almost everything they produce under a localised market system given that they are the same consumers of processed goods from rich countries which, if organised, African countries can process locally in order to add value to them; and thereby make more money. For instance, under Localised Market Theory, Nigeria, which is a big producer of crude oil but ironically still imports processed oil at a very high price can start process its oil and sell it to African countries which many still imports processed oil from abroad. Why can't African countries raise capital to have their own processing plants in Nigeria which in turn can supply them oil as it pays back the loan it acquired to establish its own processing factories? Why can't say Ivory Coast, the world biggest producers of cocoa, *a fortiori* become the home of chocolate making factories?

Essentially, African countries need to copy what Western countries did in "cartelisation of the market" John, Robert and

Lande (2012) argue that cartels have always been the highest concern of antitrust due to overcharging customers many billions of dollars annually. Under Localisation of Market Theory (Mhango 2015), just like the West, Africa needs to protect its markets as it deters unregulated entry of goods from industrialised countries by applying many conditions among which is for them to secure preferential treatments in such countries as *quid pro quo*. Without forming its cartels, Africa should not expect to develop *ex nihilo*. It cannot be. In the same breath, Jeong (2000) argues that thanks to structural limitations, poor or periphery countries have no choice except to accept the devaluation of their commodities on the world market. When we talk about market, we must specify which market. For, the market established by imperialist countries in London, Paris and Washington will never benefit poor countries in Africa save that they will create more conflicts. Smith (1904 cited in Tencati and Zsolnai 2012) succinctly maintains that "it is not from the benevolence of the butcher, the brewer, or the baker that we expect our dinner, but from their regard of their own interest" (p. 352). By localising their markets, African countries will be protecting, "their regard of their own interest." And by African countries forming their own cartels and market will be able to do away from exploitation and economic. For they will become allies as noted by Sloan, *et al.,* (2010) that "people experiencing oppression, however, do not need magic spells, they need allies" (p. 93). If anything, under localisation of market theory, Africa has magic bullet in its abundant resource given that it will help it to do away with exploitative Western market. Africa needs to assure the West and the world at large that the sheer fear that led to the mistrusts between it and them is unreasonably baseless. Indeed, Africa needs to assure them that it is ready to use its resources to foster positive interdependency and cooperation.

Another issue that we need to address is to examine if the market—that allow rich countries to dump their surplus to poor country–operates legally or illegally? Smith, despite being referred to as the father of the modern economy, ironically, did not bother with such important questions due to the situation of the time he wrote. When it comes to Africa, Smith seems to be a racist. Smith (1976a: 2 cited in Kennedy 2011) maintains that "European prince does not always so much exceed that of an industrious and frugal peasant, as the accommodation of the latter exceeds that of many an African king, the absolute masters of the lives and liberties of ten thousand naked savages" (p. 56). For such a blind and racist thinker, conflict of interests existed only to be exploited and colonised. Currently we have many exploitative markets operating. We cannot talk about the commodity without probing if the said commodity is obtained legally or illegally. So we can trace this weakness from "the father" of modern economy whose bigotry surpasses his rationality. And the market he eulogised, for Africa, has been a root of structural violence in many countries.

However, feminist critique notes that "capitalism has transformed various forms of violence into economic coercion" (Jeong, 2000: 80). Indeed, this is what Smith's highly-glorified market produced for Africa and other poor countries facing exploitation from neoliberal policies. African countries need to protest such settings in order to get a good deal. Instead of concentrating on their farm produces, they must rebel, particularly by stopping the supply of their minerals that rich countries cannot do without. If anything, this devaluation is made at the market that Smith eulogised saying that it is capable of regulating supply and demand not to mention the price. To avoid repeating the same sin the West has always committed by trying to control the market, Africa must control its commodities instead of aspiring to control the market which they do not have control over. By keeping on extracting resources which are sold at lower prices, Africa finds itself amid violence characterised by structural violence perpetrated by governments in order to survive as seen in DRC under America-sponsored dictator Mobutu as we will see later. Jeong adds that "serious conflict is embedded in an inequitable social and economic system, reflected by prolongation of exploitation supported by coercion" (*Ibid.* 31). Africa has always been coerced to abide by the rules of Western market.

When we talk about market, we must specify which market. For, the market established by imperialist countries in London, Paris and Washington will never benefit poor countries save that they will create more conflicts. By localising their markets, African countries will be protecting, "their regard of their own interest." And by African countries forming their own cartels and market will be able to do away from exploitation and economic. For they will become allies as noted by Sloan, *et al.,* (*Ibid.*) that "people experiencing oppression, however, do not need magic spells, they need allies" (page not provided) and these allies for African countries are themselves through unifying Africa. If anything, under localisation of market theory, Africa has magic spells given that it will help it to do away with exploitative Western market.

Is the market operating legally or illegally? Smith did not bother with such important questions due to the situation of the time he wrote. When it comes to Africa, Smith seems to be a racist. For such a blind and racist thinker, conflict existed only to be exploited and colonised. Currently we have many exploitative markets operating. We cannot talk about the commodity without probing if the said commodity is obtained legally or illegally. So we can trace this weakness from "the father" of modern economy whose bigotry surpasses his rationality. And, the market he eulogised, for Africa, has been a root of structural violence in many countries.

The era under which Africa allows its resources to be exclusively being managed by foreign entities must became the thing of the past whereby Africa should reclaim this exclusive rights of managing and supplying its resources in order to benefit and gain from them. De Beers provides an ideal example in which it controls over 65% (Richman 2006) of all diamonds in the world in which African diamond mined from Africa makes a big percentage. Why should De Beers control our diamond as if we cannot control it ourselves? Africa needs to rethink about making new laws that give it exclusive rights of controlling all of its products. Currently, Africa, if it decides, it has enough experts who can manage its resources shall continent puts its house in order. This is Africa's challenge.

Chapter 6

What Africa Should Do Politically?

Rule of Law and Good Governance

After gaining their independence, many African countries cascaded to one-party dictatorship that the Cold War supported and enhanced for the interests of the superpowers up until the enervation of the Cold War Levitsky and Way (2007) in 1991 after the fall of the Berlin Wall that resulted to the collapse of the Union of Soviet Socialist Republics (USSR). At this particular time, almost all African countries were divided right in the middle along capitalism and the then communism the then two superpowers, the United States (US) and the then USSR spearheaded. Many African leaders of the time took advantage of this schism to unconstitutionally and undemocratically stay and overstay in power throughout the Cold War era. Others used this crevice to rob their countries.

Arguably, during the cold war, there was no rule of law in Africa. Instead, Africa was under the cold war rule or cold war laws whereby whatever any country did depended on the orders of its master[s] depending on the side the country was allied with or aligned to. At this point and time, rule of law or good governance was not important for Africa provided that the masters did not like it. This makes the whole concept of rule of law to be capricious and dubious; especially if we ask whose interests does it serve in Africa. This being the case, Africa needs to rethink about introducing the rule of law based on its aspirations and needs.

The lack of rule of law which is a democratic recipe enhanced the creation of unnecessarily big governments in many African countries if not all. As if bigger governments were not enough, due to the lack of rule of law, African rulers got a loophole of not only forming big governments but also ruling accountably and irresponsibly. They involved themselves in corruption topped up with extravagance, embezzlement of public funds and securing more loans from rich countries so as to create even bigger and milliards of problems for Africa. Ota and Cas (2008) note that small states tend to have bigger governments. They found that in 2004, for example, the total expenditures in small states were 37% of GDP in average (p. 6). If you ask how much such countries spent on social services, you will find that it was less than what the governments burnt. Africa, apart from being poor, does not need big governments. Madrick (2010) argues that "sizeable government has been essential to growth and prosperity among the world's rich nations including America" (p. 7). If rich nations opted to have sizeable governments despite their economic and financial muscles, what of poor and destitute African countries which live on begging and handouts from the same nations?

When it comes to good governance, this volume will go with the definition of the concept based on the definition of the UNDP (1997: 2-3 cited in Gisselquist 2012) which defines governance as:

> The exercise of economic, political and administrative authority to manage a country's affairs at all levels', which 'comprises mechanisms, processes and institutions through which citizens and groups articulate their interests, exercise their legal rights, meet their obligations and mediate their differences (p. 3).

Importantly, it must be underscored that good governance as a concept has many definitions; and it means different things in different contexts (Grindle 2007). Again, considering the above definition, in Africa, currently, good governance either is in the books or in the lips of politicians. For, there are a few governments that meet the qualifications of the definition, especially when it comes to legal rights and meeting their obligations. This is why, *inter alia*, Africa has always lagged behind in development, human rights and prosperity. In many African countries, legal lights are for the ruling elites. It is this cabal of carbuncular people that gets almost whatever it needs even what it does not need. When it comes to the common citizenry, they are but the beasts of burden that pick up the tab.

Practically, Africa has no good governance but *boob* governance. If it were there, things would have taken another turn from the worse to the better. When it comes to good governance, Africa scores poorly. I think Africa is the leading continent when it comes to lacking good governance which is very instrumental to bring about change and development. If there is anything Africa boasts of currently is nothing but having unnecessarily big and irresponsible governments with a lot of discretionary powers. Therefore, the first advice one can give to Africa is that it must underscore the fact that good governance is nothing one can import or being forced to embark on. Like any success in any family, good governance needs to emanate from internal instead of being imposed by external forces. Africa needs to understand that there is no way it can forge ahead without good governance as one of the prerequisites for its development. With good governance, Africa will be able to manage its affairs and resources. But keeping on having uselessly big governments, Africa will keep on sinking even deeper to abjection and uselessness. African big governments, apart having a *carte blanche vis-à-vis* using resources and spending public money, they are renowned for their taste of extravagance. They spend as pleased even in unproductive and unwanted things whereas the majority of the citizenry are suffering from manmade miseries such as ignorance, poverty and lack of services the governments are supposedly duty bound to provide as one of their constitutional responsibilities.

Big governments consume a big chunk of budget through nihilism and corruption resulting from cronyism, nepotism, megalomania by those running them. What makes things ever worse is the fact that many African big governments are made of friends, relatives and courtiers but not competent people. As if this is not enough, even when it comes to employments, they follow the same line of technical know who. As if this is not enough, the same official employed based on nepotism and other evils are renowned for their notorious rent-seeking behaviours, embezzlement, not working, and the likes.

When the fifth Tanzania president John Pombe Magufuli came to power in 2015, he shocked the world to find that some government officials were spending public money on ferrying their girlfriends to Dubai to spend weekends not to mention other members of public boards convening their board meeting abroad which is but a typical replica for many African countries suffering from endemic and systemic bad governance and corruption. On this, Magufuli advised board members not only to travel abroad but also to stop convening board meetings in hotels whereas the departments or parastatals they oversaw had boardrooms. He advised them to convene their board meetings under trees if need be. Interestingly, such trips were booked in first class which even officials of rich countries do not use. To arrest this problem, Magufuli put a stop on foreign trips. The *Daily Nation* (9 November, 2015) quoted Presidential Press Secretary as saying, "Unless there is an urgent undertaking abroad one could be allowed to travel after getting permission from the President or the Chief Secretary." What made this criminality even abhorrently nauseatic is the fact that such girlfriends and their cucklods used to scoop *per diems* for committing such crimes against poor citizenry of their poor country. The paper added that *per diems* for a foreign travel in Tanzania ranged from US$365 for mid-level managers and senior officers to US$420 for directors and principal officers. By taking on such abuses and malpractices, all of the sudden, Magufuli became a new kid on the bloc and a rare creature among African leaders if not the toast of the town in the political scene so as to be applauded the world over. It only needs resolve and daring spirit to take on such counterproductive and irresponsible behaviours. This adds another facet that such big governments are not only squandering public funds but they also are there for the only one purpose of self-serving and live large while the majority of the people are dying of preventable and treatable diseases due to the lack of funds. While a select few is enjoying such humongous amount of money, the majority of those they pretend to serve lives under a dollar a day. Essentially, there is nothing miraculous or magical that Magufuli did. It is only the acceptance and understanding of fulfilling his responsibilities to his people as their president that enhanced his actions towards graft and self-serving habits. Africa needs such new awakening aimed at fulfilling the dreams of being independent, truly independent. Africa is on its trajectory to development if a new crop of leaders will be voted in. new blood and brains will bring new way of looking at things. They will usher in a new awakening aimed at propelling Africa to its place in the future. Awiti and Scott (2016) note that "in Tanzania President Magufuli campaigned on a platform of integrity and the restoration of the ethos of hard work" (p. 4) which he seems to deliver within a short time shall he stay the course. Warunga (2016: 21 cited in Chingono 2016) notes that the new Tanzanian president, John Magufuli, who has "shaken Tanzania to its core as [he] went in search of" corrupt public officials, and who has substantially cut down government expenditure" (p. 208).

To move forward reliably, Africa needs to mercilessly and seriously arrest malpractices in public offices. Time for a select few to live in opulence while the majority is languishingly rooting in abject poverty must become a thing of the past for Africa. Rich countries were able to break away from abjection by the way of accountability based on good governance and frugal tendency in spending public money and using public resources.

Divorce the Demigods and Fear Tigers

To do away with what has been going on since independence, I suggest that there must be a paradigm shift whereby the new style of leadership based on accountability and competence must be introduced continentally. African presidents have too much discretionary power obtained by the way of constitutional stipulations that put them above the law. There is no doubt that a president or prime minister who is above the law can deliver. Human nature dictates that whenever a human is put above the law, he or she will use it for personal gains. Here is where first families become undeservedly rich while those they lead suffer thanks to this legalised illegality. In addressing Africa's fate, African politicians and the burden the put on the shoulders of their people for their extravagance, Meredith (2005) observes that "African governments and the vampire-like politicians who run them are regarded by the populations they rule as yet another burden they have to bear in the struggle for survival" (page not provided). Indeed, this is the evil Africans need to fight in order to forge ahead. There is no way Africa can develop with and under such irresponsible, corrupt, greedy and myopic governments that use power as a conduit for self-serving and robbing the citizenry. However, Rose-Ackerman and Palifka (2016: 263) argue that open economies with greater participation in international trade tend to have big governments that may not necessarily encourage corruption. The main arguments that Rose-Ackerman and Palifka make is that big and developed economies are the ones that need bigger governments based on liberalisation and international trade that many African governments lack. Although African government participate in international trade, they end up becoming losers; thereby a burden to their people due to trade in raw materials without added value. Plümper and Martin (2003) differ with Rose-Ackerman and Palifka arguing that their conclusion lacks the theoretical model. I, too, concur with such an argument, especially if we consider how bigger governments need bigger sources of income in order to maintain them. I think for poor countries such as African ones to have unnecessarily bigger governments are one of colonial hangovers and signs of greed myopia and selfishness. For, it is only possible and suitable for an insane person to have bigger expenditure than income. This is simple to comprehend. It does not need a degree in economics or commerce. Conversely, Spear (2007) argues that despite carving Africa colonial powers neglected it especially in the early colonial times by neglecting; and not investing in their colonies substantially something that has gone one up until modern times with the exception of oil producing countries.

Apart from South Africa which is also struggling, there is no African big government that fits in this assumption. Even countries such as Equatorial Guinea, Gabon and Nigeria that produce oil, still do not fully participate in international trade at the tune of their Middle East counterparts. Instead, they seem to be an antithesis of the argument that of the spirit of the unification of Africa that many African founders envisaged to end up felled by their successors in many countries due to political greed of every president wanting to lord it over his country not to mention foreign manoeuvers against the idea that would deny foreign powers easy freeloading of African resources.

Underscoring the extravagance and bigness of African governments, Africa needs to trim them down in order to save the money that will be invested in other important areas such as commerce, education and health among others. Goldsmith (2000) argues that African states do not spend large shares of GNP in employing high ratios of population in governmental jobs (page not provided). When it comes to well-paying jobs, many African governments, especially corrupt ones, prefer to employ foreign expatriates that they can manipulate to do as pleased provided they are getting their cuts. Factually, Africa has have *experts* of almost everything. Ifejirika (2014) argues that historically "Africans were seen as mental Lilliputians or dwarfs, halfwits, adult-children and emotional idiots who often engaged in crying, weeping laughing or quarrelling" (p. 48) so as to need foreign expatriates to nurse and look after them especially during colonial times. Now Africa has been independent for over a half of a century. Why should it keep on depending on foreign expatriates instead of creating its own? Arguably, by depending on foreign expatriates while their own people are expatriates abroad, such governments are no different from Lilliputians, halfwits and zombies that need to be kicked out of power so that they can give room to competent people to run the business of their countries. If there is anything such corrupt and clap governments are experts in and good at is nothing but begging, embezzling and squandering public funds. This is why many African governments have never felt pity of begging and self-dressing down.

In a nutshell, Africa needs rule of law, good governance and sizeable governments made of competent and probable people but not political quacks, stooges, self-seekers, self-servers, corrupt dictators and their cronies who for over five decades have squandered a lot of resources and money Africa would have spent on providing social and developmental services. The only way for Africa to do away with big and do-nothing governments is only through empowering the common people by giving them the power to install and sack governments as they deem fit. This way Africa will be able to leapfrog from where it has been confined since parasitic colonial systems were introduced. Checks and balances must be applied to letter and spirit of the law. All constitutions that put presidents above the law need to be amended to see to it that everybody is being under the law but not above it. Leaders should be evaluated now and then to see if they have delivered on their promises and the expectations of their constituencies. And this is not difficult to do. Africa can learn from Western countries whose leaders are always probed by their constituency.

Rethink African Democracy

Democracy is not a new concept to Africa. However, Africa has always imported democracy despite having its brands of democracy. There has always been a problem in defining democracy by only aping Western societies that are wrongly viewed as the harbingers of democracy while they are not. Gibbon, Bangura and Ofstad (1992) maintain that "theorists tend to work their way backwards by identifying the end values of democracy in Western societies" (p. 49) blindly and dubiously so to speak. Such backward-looking approach has also been applied in many concepts such as economy, behaviour and many more. Africa can use this approach only by revisiting and exploring its history but not that of the Western countries that seek to use their trajectory to wherever they go or they are as an international standard through their universalisation gimmicks as were started by Durkheim, Hegel, Kant, and others. I do not think that there can be a single prototype in everything. In dealing with democracy, I will seek to challenge such thinking by proving that the source of democracy is not in the Western society but instead it emanates from all societies to mean different things. My hunch will dwell on Africa given that this volume is about Africa. I have taken this angle due to the fact that meanings we give to concepts are naturally relative depending on what we want to achieve or deal with. This is why Western democracy has never worked well in Africa. This is why, despite having strings attached to it, Western democracy is still wrongly viewed as the ideal and universal one.

161

I will tackle African democracy this in this chapter. Before going into details on how democracy has its home and origin in Africa, It is noteworthy to briefly revisit the history of the current Western democracy that Africa has had since attaining independence. Etymologically, the word democracy comes from two Greek words namely *demos* or people (qua "native adult male residents of a polis") and *kratos* (Ober 2008: 3) or rule to mean the power of the people or the rule of the people, the majority but not the minority. Mphele in Theletsane (2012) concurs saying that "'democracy' comes from the original term dēmokratía which was coined between the 5th and 4th century BC by the Greeks from two words: dêmos which denotes 'people', and kratos denoting 'power'. The word dēmokratía means that the ruling power shall rest with the people.

However, after Greeks used democracy to no avail, it was popularised by colonial Europe in the era they invaded and occupied other continents such as Africa, the Americas and others. Mann (2005) faults this democracy blaming it for committing crimes against humanity such as colonialism, slavery, genocide, massacre, poisoning and others which he calls murderous cleansing. Yes, it is this democracy that perpetrated genocide in Rwanda where the so-called democratic countries such as France provided support in the preparations genocide not to mention Western democratic countries that turned a blind eye on Rwanda when the 1994 genocide was committed. It is very same democracy that has enabled Western countries to perpetually exploit Africa. It is this exploitative and suspicious democracy I am trying to question in order to get the answer that will help Africa to go back to its democracy. Given that the essence of this volume is to show how Africa can turn various things around for its development, I am not going to dwell on the origin of Western democracy.

When it comes to the current crop of democracy that Africa has it can be traced to the end of the cold war. Due to this abrupt fall, the early 90s saw a changed world after the fall of the Berlin Wall which installed the US and the West in general as a sole hegemony of the world. Since then, democracy became synonymous with aid the West offers to Africa in particular Barya (1993). The crowning of one hegemonic power saw the rise of the influence of the International Financial Institutions (IFIs) as the economic mouthpieces of the West. Before the fall of the Berlin Wall democracy was a very expensive item on the menu. Countries that were allied with the East were not necessarily exposed to democracy; and, like their boss, the USSR, did not need democracy but instead, they needed either communism or socialism but not democracy. Ironically, even countries that were allied to the West that is now hollering about democracy did not have or need democracy but instead all they needed was capitalism. This is why tin pot dictators such as Joseph Mobutu (Zaire then the DRC), Idi Amin (Uganda), Omar Bongo (Gabon), Jomo Kenyatta (Kenya) and many more burst into the scene; and thereafter the West mollycoddled and supported them conditionally the help it in exploiting their countries up until the fall of the Berlin Wall. Some of dictators brought the independence of their countries while others were just cloned by the West to serve its interests. After the introduction of multiparty politics that despots seem to have easily hijacked, the West led by the US still preach democracy tied on free markets and liberalisation of economies of African countries. Essentially, this is what the West envisaged after the fall of the Berlin Wall. Bond (2006) maintains that "the role of the US state in Africa–prior, during and after the Cold War–is invariably tied to corporate extraction of resources and backed by military might" (p. 30).

If there are any political relics that the two camps through their clientelism and patronage left for Africa are nothing but corrupt and dictatorial regimes either made through the shoddy ballot box of *coup d'états*. History has it that during the cold war stint there were dictators on both sides of the divide. Call them notoriously benevolent or malevolent dictators, the truth is that they were there doing the same thing under different banners. The first thing these dictators did was overstay in power messing and squandering the resources and finances of their countries in order to unconstitutionally remain in power. It is at this time the culture of keeping big armies was cultivated so as to haunt Africa up until now. Thanks to the proxy enmity and wars of the two master camps, African countries became sworn enemies without any logical reasons emanating from their plans, programs and desires. The two superpowers of the time seized the chance; thereby selling weapons on top of ideologies. They added more spice in this antagonism by selling two opposing ideologies namely capitalism and socialism or communism. African conmen took up these ideologies and ruined their countries. There were those who were more fanatic than their masters such as Ivorian former president Felix Houphouet Boigny, Kenyatta (Kenya), Hastings Kamuzu Banda (Malawi) and many more who hated whoever that did not subscribe to this exploitation made in West. Others became staunch followers of socialism. Such were Kenneth Kaunda (Zambia) Julius Nyerere (Tanzania) Ahmed Sekou Toure (Guinea), Kwame Nkrumah (Ghana) and many more depending on the side one was stationed in this cold war era. Although both side accused each other of being stooges of colonialism, with the exception of Nyerere, almost all ideologies were exploitative and foreign to Africa.

On their side, dictators, be they benevolent or malevolent, they defined democracy according to their wishes and terms. They used to convene shoddy elections and won with 99.99% percent. I remember when I was young, our first president used to compete against darkness. Whenever the results were announced, we could go to the streets to celebrate the victory of the president. You would see people coming from up country hundreds of kilometres to congratulate the winner even if they knew that they put a wrong person in right place to end up turning things around for his advantage. Huntington (1996) maintains that democracy is responsible for making a society more parochial but not more cosmopolitan, as it has been maintained due to the coloniality of those believing so. Despite such underperformance, the same is still referred to as a modern concept while what it does, especially for Africa is as archaic as the crimes it brought in.

When it comes to the modern democratisation we are evidenced in Africa there is nothing democratic but the extension of colonialism in a different style. Barya (*Ibid.*) notes that "the new political conditionalities have nothing to do with the desire of Western countries to actually encourage democracy in Africa" (p. 16). Instead, democracy is used as a ruse to help imperialistic and hegemonic countries to get away with murder. If democracy was *sine qua non* with the current world dispensation, the first countries to need it would have been China Middle East emirs and kingdoms and Russia but not Africa that has, for some times, partly exercised it.

Due to the deficit and abracadabra of the current regime of democracy as the West superimposes on others, I would argue that Africa needs its typical African democracy that enhanced it to thrive. Before the introduction of colonialism, Africans were ruled by kings and chiefs as the United Kingdom, Denmark and other countries are ruled. The difference however is that kinghood and chieftainship in Africa came with the responsibilities for those bearing them to make sure that they look after their subjects. In many African kingdoms and chieftainships kings had to make decision based on the consensus. Julius Nyerere cited in Wiredu (1995) maintains that "in our original societies we operated by consensus" (p. 53) Nyerere's claim is supported by Kenneth Kaunda cited in the same noting that "in our original societies we operated by consensus. An issue was talked out in solemn conclave until such time as agreement could be achieved" (p. 53). And indeed, democracy is about consensus based on majoritanism.

Furthermore, Kanu (n.d year) maintains that democracy existed in Africa long before the arrival of Europeans (p. 1) who also did not bring any democracy but colonialism. He cites the Oyo Empire, and Igbo of Eastern Nigeria that had many democratic institutions such as oyomesi, the council of seven non-royal wards of the city of Oyo whose leader was known as Boshrun, the Ogbon, the second council that was responsible for checks and balances of the empire, and Are-Ona-Kakanfo, the military commander of the Empire; also see Louw (1998) who ties democracy and the concept of African Ubuntu or humanness. Arguably, democracy, just like any other concepts, is a human trait based on the fact that humans' lives revolve around agreements and disagreements reached through dialogue. I view democracy like food which its preparations differ from one society to another. However, its role to human sustenance is always the same. Some spice their foods while others do not. Again, food is food and nobody can lay claim to have discovered it. This is why in many African languages; democracy is not a new term like computer and others. Khama (1970: 6 cited in Mhango 2016) traces the concept in some African societies citing examples such as Tswana who called it *Paso ya batho ka batho* or the "rule of the people by the people" (p. 139). Mhango goes ahead by finding the meaning of democracy in Zulu which is called *Yeningi* while in other languages; the concept is adopted so as to sound as it is. Swahili call it *demokrasia* to show how this word is new in their language.

Essentially, Western democracy–thanks to the backing of colonialism and neo-colonialism–throve over others by either denying the existence of the concept in other non-Western societies or demonising them so as to look undemocratic. Again, if democracy existed only in Western societies alone, why had it taken long time to be exercised? I think; if Western societies were democratic, they would not have colonised others due to the fact that democracy is not only against dictatorship but all types of exploitation, inequality, colonialism, hegemony and many more.

Looking at the above example, you can call this African democracy that was suitable to its environment provided that it functioned well apart from showing the existence of a political system that catered for the population. Skinner (1998) maintains that "some African scholars declare that there were traditional forms of democracy, autocracy, monarchy, and oligarchy in state-organized societies as well as stateless societies in their pre-colonial history" (p. 21). So, too, this democracy was not as conditional, expensive and elusive the Western is. Again, if the UK can be deemed as a democracy, scholars who claim that African kinghood and chieftainships had some elements of democracy are dead right. Olutunji (2011) maintains that there are different forms of democracy. This is obvious, especially when it comes to the application and interpretation of the concept. It is the simple logic that the UK is under the monarch and yet it is referred to as a democracy. This is controversial and a double standard in that what the UK kinghood saves as the symbol of the nation is the same African kinghood saved. Ironically, the same British monarch sabotaged African kinghood and chieftainships simply because they were not democratic. Who voted for the queen of England? Why was it logical and important for the UK to have a queen or king but not African societies? I am not intending to defend African kinghood and chieftainships. But when I look at the history of their services, I find that, sometimes, some were better than the current corrupt so-called democratic governments that spend much money to convene shoddy elections that end up being rigged.

As it has proved to be, Western democracy is suitable for the West based on its traditions the same way African democracy

167

was for Africans in their environment. This is why on the one hand the British still revere their monarch while on the other hand demonises other monarchies as if monarchies are different.

What those who impose their democracy on other forgot is the fact that if they were able to rebel against undemocratic systems in Europe, Africans too would rebel against theirs so as to come up with their unique form of democracy suitable for their environment and interests the same way the Western democracy does to the West. Mhango (2015) wonders how Africans allowed colonial powers to abolish their kingdoms while maintaining theirs. Africa was colonised under the British, Portuguese and Spaniard kinghood. I am sure Africans would rebel and come up with their own democracy with roots in their traditions the same way they rebelled against white supremacy when they interacted with white people and discovered their brutality and uncivility so, too, claim the rights of equality. Whites too did not think Africans were as equal human beings as they were. But slowly, after intermingling and interacting with them and discovered their generosity and sense of equality, they rebelled against their racism and supremacy.

Before being forcefully taken to the world wars, Africans used to wrongly perceive a white person as a unique creature. But after fighting with, sleeping with their women and witnessed them dying like them, they realised that they were all mortals something whites were not able to appreciate and discover.

Another way of looking at democracy is through looking at the US and France that are touted as the champions of revolutions that brought democracy to the world (O'Kane 2004: 89-11 cited in Olutunji, 2011). Ironically, these two countries are renowned for their racism against Africans. You wonder; if really democracy meant equality, equity, equal rights and humanity, why did it take generations for these country to abandon racial discrimination not to mention colonialism and neo-colonialism we currently still face. You can see how hypocritical and chimerical this democracy the West propagates is. Ruetschlin and Asante-Mohamed (2013) note that Americans always claim that their "nation's highest challenge is to create a democracy that truly empowers people of all backgrounds, so that we all have a say in setting the policies that shape opportunity and provide for our common future" (page not provided). Is there any meaningful that America has ever introduced to any country? Refer to its toppling of patriotic leaders all over the world who refused to be in the same bed with it selling their people.

After suffering from many coup *d'états* be they military or competitive authoritarian regimes (Levitsky and Way 2010) which became an extension of one ruling party or stolen multiparty elections, the West made the world to believe that elections are the magic bullet to these problems. After superimposing its brand of democracy to Africa, the West knew how expensive their democracy will be, especially for poor African countries. So, too, the West knew or if it did not, saw how elections were stolen so as to lack fairness and freedom yet, they kept quiet as long as their interests were safeguarded. Some regimes were allowed to rig elections as a temporal reprieve for the West to find suitable stooges that they would trust and use in this new and post-cold war dispensation. Arguably, despite its beauties and goodies, Western democracy has always been expensive for Africa so as to force it to pointlessly depend on the West that uses the same opportunity to control African governments. The West has taken advantage of the expensiveness of their democracy to tamper with African affairs in order to safeguard their interests. Huntington (1996) maintains that "politicians in non-Western societies do not win elections by demonstrating how Western they are" (p. 39); instead, for those who rig elections, demonstrate how adaptive and manipulative they are. You can see this in Africa, especially in the early 1990s when stinking despots all of the sudden transformed themselves into democrats after the fall of the Berlin Wall that offered the West the ruse of superimposing multiparty politics in Africa (Sklar 1983). In Kenya in 1992, a long time despot, Daniel arap Moi, convened the first multiparty and won so as to win again in 1997 thereby serving two terms the multiparty constitutions stipulate. In the following year in Gabon, its former despot, Omar Bongo did exactly the same and thereby survived up until he died in power in 2009. In Gabon and Togo, manipulations of multiparty democracy did not end up with long time despots. They were able to die in power and pass the baton on to their children who are still in power even today. In the above mentioned countries where long time rulers do not think about relinquishing power, the situation was the same. For Africa to turn things around for the better, it needs to bring such dynasties to an end. Doing so will allow new blood and brains to come in and change the countries hugely mismanaged by such dynasties for a long time.

Basically, African despots beat the West at its game. However, the loser here is none other than the citizenry that has gone on being under either the despots themselves or their children. So, too, the West has never lost in this game of political gimmicks. Like African despots, the West used democracy and elections to entrench itself in African politics. Elections based on multiparty politics were used as a reminder and shake up for African rulers. The West wanted them to understand that the new sheriff was in the town as far as safeguarding the interests of the West was concerned. This shows how the West used democracy to force despots to toe their line without bothering about the interests and wellbeing of the citizens in countries under corrupt and despotic rules.

If there are leaders who can push their countries ahead economically they can be left to rule for a long time provided that they are not becoming dictators or corrupt.

Africa Must Rethink about Cutting down Milex

If there is any lossmaking investment that Africa has for a long time undertaken is nothing but its armies. It is not only armies but big and do-nothing armies. If they have anything they do, many armies in Africa are used by rulers to intimidate and silence dissent voices. Many African countries spent much money on weapons (Stroup; Gupta, De Mello and Sharan 2001 cited in Hopkin and Rodriquez-Pose 2007). We know that African countries spend a lot of money purchasing weapons and maintaining big and do-nothing military whose job is nothing but protecting sitting despots. I say African militaries are do-nothing due to the fact that the enemies they are created to confront are either imaginary or colonial imposed than real. Although many African armies think they are there to repel enemies, they are themselves the enemy of the people due to how they treat them. What do you call or define the armies that intimidate and stop citizens to voice their angers or opposition to the ruling governments or ruling parties that abuse their mandate in power?

Arguably, Africa's enemies are within itself but not outside of it. Those who keep such armies are the very enemies Africa needs to fight tooth and nail. For, they use and spend public money to remain in power while exploiting and terrorising the same people they purportedly claim to protect. I do not know if the armies and police that unconstitutional governments that have been in power for a long time use to intimidate and silence the population are what Africa deserves for its security. Whose security if at all they are using to serve a few dictators who have turned their countries into private estates as it currently is in the case of Angola, Burundi, Chad, Congo, DRC, Equatorial Guinea, Eritrea, Ethiopia, Gabon, Gambia, Lesotho, Mauritania, Swaziland, Sudan, Togo, Rwanda, Uganda, and Zimbabwe where long time rulers do not think about vacating the reins of power? Again, when you confront such rulers to step aside after exploiting and failing their countries, they will call you the enemy of the nation. For them, national security is about their survival but not about their countries. What they call national security is nothing but their own security even if it comes and means the insecurity of their countries.

Another farfetched enemy is nothing but the division among African countries. However, corrupt and inept rulers like it and do not see it as an enemy given that it enables them to remain in power illegally. After dividing Africa into modern-day weak states in Berlin Germany in 1884, colonial powers created enmity and disharmony among African countries so as to use it to perpetually exploit them. This was purposely conceived and done aimed at creating future clients for weapons Western and other military advanced countries produce and sell to Africa to stagnate and arrest its development. Former colonial powers knew that enmity created would unendingly force African countries to hate and suspect one another. They experienced this in Europe before the break of the so-called world wars I and II even if they actually were not. Mhango (2015; 2016) tackles this issue deeply. Thies (2007) argue that there are several ways to reconcile the existence of relatively weak states in Africa, despite the fact that predatory theory would expect increased extraction as a result of the competing internal and external pressures. Ironically, thanks to the enmity colonialism created and external threats, many African countries' enemies are none other than their African sisters in the neighbourhood. This is why most of them are spending much of their GDPs on purchasing weapons from the same colonial masters that divided and partitioned them. African countries need affinity and connectivity but not enmity and detachment. So, too, military expenditure can nicely be measured by comparing what it consumes to the country's GDP in order to see how a burden it is. How much do African countries spend militarily? Perlo-Freeman, Perdomo and Sköns (2011) answer the question disclosing that:

On average, military spending in African countries was 1.8 per cent of GDP in 2007, down from 3.7 per cent in 1999. A few countries had shares well above the 2007 average, such as Burundi (4.9 per cent), Djibouti (4.1 per cent) and Angola (3.9 per cent). The military burden of some countries—including Angola, Burundi, Ethiopia, Rwanda and Sierra Leone—has fallen heavily since 1999 (p. 199).

If you look at countries that heavily spend on the military you find that they are among the poorest and less developed compared to other African countries. Yet, despite that, they spend heavily on a lossmaking area. Apart from causing inequality in the distribution of country's budget, the same is exacerbating poverty and insecurity, especially by creating home threats resulting from disgruntled populations. To avoid this threat, rulers in these countries heavily and solely depend on the military they prefer to remain in power illegally and unconstitutionally. Yet still, donor countries still offer them aid and loans to waste in such expenditures provided that such countries keep on receiving orders from them not to mention keeping them divided. This is obvious due to the fact that some countries have no resources or geopolitical meaning. Again, if and when African countries are kept divided the fear of their neighbours and of unknown will be perpetuated for the weakening of Africa even further. As indicated earlier, when African countries are kept as divided as the colonial powers created them, they will surely keep on purchasing weapons from the same countries that weakened them. Given that arms selling is a "money making business" (Young and Godlee 2007) former colonial powers, and other arms-producing companies and countries would not like to see it affected in any way. For, doing so, does affect their countries economically and financially due to the fact that arms-making industries employ many people not to mention those who benefit from selling arms.

One of the ways of reducing military spending for African countries is through harmonising their relationships. This means; they need to turn around their colonially-divided setting that was purposely created to weaken and force African countries to purchase weapons from their ex-colonial masters and later other arms-producing countries for their self-destruction. Africa needs to beat swords into ploughshares shall it want to turn things around for the better. Historically, this is what made Europe survive its warring past so as to become a world economic power house. After fighting two big wars Europeans called World War, they decided to cooperate so as to survive. This did not come out of choice but necessity. Africa too needs to learn this in order to survive. Doing so will avert the threats and fear of the unknown of one country pointlessly confronting one another militarily. Normally, it is enemies who fight but not friends. By harmonising their relationships, African countries will not only avert conflict; and thus cooperate but will also deconstruct the division and animosity colonial powers created for their detriment. Also, by harmonising their relationship, Africa countries will be able to invest the money they would have to spend on unnecessary wars to other service. I know very well. It is difficult to convince African countries to reunite and form one big and powerful country. However, they still can harmonise their relationships in order to eliminate unnecessarily and megalomaniac military expenditure which the fear and suspicion of each other have always engineered. I am sure; after experiencing the rewards of harmonised relationship, African countries will be able to see the bigger picture of the unification of Africa as a step towards Africa's total emancipation from the miseries it has faced since colonial era.

Apart from cooperation and harmonisation of relationships, African countries need to introduce or strengthening already-existing true democratic systems of running their states. For, doing so will make dependency on military muscles redundant in many countries ruled by despots supported by the military. Dunne and Perlo-Freeman (2003 citing Rosh, 1988; Hewitt, 1991; Maizels and Nissanke, 1986) maintaining that democratic countries tend to spend less on military than non-democratic one. Therefore, democratic states should put their military to production of other non-military projects. Fan, Yu and Saurkar (2008) note that military capital bears a little in relations to productivity whereby Africa spent more in military since 2000 compared to other continents such as Asia and Latin America at the tune of roughly 27–34 percent of GDP. To avert such wastage of money and resources to keep do-nothing armies, Africa needs to divert its military personnel to productive projects such as agriculture, construction of infrastructure, research and others. You can see this on many African soldiers. Most of them–thanks to doing nothing–have grown tummies as the sign of not being well utilised mentally and physically. Bellied soldiers cannot do anything as far as the protection of the country is concerned. For those who care to look at African military and police personnel will agree with me that most of them are obese thanks to be well fed on top of soliciting additional monies by the way of corruption and extortion. Compare them with their counterparts in the West. They are two different creatures ethically and physically.

Keeping do-nothing armies dry the treasuries of African countries so as to reduce the monies that would be allocated to other important social services and other productive areas such as infrastructure, trade and investment among others. Smaldone (2006) that "nevertheless, in Africa–as elsewhere–milex not only competes with other public spending programmes, but also affects the allocation of available public goods and broader socioeconomic conditions" (p. 18). Here we are talking of misdirection of monies and resources. There is yet another facet of keeping do-nothing armies, especially in the countries heavily suffering from endemic and institutionalised corruption

(Hellsten and Larbi 2006). Much military procurement tenders and expenditure in many African countries involve corruption due to the fact that military budgets are not audited just like other ministries' budgets; they always involve a closed process (Henk and Rupiya 2001) which offers some motivations for corruption and rent-seeking practices in the armies. This is why when you look at budgetary distribution in Africa you find that military expenditures are assigned more money than social services. This led (Nafziger and Auvinen 2002) to draw the conclusion that increasing military allocations in very poor countries may produce downright starvation and destitution which is imminent in many African countries ruled by corrupt and predacious rulers who use the military to protect them and thereby remain in power unconstitutionally. All this is done under the pretext of national security. d'Agostino, Dunne and Pieroni (2012) maintain that allegations of corruption in the military in Africa are neither infrequent nor unexpected; also see Tiongson and Davoodi (2000). In many corrupt countries, such allegations have become the face of the military. Many African armies are as corrupt as those they defend. And they know too well the dangers of what they do. So, too, they know how civilians know the role they play in their suffering not to mention the hatred the general public has against them.

Furthermore, military expenditures affect economic and human development adversely. To remedy this, Africa needs to not only cut down military size but also reduce the reliance on military based on fabricated fear. Deger and Sen (1991 cited in Murshed and Sen 1995) maintain that there are trade-offs with education and health which negatively affect human capital in many African countries. For Africa to advance, it needs to turn such expenditures around; and thereby invest heavily in human development as opposed to military maintenance that for a long time has never produced any momentum for development. For, there is no way Africa can keep on begging and borrowing to end up investing in and spending on such unproductive projects. Africa's past military expenditures must act as a catalyst to changing things to its advantage. If Africa decides, the big chunk of its budget that is spent on military can be directed to other important expenditures. This is feasible now, particularly after the African Unity (AU) declared *coup d'états* illegal in 1999 (Omorogbe 2011). Africa needs to use take this opportunity to put its armies to other uses just like the developed world in which armies are always involved in invention and doing other productive activities such as saving people during calamities and other such uses.

Another important thing that Africa needs to do is re-educate its military so that they can assume the new roles they are going to be assigned.

Chapter 7

Africa Still Has the Wherewithal for Development

In my book *Africa Reunite or Perish*, I generally addressed various striking issues pertaining to how Africa has been underdeveloped. To the contrary, this volume aims at unravelling what Africa can do to turn things around; and therefrom become prosperous just like other continents. Such leapfrog may enable Africa to play a crucial role in international affairs. However, Africa may turn things around for the better conditionally that Africa must change the way things are now. If Africa meets this condition among others, arguably, I see all possibilities for Africa to tip the balance in international affairs. Africa will not only tip the balance of the world economy if it does its home work well and carefully but also will become prosperous and respectable. It will do away with the beggarliness and desperation it has suffered for long simply because it allowed itself to become the backyard of the world. Many hyper-iconised and eulogised European racist scholars such as G. W. F. Hegel, Darwin, Ibn Khaldun, François-Marie Arouet (Voltaire), Ibn Sina or Avicenna, David Hume, Emanuel Kant, Ibn Qutaybah and others, viewed Africa as an android that will never do anything meaningful for itself while at the same time it has for many years contributed immensely for the prosperity of the world. Nonetheless, things have now changed. Africa is evolving accidentally. I am saying accidentally due to the fact that whatever levels of development achieved are not the creatures of Africa's plans or making. On its side however, the *Economics* (November 2, 2012) differs from such racist thinkers noting that "plenty of pundits foresee a bright future for Africa south of the Sahara" due to the fact that resources and demographic dividends will propel Africa to the future so as to make what was thought to be Asian century to be African century. The paper cites China's rapidly aging population that will get old before getting rich. Despite such accolades, the *Economics* adds that Africa will become what is predicted conditionally that it must have good governance that will stop conflicts and corruption that have, for a long time, destabilised the continent part from robbing it. If Africa seriously takes on those evils and others, it is not about if it will develop but how and when. This is where a major challenge for Africa lies.

Once again, this volume aims at specifically addressing some areas in which Africa can put its house in order; and thereby turn things around for its bright future. Historically, no country or society started automatically developed. Naturally, human beings are changing creatures who have always aspired to better their lives throughout their existence on earth. Further, human history shows human evolution trajectory that almost all humans went through to overcome natural barriers such as disease, poverty and other miseries (Bem 1996) to primarily depend on and need societal efforts and readiness in so doing. Essentially, there is no way a society or country can develop by depending on others to export development to it. Instead, such a country or society can adopt some strategies to top up to what it naturally is endowed with. Therefore, development is a result of an internal spur that squarely emanates and rests in the hearts, minds and on the shoulders of those who aspire or want to develop themselves to top up to whatever external forces can offer. Therefore, it is not a wishful thought or daydreaming or being disingenuous to suggest that Africa, just like any human society, will one day sprout and catch up with others shall it decide and desire to do so scientifically and realistically. I still have hope in Africa, especially when I look at the challenges it faces at the moment. It needs a stroke of genius and readiness for Africa to take its destiny in its hands instead of keeping on allowing foreigners to define it and decide for it. This is where

180

the essence of investing in its people becomes *sine qua non* to Africa's proclivity to development.

Importantly, Africa needs to learn from its history and that of others who made it out of socially-constructed-and-enforced backwardness economically. It requires Africa to see things by its own eyes; and thereafter decide on how to tackle its problems. There is no donor that will come to solve African problems. If there is any, to larger extent, he will come to make things even worse than they are currently. When it comes to development, it is squarely on the shoulders of who wants it. It is like life and death. Nobody can live anybody's life or step in somebody's grave. What one can do is help to either make one's life better or worse or get in the grave to fix that person in it well when death knocks on the door.

Thinking about and suggesting that Africa will one day wake up from its slumber is one thing; and doing exactly that is another. All depends on how Africa and Africans will take up the challenge and recast its nets (Mandela 1993) all aimed at either being a formidable or a deplorable force in international affairs. So, too, if Africans seriously become aware of their problems *in situ,* they are able to turn things around for the better of their continent. I must warn here; whatever Africa envisages, must originate from home not from abroad. This because for the whole period Africa has relied and depended on foreign forces to develop it has not worked to its favour. It has always been minatorial for Africa. Dependency on foreign programmes has not worked for the entire time and umpteenth reasons Africa tried them. Africa must stand and reclaim its place in the world by aiming higher. Africa has what it takes to do this. I have a couple of reasons why Africa will overcome the desperateness and antics it is in because it has what it takes to do so shall it decide to do things differently and rightly from now on.

First and foremost, Africa needs to draw from its history, especially after some Africans returned from the world wars with new changed personae (Collier 1982) so as to influence the liberation of Africa from colonialism. Despite bringing new personae into African politics and struggle for emancipation, the results were not totally attractive. For, soon thereafter, dictatorship kicked in so as to dent the job well done of liberating Africa. Africa was wrestled from European colonial monsters to end up in the hands of homemade African colonial monsters who misused more miserable than those they kicked out of power.

Secondly, now Africans are scattered all over the world doing various activities in academia, art, business, science and whatnot. Shall African governments tap in this pool of brains, chance of using them to push Africa forward are higher. And there is nothing unique for Africa to use its brains for its development. Almost all countries that attained their development did the same. For example, China, India and the Middle East are still doing the same by sending their people to advanced countries to learn and go back home and apply the knowledges and skills they obtain. Stark, *et al.,* (1997, 1998 cited in Lien and Wang (2005) observes that "skilled migration can be the source country to a higher average level of human capital per worker" (p. 154) which is good for the development of the country; also see West and Dasgupta 2011. There is no way Africa can develop either by ignoring its own diaspora brains or by depending on foreign expatriates. Zweig, Fung, and Han (2008) maintain that from 1992 China under what is known as *wei guo fuwu* or 'servicing the country' embarked on concerted efforts of encouraging its skilled diaspora to go back home and develop their countries in conjunction with either those who have already returned or those produced at home. Essentially, this project asks Africa to make sure that its brains near and afar are utilised for its development. As well, we need to appreciate the fact that development is the result of internal desire and drive to attain it depending on how those aspiring to attain it analyse, define and view it. Gow (2008) maintains that "development as we currently know it is imposed and does not work, at least for poor and marginal" (p. 9). This means, when we aspire for development as a continent, we must make sure that we know the definition and meaning of the development we want based on our needs. For example, the West puts many premiums on material development as opposed to moral one. We need to know and choose what we need and want. Gow (*Ibid.*) sheds more light on how we must address development saying that there is a "tension between the 'inside' and 'outside' between the 'old' and the 'new', between the 'proven' and the 'unproven' is reflected in the contentious debate over "local knowledge" and its potential "contribution" to development and modernity" (p. 13). By understanding the tension[s] in addressing and defining development, we will be careful to avoid falling on the same trap that Africa has always been in for generations, especially after being occupied and colonised. Nadasdy (2005) concurs with Gow arguing us to not accept some claims at face value if we surely need to comprehend what we need and want. I will address this aspect in detail when I talk about investment, sound investment Africa has to make in order to pull together and move ahead.

Third, there is no miracle [s] about using diaspora brains to develop their countries. First of all, despite living abroad, the diaspora still understand how east and west home is the best. Secondly, they accept and appreciate the role they have to play back home. This is why remittances have become the backbone of some countries.

Fourth, most of diaspora thanks to how Africa is viewed and treated are likely to be nostalgic at certain if not all times. This is human nature. We all belong to a certain place we call home that we miss dearly. Therefore, there is no doubt about the role the diaspora has to play for Africa's development if they are fully and unconditionally enticed, consulted, empowered and listened to. Once the country entices and encourages its diaspora brains to return home and apply their knowledges and skills, this country is surely posed to reap the rewards of such an undertaking. China and the said countries above sent their skilled persons abroad to the US (Silicon Valley), Canada and other countries to learn. When they went back, they changed the dynamics of the economies of their countries. This is why now China is among the leaders in economics, electronics, avionics and other specialisations. Basically, the miracle we currently see China performing economically can be attributed to this mission of seeking knowledge in order to develop. Apart from China and India, the Middle East has emulated this strategy by sending its brains abroad to learn and bring back knowledge. In Canada, after Chinese and Indians, I see many Arab students in various universities. I think the Middle East has realised how vulnerable it is without its own brain to manage the wealth, especially oil, it is endowed with. The Middle East did not reach this stage without exploring its past history whereby everything technical was in the hands of foreigners. The life of just enjoying for many Middle East is a thing of the past the same way the era of dependency for Africa needs to become.

Fourth, the idea of investing in brain regain based on diaspora is real and viable for Africa, mainly at this juncture when Africa needs all sorts of expertise almost in everything. Take Kenya, for example. Despite suffering under long time dictatorship and having less resources compared to its neighbour Tanzania, its economy is more stable than Tanzania's that has more resources and land mass than Kenya. Why? It is simple! Kenya sent many of its brains abroad to learn. Thereafter, it enticed and invited them to come back and apply their knowledge. Ghana too, despite suffering from a long time of *coup d'états* is doing fine simply because it has hugely invested on its home and diaspora brains. These two countries are not only investing in diaspora students, they too invest at home.

184

According to the *Ministry of Foreign Affairs of the People's Republic of China* (28 October, 2006) Kenya increased its primary-school enrolment by 1 million students after abolishing tuition fee in 2003. The same measure has made Ghana's primary-school enrolment rise up to 14 percent. Such are the investments that Africa needs to undertake in order to leapfrog in respect to development. For, no country can develop without investing in its people.

Fifth, African countries need to exchange people in various areas of expertise. Why should someone go for education that he or she can obtain in Africa? To attain this, African countries need to establish their own high institutions of learning. They can start with the already produced manpower or hire some from abroad so as to offer knowledge in Africa instead of sending people abroad to study for the fields that can be obtained locally in Africa. When it comes to education fitting African environment and needs, Africa needs to plan and program it. Fielding and Moss (2011) define education as "a long-established concept of education that understands education as fostering and supporting the general well-being and development of children and young people, and their ability to interact effectively with their environment and to live a good life" (p. 19). Yes, Africa has failed to give good life to its majority because of depending on the West almost in everything including education. To do away with this, Africa needs to recalibrate its syllabi based on time and its needs. So, too, Africa needs to heavily invest in education to see to it that it has educated society that can run and manage it professionally and competently. Currently, investment in education is dismal. Moyo (2009) tersely maintains that in many African countries the education or health care share of government expenditure is something like less than 2 percent, whereas military is something more like 40 percent, with the rest going largely to debt payments. This way Africa cannot forge ahead pragmatically. I think Africa needs more educated people than militias. Therefore, to turn things around, Africa needs to turn this trend on its head. Time of keeping fat armies is long gone. Instead, Africa needs to create an educated society.

Tanzania provides an ideal example when it comes to addressing some anomalies that are chronically endemic in many African countries. After spending a lot of money sending its people to India for medical purposes, it brought some experts from China and India to train its own experts and offer the same services locally; thereby gaining knowledge and serving forex. The *Daily News* (6 September, 2015) quoted Minister of Health and Social Welfare, Dr. Seif Rashid as saying "this is a modern facility and the government allocated 10bn/-to make sure that heart patients receive treatment locally. Heart diseases cause death to many people globally followed by communicable diseases." In establishing this state-of-the-art institute at Muhimbili National Hospital (MNH), Tanzania will save Tshs 2.5bn it used to spend on sending patients to India. Such an investment is not important only for Tanzania but also for the region, especially Central and East African countries. How much a Congolese patient who used to spend thousands of dollars on airfare to India will save? How much will the DRC save by sending its patients to Tanzania instead of India or China? Suppose other facilities of this nature were opened zonally in Africa to cater for its needs. Suppose Africa goes on establishing other facilities such as those dealing with researches on cancer, malaria and chronic diseases that cost Africa a lot of money and lives.

Seventh, on top of opening new facilities dealing with various diseases, Africa needs to ponder on opening other facilities charged with researching African traditional medicines. How come Africans were able to live with sound health up until the coming of colonial powers but now cannot do without depending on them? For Africa to have reliable health services it needs to invest in both Western and African aspects of health science. Africa is rich in herbs that can be used to produce various types of medicine that ancestors used to rely on cure themselves. Herbal medicines play a very important role in the lives of Africans (Fennell *et al.*, 2004) even after embracing Western medicines which however have become expensive and some face resistance from bacteria and viruses. So too, due to the important role African herbals play in the Western pharmaceutical success, Africa needs to enact laws that will prevent foreign companies to use its herbs without paying for them. This must include even patenting of its products in order to avoid modern theft that many pharmaceutical companies commit, especially against countries that either have patent and copyrights law or have weak ones. Having laws in place will avert conflicts with Trade-related Aspects of Intellectual Property Rights (TRIPS Agreement) (Hestermeyer 2007), especially when they seek access to certain types of herbs.

Eighth, despite being smaller, Ghana and Kenya send many more students abroad to study than many other African countries. And, this has huge positive impacts on the economies of these countries. Kenya now, is a hub of Information Technology in Central and East Africa followed by a tiny country of Rwanda which invested in IT vigorously so as to shed its genocide image. These two countries also enjoy economic boost through investing in their education so as to attract neighbouring countries. The Nigeria *Vanguard* (22 October, 2015) observes that in 2014, about 75,000 Nigerians were said to be studying in Ghana, paying about US$1 billion annually as tuition fees and upkeep, as against the annual budget of US$751 million for all federal universities which is equivalent to the remittances Ghanaians living abroad sent back home in 2004, *Migration Policy Institute (MPI)* (1 March, 2006). I am an advocate of African intra-trade and intra-cooperation. If all African countries can hugely invest in educating their people, chances of turning things around are high and viable. For, having educated and skilled manpower does not only assure the country of skilled and educated people to employ but also enhances such a people to create jobs by involving themselves in private sector. One thing Africa needs to ponder on is the fact that many countries are satisfied with remittances their diaspora people channel home. The *Mail and Guardian* (2 June, 2015) maintains that some countries, especially the poorest based on their GDP depend heavily on remittances. For example, when it comes to dependency on remittances Eritrea stands at (38%), Cape Verde (34%), Liberia (26%) and Burundi (23%). Statistically, the above counties heavily depend on remittances. And, this has its ramifications in that poor people who receive such money from the diaspora relatives cannot take to the streets to overthrow their long time dictatorial regimes. So, it can be said that remittances have become another reprieve for despots due to the fact that those receiving them see no reasons of risking their lives to take to the streets. Some failed states such Somalia and weak ones such as Zimbabwe have survived on remittances. The *Mail and Guardian (Ibid.)* estimated that Africa receives about $ 160bn annually. This money is huger than aid that rich countries extend to Africa. Again, should Africa be satisfied with this huge chunk of money? What we need to ask ourselves is: if African diaspora can send such a huge amount of money, how much do they make out there? What if we bring them and use them at home? Answers are obvious that they will make more money than they remit back to Africa. Here we are talking about $ 160bn without including the amount countries they are in and the couriers that transfer such money charge those remitting the monies. How much do they pay in terms of tax, rent, visas and other essentials for their lives and legality to stay abroad? This shows how Africa has practically what it takes to turn things around for the better; shall it committedly aim higher. Arguably, Africa is like a fish that dies of thirsty while it is in the middle of the lake. Africa sits on humongous resources plus having the manpower that is not well utilised. This if turned around, shows how Africa has the wherewithal for its development shall it seriously will to do so.

Africa Must Face It in Turning Things Around

I think Africa needs to think positively and boldly *vis-à-vis* its diaspora brains by welcoming them back home so that they can develop it.

First, hypothetically, Africa has been changing however not with a corresponding pace compared to its challenges and others. MacMillan, Rodrik, and Verduzco-Gallo (2014) note that the beginning of the twenty-first century saw African economies grow as faster as, or faster than the rest of the world, especially in the century that evidenced many economic shrinkages. This observation, *inter alia,* is encouraging; however, it is not clear as to whose interests such economies have been growing faster provided that they heavily depend on exporting law materials and importing processed materials. Can such growth be seen in the lives of Africans, mainly in rural areas where many Africans live or just statistically as the trend has been in many countries? Nevertheless, despite such statistical growth, much is still desired when it comes to improving the lives of millions of Africans in rural areas. Importantly nevertheless, Africa can still stand economically as it did during the 2007 Credit Crunch that left many advanced economies shaken while others sank as it happened in Greece, and Iceland not to mention the bailout that was introduced to save many economies in the West. Cramer, Johnson and Oya (2009) observe that African weakly integrated banking systems to the global financial markets became a blessing for Africa countries so that the financial crash did not severely affect African banks and financial institution as it did for Western institutions. The nature of African traditional life for the majority of people who live in rural areas has a lot to do with African financial institutions that do not depend on purely Western ways of running them. African traditional life did not encourage pointless consumerism as the Western do. Therefore, whenever there is a shortage of anything, based on collectivistic nature, Africans are likely to easily share and make do with whatever available.

Another thing that Africa needs to address is the current regime of business. Mhango (2015) argues that African countries do not do business among themselves compared to how they do with foreign countries. Business, just like any other concepts, is not a new concept to Africa. Africa used to do business with the Far East a long time before the arrival of colonialists. It had a very thriving economy at the time. Conversely, its's economy was non-monetised in that it did not basically depend on Ponzi-scheme-like system the European economy had that is now causing a lot of problem to the world. Credit in African system was totally different from the one we know today. Hopkins (2014) argues that all societies have an economic system that helps them to produce and supply their biological and social needs and he goes on arguing that for example, agriculture which is the first human economic activity started in West Africa 5,000 BC. Here we are talking about agriculture at its early stage. There is yet another trade system that was completely free of European interference or cooperation on top of the West African trade. This is the trade along the East African City States that traded with the Persian Gulf and the Far East many years before the arrival of Europeans who attacked and robbed these cities in 1498 (Burton 1872; Lodhi 1994; and Mancke 1999). Also, Africa, especially Bantu speaking people (de Maret and Nsuka 1977) is believed to be the harbinger of metallurgy in the world (Excoffier, *et al.,* 1987; and Selin 2013). Africa had its own mature way of doing things scientifically and mathematically. Selin (*Ibid.*) argues, for example, that Africans South of Sahara used probabilities under the game of chance, to determine things. Swahili, Sukuma and other many African communities have the so-called bao an African chess-like game which involves two people who fill some stones or dices in the holes to determine the winner. This sport needs high mathematical ability just as it is in the chess for one to defeat her or his opponent. It is purely mathematical just like chess or Asian Toguz korgol or "Nine sheep droppings" Adilova (n.d year); also see Campbell and Chavey (1995).

Secondly, as it is for vacuum, nature does not allow stasis in human society. However, Ntuli (2002) argues that for Africa to bring about the renaissance needs to dramatically change, in fundamental ways, by making sure that its thoughts and ideas work in in "a totally new and radical way" (page not provided). Arguably, Ntuli maintains that Africa can apply its traditional knowledge, mechanisms and systems that enabled it to live for millions of years without depending on anybody up until some European colonial powers colonised and destroyed it and its way of doing things. Again, this is not the time to cry for the spilled milk. However, this does not mean that we must forget the past wrongs that colonialism and slavery caused, especially to Africa. Slavery in particular became the foundation on which Europe built its prosperity that acted as a capital for the wealth we see today in Europe (Wolf and Eriksen 2010). Instead, this is a time for Africa to stand up again; and thereby reclaims its lost glory based on the realities of today. One thing that cannot be opted out of the table is for Africa to seek redress for the evils and wrongs it suffered and is still suffering even today. As we will see later, Africa still has precious resources, people and wherewithal to move forward shall it rethink its future based on its needs and aspirations as a continent and as a people.

And thirdly, Africa, just like any society of a people, cannot always be an exception to the general rule as far as human dynamism for change and improvements are concerned. Africa is not static. It is dynamic just like other societies. Maslow (1954 cited in Uduji 2013) expands human on behaviour *vis-à-vis* needs and behaviour noting that man is a wanting animal that will never be satisfied with whatever achievement due to the fact that whenever one need is satisfied; another appears in its place. Africans are humans just like any other humans of this world. Africa needs to take this challenge up and prove wrong all those who think that Africa will forever be the back of beyond. I usually like to say that Africa can use its history and experiential knowledge as its tools of development. We all learn from our mistakes based on our pasts. The same way, Africa still has what it takes to learn from its past history.

Fourth, historically, countries deemed to be advanced; and thereby developed today were languishing in poverty at certain times of their existence. Take Europe, for example. There were times Africa and China among others were better off in development than Europe (Hui 2004: 184). Again, through concerted efforts based on experience and the drive for the future, such countries overcame and here they are blossoming. If other were able to change, why should Africa not change and leapfrog really? Freeman (2015) maintains that the Greeks merely built on and improved sometimes somewhat what the Egyptians invented. If anything, this one of the impetuses that saw Europe advance technologically. Nothing contributed to the prosperity of Europe like gunpowder whose technology Europe copied from China (Hoffman 2011). For, without ships Europe would not have been able to conquer; and thereby colonise the world in the 17th century. What is wrong for Africa to copy from others if doing so will help it to turn things around just like the British did? Even when it comes to seafaring China was ahead of Europe, especially under its dragon like Admiral Zheng He who enabled China to rule the oceans not to forget overthrowing the Mongols in 1382 at the time European ability to embark on exploration was a century abaft comparably (Viviano 2005). You can see how China became the harbinger of sea knowledge. Xu (2006) concurs with Viviano noting that "China's field of vision was strictly limited to its own territory and borders, [although] the Ming dynasty [Adm.] Zheng He's seven voyages into the Western Ocean opened up a maritime silk route, which preceded the Western Great Age of Discovery by a century" (p. 53). This shows how nobody can stay on top on development. What is needed is for those who are underdevelopment to learn from those ahead of them *vis-à-vis* development. Importantly, this needs awareness, fortitude, ideas, mojo and whatnots. Again, Europe had an advantage of colonising other countries. For African though, there is no country left to be colonised. Instead, Africa must colonise its own resources in that it must utilise them after adding value to them. How can this be done? Invest in Africans by making sure that they are getting worthy education. Curb graft and maladministration not to mention colonial legacies that have always made Africa dependent pointlessly. Africa has everything as a capital needed for its development.

Typically, Europe's story above is true; and can act as a catalyst for Africa to turn things around. History has it that Egyptians discovered irrigation–which became instrumental for population growth–before anybody had ever tried a hand on it. King and Hall (1906) observe that:

> With the exception of a few palasoliths from the surface of the Syrian desert, near the Euphrates valley, not a single implement of the Age of Stone has yet been found in Southern Mesopotamia, whereas Egypt has yielded to us the most perfect examples of the flint–knapper's art known, flint tools and weapons more beautiful than the finest that Europe and America can show (p. 4).

However old this work may seem, it still shows how things used to be in the light of discovery and advancement of human society as Africa championed and pioneered many inventions. The history of Africa as the harbinger of technology does not only end in irrigation but also in medicine. Herodotus (1890; and von Staden 1989 cited in Blomstedt 2014) maintain that "the art of medicine might be said to have first seen the light of day in Egypt, and the Egyptian doctors were well respected and sought after by foreign rulers" (p. 670) which is indicative that there is nothing new that Africa did not have before its civilisation was felled after the introduction of colonialism.

This proves to us that there is no limit as far as Africa is concerned when it comes to advancement and development. What is needed is for Africa to take the challenge up and turn things around by borrowing from its institutional history that shows that Africa lost its mojo soon after the legitimisation of the colonial state that resulted into the lack of congruence of the African post-colonial state with respect to pre-colonial institutions so as damage its capacity to manage development (Englebert 2000) thanks to being superimposed to Africans for the benefit of the colonisers. History has the tendency of repeating itself. We have seen how Africa pioneered many innovations for human development. Again, should Africa wait for history to repeat itself *vis-à-vis* its development or Africa must cox its history to be used to bring about change instead of waiting for it to repeat itself? If Africa is to develop, it has to make sure that turning its history into a tool of its emancipation must be done urgently instead of waiting it to act on its discretion in repeating itself.

Further, Africa has what it takes to turn things around based on its history. Historically, Africa is the cradle of many things. For example, Africa boasts of the oldest city of Cairo whose advancement at its heydays was second to none; also see Mitchell (1991; and Sutton and Fahmi 2002). Even the ruins of the Great Zimbabwe are older than London (Huffman 2004); also see Chirikure, *et al.,* (2013). All such findings show how Africa has more propensities in its past history that can be used as a motivation in facing the challenge of turning things around for the better. Why was it possible for Africa then to do all such earth-breaking things but not now? Therefore, Africa needs to take a leaf from Europe that later became the champion of modern development in the 18th century despite being once more impoverished than Africa. After knowing its problems, Europe decided to take on them by sending various people to explore the world so that they could get some alternatives and opportunities that later paid back. Refer to how Vasco da Gama was wowed to see East African City states and thereby benefit from their gold trade. So, too, when Europeans visited Ghana Empire, they were astonished to see how rich the empire was with gold and opulence not to forget complexity in its administrational settings. Nevertheless naïve and controversial as it is, the same happened when Europeans saw Zimbabwe stone ruins for the first time so as to end up speculating and misconstruing them as King Solomon's (Carrol 1988: and Kaarsholm 1992) which implies that they had never owned or seen anything like that. Despite their malice against Africa, there are some traces that can tell the truth they hid in order to easily colonise Africa and bloviate that they civilised it while they actually desecrated it.

In Ghana, the king was sitting on golden stools. Comparably, even biblical King Solomon whom–the Europeans eulogised and were in awe of–did not have such lavishness and copiousness. However, the difference is that Europe criminally made mountains of money which created the propensities for its development–we see today–by robbing others through slavery, piracy and colonialism which are not suitable today (*People's Daily*, April 26, 2006 cited in Taylor 2009) which ushered in underdevelopment for Africa. Frank (1966, 1967 cited in Wolf and Eriksen 2010) argue that development and underdevelopment are bound together. Therefore, there is no way one can talk about the development and advancement of Europe without talking about the underdevelopment of Africa that caused the development of Europe (Falola and Archberger 2013). Essentially, the development of Europe is nothing without the contribution of Africa. And this is how Europe underdeveloped Africa and how Africa developed Europe the role Africa has religiously played ever since.

Again, China is now advancing vigorously without colonising anybody save exploiting some poor countries as Taylor (*Ibid.*,: 31) maintains that "China actually makes things worse for some in Africa" thanks to its thirsty for resources that Africa has abundantly and offers without any conditionality whatsoever.

Another difference is that China does not export missionaries to colonise Africa. Instead, it dispatches its army of jobless to invade Africa and "steal jobs" (Morapedi 2007) from Africans. Morapedi cites the situation in Botswana where there is a belief that Chinese and Indian immigrants cause more unemployment nonetheless even Africans from neighbouring countries such as Malawi, Mozambique and Zimbabwe are accused of stealing jobs in Botswana and South Africa though not overtly so due to doing many menial jobs compared to Chinese and Indians who do highly paying jobs resulting from their interconnectivity. Africa can learn from such groups and use their own methods to turn table against them when it comes to depriving Africans jobs in their countries due to the myopia and ineptness of their governments that were colonially cloned to serve the interests of their masters and other foreigners. To turn things around for Africa, there must be true and practical reciprocity in whatever dealings African countries are involved in. they need to equally and equitably give exactly what they are given. If anything, this is the areas in which Africa needs to create strategies to address in order to avoid wasting a lot of time and money on addressing its consequences resulting the corruption, myopia and selfishness of its rulers. Crush, Chikanda and Skinner (2015) claim that Chinese employ family members under what is known as guanxi (or personal relationship) networks something that creates more sufferings for their hosts so as to hate them. Furthermore, China does not sell weapons to Africa. Instead, it exports all sorts of booked solid products genuine, fake and substandard. In return however, China depletes Africa's resources so as to cause some types of animals to become extinct. Udeala (2010) cites Nigeria where he says that "the incidence of flooding of the Nigerian market with substandard goods from China and inability to implement various bilateral agreements between the two countries among other problems" (p. 73). If anything, this is the typical replica of what has been going on in Africa for a long time since China economically burst to the scene. This however should not be misconstrued to mean that China is the only exporter of substandard goods. India does the same (Vasudevan 2010) by flooding Africa with substandard goods not to mention many economic immigrants that can now be seen in many African countries either doing business or jobs that Africans are able to do. I must make this absolutely clear. The nuance here is not racism or anything closer. Why should Africa accept the armies of jobless from some Asian countries while the same do not reciprocate in any way? Why is it possible for the United States and other developed countries to limit the numbers of illegal and economic immigrants in their territories while it becomes racism for Africa to do the same? To show how Indians treat non-Indians especially African, the *Telegram* (I October, 2014) quoted professor Zubair Meenia of Delhi's Jamia Milia University responding to attacks on Africans studying in India saying "there is no doubt about it. Indians are racist and the irony is we are not aware of it and hence no sensitisation and acceptance. We have a history of racism", especially against Africans and untouchables. Imagine! Africans discriminated against are students who contribute to the economy of India. What would happen if they were mere economic immigrants? I think Africa needs to learn the law of reciprocity by treating whoever it interact with the same way that person or country treats it and its people. This is a sacred duty for any government and country, to protect its people.

Africa needs to protect its job market just like any other countries do. In Western countries where my experience is drawn, whenever anybody applies for a job, the first thing he or she is if he or she is asked if such a person is legally allowed to work in that country. And, no employer can circumnavigate such laws. Doing so is unthinkable so to speak due to the way authorities severely deal with such lawbreakers. In Africa, it is a different story. However, some countries have laws that bar illegal immigrants to work in their territories; still employers may ignore them and get away with murder due rampant and institutionalised corruption. African countries need to impose heavy punishment to such employers in order to protect the job market for their people. In this regard therefore, Africa needs to fully fight corruption at all levels.

By exploiting such a weakness, many criminals, cons and quacks have made huge fortunes while Africa goes on suffering simply because it is in the hands of myopic and selfish rulers. Essentially, what they do is giving predatory rulers the same money they are able to get if they work diligently hard and effectively. Africa needs to deal with its external and internal donors cautiously to see to it that it sustains itself instead of depending on handouts many made out of their own wealth. What such criminal do is like giving a chicken its eggs and make it believe that those doing so have given it a worthy gift.

Chapter 8

How Should Africa Address Economic Quandaries?

In concluding, after generally looking at areas that Africa has to address in order to aim at advanced future, I will specifically delve into what Africa needs to do in order to turn things around for its better and competitive future. I will categorise things that Africa needs to do to turn things around for its better future in three major clusters namely; economically, politically and socially. Apart from being a common way of categorising things based on social science, this categorisation makes it easy to address the issues not to mention making it easy to understand the concepts and arguments propounded in this volume. However, this is not a canon when it comes to analysing or categorising concepts. Writers choose how to address and present issues depending on their strategies and styles of doing so.

For Africa, this is a defining moment and a watershed so to speak, especially after two non-Western powers, China and India emerge. I should say it from the outset that also the rise of the said powers will help Africa only if and when Africa prepare itself to use the dichotomous business situation to bargain a good deal. Arguably, shall Africa do its homework nicely; it has what it takes to turn things around for the better.

To begin with, let us look at how Africa can address its economic quandaries that it has been languishing in for many years even after becoming independent although dependent still. I have never accepted the situation as a normal one whereby Africa, as continent endowed with resources of all kinds, is helped by a small country like Britain, Sweden or Finland while it has more land mass, manpower and resources than the said countries put together even a hundred times. Now, why is it that the said countries help Africa instead of Africa helping them? I must clarify here. When I say help, I mean being given handouts or aid. For, when it comes to the successes of such countries, especially those that colonised some African countries, Africa has always helped them to become what they are today.

In addressing such an anomaly above, I will dwell on three facets of life of any country namely economic, political and social ones. I will later elaborate these facets independently of each other soon after introducing this section. First and foremost, Africa needs to learn from its history and believe that things will never be the same or *in situ*. This is because Africa had almost whatever it takes to develop before the introduction of colonialism. As a society and a people, Africa function so well that when colonial powers arrived, they only built on what had already been established without any assistance of influence from outside of Africa. For example, Law (1977) cited in Fenske (2014) discloses that Africa used to have its own precolonial currencies such as cowries while Ake (1981) cited in Chukwuebuka (2010) names them to include gold dinars, mithqals, cloth money, copper rods, iron, cowries and manilas that which European currencies felled due to the fact that Africa was not prepared to compete with these currencies. I can argue that Africa failed simply because it did not have the culture of manipulating business, currencies and competing by ignoring moral values which lacked in Western systems as capitalism espoused them. Traditionally, Africa was a socially conscious but not profit geared society. Despite its beauties and goodies, this trait became a disadvantage for Africa when it faced off with Western ways of doing business. I will expand this when I touch on the dubious colonial treaties that some African chiefs and kings signed with colonial agents believing that they were all on the same footing. Con, deceit, and manipulations were the rules of the game for Western countries when they first came to contact with credulous Africa.

However, the existence of currencies and business structures truly show how Africa had an already-developed-business regime that many biased Western historians tend to either dubiously exclude or paint with the same brush aiming at justifying their assertions that they brought civilisation to Africa while the truth is the opposite. One point that many biased scholar miss is the fact that all human societies have some automatic and universalised qualities and intrinsic worth *vis-à-vis* survival and administration of their societies based on needs and times. Africa cannot be an exception the general rule if at all evidence is all over the place that Africa used to thrive before the introduction of colonialism. Mhango (2015), for example, argues that it is a big lie for Western countries to assert that they brought development such as in health services while they actually sabotaged and felled these services. The vivid evidence he offers is the availability of slaves that were ferried to the then so-called New World in the Americas. Mhango goes on arguing that Western slave hunters did not start slavery in Africa. They started it back home only to find that their people were not fit enough to carry on heavy duties as Africans did. Once, again, this shows how advanced Africa was in health services. There is a big lesson from the history of Africa. This being the case therefore, Africa still has somewhere to turn to in its attempt to forge ahead economically. As mentioned above, some infrastructure is still in existence in rural Africa where business—despite facing cutthroat competition currently due to the introduction of Western ways of doing it—still is done in traditional manner in which trust and morality are observed and preserved which is totally different from the Western regime of doing business. Conversely, things seem to have changed for the worse for Africa. Darley and Blankson (2008) maintain that "the rapid urbanization seems to have undermined the traditional

201

African culture so as to pose "a challenge for any discussion about African culture and its implications for business marketing practices" (p. 377). I can say that what is new to Africa is the way of conducting business but not the concept itself. Mbiti (1990: 209) cited in Darley and Blankson (*Ibid.*) sums it up nicely maintaining that:

> The essence of African morality is that it is more "societal" than "spiritual;" it is a morality of "conduct" rather than a morality of "being." This is what one might call "dynamic ethics" rather than "static ethics," for it defines what a person does rather than what he does not because of what he is (p. 375).

Perennial morality and malleability helped Africa and its institution to develop rapidly according to the need and plans of the community. Michalopoulos and Papaioannou (2013) maintain that their analysis shows that the complexity and hierarchical structure of pre-colonial ethnic institutions in Africa correlate significantly with contemporary regional development. The claims above are very obvious that business in African traditions is about relationship and profit. However, profits are made conditionally that they are based on strengthening relationship and society coherence. This means to compliment and compound each other. And this is why, the market or marketplace in many African societies acted as business-cum-social arena where people would meet and exchange goods, news and views pertaining to their community and communities beyond (Achebe 1958) while Europe traces the origin of the institution of the marketplace at around 7000 BC in ancient towns such as Catalhöyuk as well as the Greek and Roman towns (Mbisso 2011) this institution, in African societies, is as old as the societies themselves. Arguably, the marketplace, as a fundamental traditional institution dealt with business and relational matters the same way the modern market does when companies seek to know the information of their customers so as to entice them to buy their products. Such practices and philosophy are evidentially found in Ubuntu which Karsten and Illa (2005) note that "Ubuntu has strong moral overtones. It is being defended as a new view on business based on a concept, which is anchored in a long-standing cultural tradition" (p. 614) in many African societies, chiefly in the Central, East and South African regions. Karsten and Illa go on citing an example whereby South African government introduced the concept of Ubuntu in business soon after the demise of Apartheid which they say "Ubuntu as well as other dimensions of African culture where introduced as positive resources for catalysing the business transformation in South Africa" (p. 612) soon after the new democratic government kicked in. additionally, Mphele cites Wal and Ramotschoa (2001:4 in Theletsane 2012) notice that Ubuntu is sometimes popularised in business books reflecting the tendency to align it with productivity improvement and worker motivation techniques. This shows how Africa has something to offer in business continentally and globally based on its own philosophy and practices as evidenced today in Ubuntu.

For Africa to pragmatically and quickly move ahead and turn things around, it must embark on the following undertakings:

Apart from revisiting and resuscitating some its traditional institutions so as to advance and advance them, fundamentally, Africa must have its own homemade programs for its development; economy and whatnots based on its cultures, needs and traditions to top up to the Western ones shall it aspire to move forward quickly and sustainably. And this is possible due to the fact that Africa currently has all sorts of experts in many areas. Africa has to have institution, structures and systems that resonate with its aspirations and desires. Shall African experts be well and fully utilised, chances for Africa to turn things around for the better are high. Instead of depending on the World Bank and the International Monetary Fund (IMF) to tamper with its economy with their controversial policies despite being inadequately represented in this organisations touted to be international while the actually are Western (Grabel 2011) which beg for Africa needs to have its own economic programs and plans aimed at serving the interests of its people. On this, Africa should not worry or feel that it cannot plan for its own development. On his side, Batts (2013) cites a Chinese proverb that says that "if you don't know where you are going, any road will take you there" (p. 1). One of the roads that can take Africa where it needs to go is by revisiting its past, especially the time before the introduction of colonialism. At this time, Africa was able to feed itself without necessarily begging or borrowing so as to have strong people suitable for slavery. Evidentially, this shows how developed and successful Africa was. Again, where did this muscle go? The answer is obvious that colonialism chopped it so as to fell Africa's propensities to the future. Such a journey to the past that aims at propelling Africa to the future needs to be taken by academics in particular so as to generate knowledge for the consumption of Africans that are required to fully make this sojourn to development. Such a role needs freethinking academics that can deconstruct and demystify the lies Hegelian academics pummelled in the academia.

One important question Africa needs to ask itself is this; why the IMF and the WB only dictate and tutor Africa but not all countries equally. I have never heard these international financial institutions setting conditional and stern conditions to the economies of countries like Canada, Russia and other so-called developed countries. So, too, experience shows that these IFIs have always helped the Multi-National Financial Institutions (MNIFs) in exploiting Africa. Again, the IFIs and the MNIFs have always forced poor countries to swallow, hook and, sinker their programs while some researches show that their policies are negative to economic growth in the countries that enter into agreement with them. For example, Przeworski and Vreeland (2000) conducted research on countries that entered into agreement with IFIs and those that abstained. They drew this conclusion maintaining that "indeed, what is striking is that IMF programs have a negative effect on growth even if we assume investment to be exogenous with regard to participation" (p. 410); also see Dreher (2006). Many of the IFIs' priorities have always been to encourage Africa to open its markets to supply the West and consume from it. Since independence, African countries have been encouraged, for example, to produce cash crops they cannot eat or alternatively sell to another buyer apart from the West. This puts African farmers who re the majority in corner. Mhango (2015) maintains that African farmers will always be vulnerable as long as they depend on cash crops he calls crush crops due to the fact that they cannot eat them once Western countries refuse to buy them or drop their prices as it has always been. Mhango equates Africa's tendency of depending on cash crops to the chicken that produces what it does not eat and eat what it does not produce.

There is no way Africa can develop while it keeps on depending on Washington, New-York, Paris or London made policies even on what to produces and consume as it has applied them for a long time to no avail. Arguably, the West has always turned Africa into an experimental object for their policies. There is no way a guinea pig will benefit from the role it plays in seeking a solution to any ailment of problem. Once the solution is available, the guinea pig is left to die. What did the Economic Structural Adjustment Policies (ESAP) achieve for Africa? Didn't they send many countries to more poverty by pumping much money to them to end up being misused thereby expanding national debts in many African countries? Mosley, Subasat and Weeks (1995) provide answers to the two questions above noting that structural "adjustment in Africa points to the "road ahead" as more of the same. We have argued that the journey to date has proved an unsuccessful route by which to arrive at the goal of recovery in Africa" (p. 1470). This proves how Africa has been subjected to the obnoxious role of an experimental object if not a guinea pig for the West. To the contrary some pro-Western scholars tout structural adjustment as a good thing for Africa even though it is not. Corbo and Fisher (1995) sum structural adjustment up arguing that "… structural adjustment policies aim to restore macroeconomic balance, to integrate the economy into the global economy" (p. 3) which is good for rich countries but worse for poor countries. Here the question we need to ask is how does Africa actively participate in the so-called world market; and what is the world or international market? Mansfield and Busch (1995) answer this question maintaining that:

> The American vision for the postwar trade regime was originally outlined in a plan for an International Trade Organization (ITO), which was intended to complement the International Monetary Fund. As presented in 1945, the American plan offered rules for all aspects of international trade relations (p. 299).

The quote above shows how current trade regime is purely American for the interests of the West led by America under its capitalistic and neoliberal policies that have nothing when it comes to the interests of poor countries. This is evident on how such policies have affected the market that the West controls for its advantages as opposed to the interests of others. If this is not addressed, Africa will be perpetually exploited as continent as will its people. Nonetheless, Baker (2006) defines the market as "a collection of products and geographic locations" (p. 130) which obviously denies the US and the West the jurisdiction of making any world decision on any market[s] or location[s] that is not within their jurisdiction. If there is an area where Africa

206

needs to do its homework well is on the market. For, the so-called world or international market has never favoured Africa when it comes to supply it. Western countries have always protected their markets and products while at the same time force other non-Western countries to liberalise their markets. This has always been detrimental for Africa; and indeed, apart from colonial legacies, it is another major of poverty and underdevelopment for Africa.

Africa needs to revitalise its traditional market based on its needs and demands. On his part Massey (2000) argues that "traditionally market definition was based on the cross-price elasticity of demand, which measures the responsiveness of the change in demand for a product, to changes in the price of another product" (p. 314). This shows how the market is supposed to regulate itself which means it can either be liberal or protective all depending on the supply and demand but not on the *diktat* and policies of one group as it currently is where neoliberal policies force poor countries to subscribe to Western policies and discretion.

By considering the nature of the market, Africa still has the right to decide how its products should be traded all based on its interests, needs and wishes. By the way, who gave America the power of deciding and planning trade regime for the whole world? It is obvious that the US was starting the experimentation of its newly-acquired superpower position not to mention trying to secure the legality of denying its then competitors access sensitive products such as uranium that many countries would like to put a hand on so as to produce nuclear weapons which guarantee them the place in international affairs. You can see this in recent kerfuffle between the West and Iran which, like North Korea, wanted to produce nukes as a bargaining chip (Litwak 2008) in dealing with the West which does not want to see the countries it calls rogue to acquire such weapons.

One of the reasons that geared the US and the West to define and prepare the policies for the world market can be attributed to the fact that after the US embarked on its ambitious projects such as making atomic and nuclear bombs which were aimed at ruling the world through its military might as it later occurred. Even today, due to the origin, trust and treaties that the US has with Europe, it opposes any country that is not toeing its line to acquire nukes. The lesson the US and the West learned after India and Pakistan acquire nukes made them reckon with whoever that wants to acquire nukes. Furthermore, America's usurp of power shows how its major policies such as conditional aid and democracy, market liberalisation and structural adjustment, *inter alia,* are aimed at becoming a modicum through which to access African markets and resources. I think this is why structural adjustment has never worked for Africa. The question we need to ask and answer is: When we open our markets, do they as well open theirs? *The Global Policy* (12 December, 2013) notes that:

> Robert Pollin, an economist at the University of Massachusetts, estimates that developing countries have lost roughly $480 billion in potential GDP as a result of structural adjustment. Yet Western corporations have benefitted tremendously. It has forced open vast new consumer markets; it has made it easier to access cheap labor and raw materials; it has opened up avenues for capital flight and tax avoidance; it has created a lucrative market in foreign debt; and it has facilitated a massive transfer of public resources into private hands (the World Bank alone has privatised more than $2 trillion worth of assets in developing countries).

Does this need a PhD in economics to decipher and draw a conclusion that things have not worked for Africa under the current international system? What should be done then? Some scholars think that Africa needs to truly democratise so as to do away with conflicts that cost it a lot of resources and manpower. This is right and true that Africa loses a lot to conflicts. However, conflict is the tip of the iceberg given that Africa suffers from many problems mainly resulting from slavery, colonialism and neo-colonialism. Ndulo (2003) maintains that conflicts in Africa always revolve around struggles for political power, ethnic privilege, national prestige, and scarce resources which detrimentally act as internal catalysts fuelled by external catalysts which are rich countries' desires and greed. This is why it makes sense to tie political facet to economic one *vis-à-vis* the rampancy of conflicts in Africa. Essentially, as we will see, Africa's problems are interconnected. Some are internal' others are external and they enforce each other. Therefore, in dealing with them, we need to appreciate the multiplicity of causals and facets; and thereby come up with a multifaceted approach of dealing with them. This is why Africa is not supposed to be left alone in addressing such problems due to the fact that though they heavily affect Africa, in the long run they will affect the whole word. One of the examples is global warming. Although Africa's contribution is negligible, thanks to the population growth, soon Africa will become a major contributor to global warming if it is left alone. Although this volume will not go in details as far as global warming is concerned, it will specifically dwell terrorism to show how the world is supposed to pull together to see to it that Africa is turning things around for its better and the better of the world at large. So, too, we will propose what must be done for the world to solve these problems hand in hand with Africa.

In concluding, the conflicts we evidence in Africa, if they are left to Africa alone as its problem, will affect the whole world. We all have a fair share in the conflicts that are currently going on in Africa either directly or indirectly. Sadly though, while Africans have invested heavily in finishing each other geared by greed, rust for power and myopia, rich countries are scheming and negotiating on how to take over Africa's resources without necessarily resorting to wars. In the beginning, they used the Berlin conference 1884 to divide Africa. To the contrary though, currently, they are using Africa's greed, myopia, division and its refusal to learn from history as swift means to keep on exploiting it. Malan (2015) maintains that there is no way we can move to the destination without knowing and acknowledging the sound role our history and environment provides. We will touch on new emerging powers which are non-European, namely China and India; and the way they are scheming to join the spree of eating Africa up. Pity as it may sound, Africans, sometimes are to blame even more although not all. By heavily investing in conflict, they make the job of taking over their resources much easier for rich countries. What rich countries do is playing double roles of supplying them with weapons first; and thereafter come in to resolve the conflicts they have always fuelled and financed. As if this is not enough, Arms are not cheap toys. Some countries spend money they get by means of loans to purchase them or add to the military budgets (Yakovlev 2007) instead of investing in other social services such as education and health not to mention economic sectors such as infrastructure, industrialisation and banking. We are talking about democratisation. Again, is democracy that has no roots in Africa a viable solution to Africa's problems? How can it be while it is superimposed and financed by the same enemies who pushed Africa to the abyss? For, African economies to perform well for the benefit and welfare of Africans, democracy must have roots in Africa. African countries should create the need for democracy instead of waiting for the West to superimpose its brand of democracy. In the coming chapters I will try to show how democracy is not a new thing to Africa.

Conclusion

In winding up this volume, I must sincerely argue that Africa has; and needs to drastically change from being a backyard to being an important player in world affairs. Therefore, it needs to skedaddle from this situation by all means possible shall it aspire to turn things around pragmatically for the better. Africa, of course, needs to committedly, fully, purposely, strategically, and, above all, wholeheartedly change and take on all challenges it is facing currently. How will this be done? This is what this volume is all about. How will this be achieved? You can write tons and tons of books on the topic in exploring issues that we need to seriously look into for Africa to turn things around for the betterment of its people. Nothing important that Africa needs, *inter alia*, like changing the mind-sets of its people and the world based on the way they view others and Africa in general.

God bless Africa and whoever aspires to see Africa turning things around for its furtherance and the betterment of the world becoming a reality. As Bob Marley puts it, emancipate yourself from mental slavery; and nobody can emancipate us except ourselves. So, it applies to Africa and the world at large. For many decades, Africa sought answers to its problems be they internal or external to no avail thanks to the international systemic rot. Now than ever before, Africa needs to turn things around by looking for the same answers from within and without. Let us try this experiment. I believe that as Africans lived for thousands of years without necessarily depending on handouts and favours before colonialism was introduced, Africa still can replicate its resilience, successes and above all, its wherewithal; and thereby turn things around for the better. Warning: ignorance is the tool of a fool while curiosity is the bat of a theorist.

References

Abadie, A., (2004) *Poverty, Political Freedom, and the Roots of Terrorism* (No. w10859). National Bureau of Economic Research.

Abuzeid, F., (2009) Foreign Aid and the "Big Push" Theory: Lessons from Sub-Saharan Africa. *Stanford Journal of International Relations, 11*(1), pp. 16-23.

Acha, I., Akpanuko, E., and Unuafe, O. K., (2013) "Illicit Financial Outflows from Africa and Their Developmental Implications: Experience from Nigeria." *Management 3.7* (2) pp. 417-426.

Adelman, H., and Suhrke, A., (1996) Early Warning and Response: Why the International Community Failed to Prevent the Genocide. *Disasters, 20*(4), pp. 295-304.

Adilova, G., Kyrgyz Traditional-Folk Games and Its Influences on Education. *Редакційна Колегія*, p. 85.

Aghedo, I. and Osumah, O., (2015) Insurgency in Nigeria: A Comparative Study of Niger Delta and Boko Haram Uprisings. *Journal of Asian and African Studies, 50*(2), pp. 208-222.

Aidt, T. S., (2003) "Economic Analysis of Corruption: A Survey." *The Economic Journal 113.491.* F632-F652.

Al Jazeera. 2015. Television Documentary, August 1.

Alemazung, J.A., (2011) Leadership flaws and Fallibilities Impacting Democratization Processes, Governance and Functional Statehood in Africa. *African Journal of Political Science and International Relations, 5*(1), p. 30.

Alford, R.P., (2012) A Broken Windows Theory of International Corruption. *Ohio St. LJ, 73*, p.1253.

Altheide, D. L., (2006) "Terrorism and the Politics of Fear." [*Cultural Studies? Critical Methodologies* 6 (4), pp. 415-439].

Alves, A. C., (2008) "China and Gabon: A Growing Resource Partnership." Braamfontein: The South African Institute of International Affairs (SAIIA).

Andrews, N., and Okpanachi, E., (2012) Trends of Epistemic Oppression and Academic Dependency in Africa's Development: The Need for a New Intellectual Path. *Journal of Pan African Studies*, 5(8), pp. 85-104.

Anyanwu, J.C., (2014) Does Intra- African Trade Reduce Youth Unemployment in Africa? *African Development Review*, 26 (2), pp. 286-309.

Appel, H. C., (2012) "Walls and white elephants: Oil extraction, responsibility, and infrastructural violence in Equatorial Guinea." *Ethnography* 13 (4), pp. 439-465.

Arezki, R., and van der Ploeg, R., (2007) "Can the Natural Resource Curse Be Turned into a Blessing? The Role of Trade Policies and Institutions."

Armstrong, E.A., and Crage, S.M., (2006) Movements and memory: The making of the Stonewall myth. *American Sociological Review*, 71 (5), pp. 724-751.

Asongu, S. A., (2013) "Fighting Corruption When Existing Corruption-Control Levels Count: What Do Wealth-Effects Tell Us in Africa?" *Institutions and Economies* 5 (3), pp. 53-74.

Asongu, S., (2014) Financial Development Dynamic Thresholds of Financial Globalization: Evidence from Africa. *Journal of Economic Studies*, 41(2), pp. 166-195.

Asongu, S.A., 2014 Fighting African Capital Flight: Empirics on Benchmarking Policy Harmonization. *The European Journal of Comparative Economics*, 11 (1), p. 93.

Awiti, A., and Scott, B., (2016) Kenya Youth Survey Executive Summary.

Bäckstrand, K., (2006) Multi- Stakeholder Partnerships for Sustainable Development: Rethinking Legitimacy, Accountability and Effectiveness. *Environmental Policy and Governance*, 16 (5), pp, pp. 290-306.

Badiane, O., (2008) *Sustaining and Accelerating Africa's Agricultural Growth Recovery in the Context of Changing Global Food Prices.* International Food Policy Research Institute (IFPRI).

Bai, C.E., and Qian, Y., (2010) Infrastructure Development in China: The Cases of Electricity, Highways, and Railways. *Journal of Comparative Economics, 38* (1), pp. 34-51.

Baker, J.B., (2006) Market Definition: An Analytical Overview.

Baker, R.W., (2005) *Capitalism's Achilles Heel: Dirty Money and How to Renew the Free-Market System.* John Wiley & Sons.

Bakke, K.M., Cunningham, K.G. and Seymour, L.J., (2012) A plague of Initials: Fragmentation, Cohesion, and Infighting in Civil Wars. *Perspectives on Politics, 10* (2), pp. 265-283.

Ballentine, K., and Nitzschke, H., (2005) The Political Economy of Civil War and Conflict Transformation. *Berghof Research Center for Constructive Conflict Management, Berlin.* *[http://www. berghof-handbook. net/ articles/ BHDS3_ BallentineNitzschke230305. pdf].*

Bangerezako, H., (2013) *"Working for the Nation": Diasporic Youth and the Construction of Belonging in the Rwandan Capital* (Doctoral Dissertation).

Bannon, I. and Collier, P., (2003) *Natural Resources and Violent Conflict: Options and Actions.* Washington, DC: World Bank.

Barya, J.J.B., (1993) The New Political Conditionalities of Aid: an Independent View from Africa. *ids bulletin, 24* (1), pp.16-23.

Batts, S., and Church, F.P., (2013) If You Don't Know Where You Are Going, Any Road Will Take You There.

Beddington, J., (2010) Food Security: Contributions from Science to a New and Greener Revolution. *Philosophical Transactions of the Royal Society of London B: Biological Sciences, 365*(1537), pp. 61-71.

Belasco, A., (2009) *Cost of Iraq, Afghanistan, and Other Global War on Terror Operations since 9/11.* Diane Publishing.

Bem, S.L., (1996) *Transforming the Debate on Sexual Inequality: From Biological Difference to Institutionalized Androcentrism.* na.

Benin, S., and Yu, B., (2012) Complying with the Maputo Declaration Target: Trends in Public Agricultural Expenditures and Implications for Pursuit of Optimal Allocation of Public Agricultural Spending. *ReSAKSS Annual Trends and Outlook Report.*

Berg, E., (2000) Why Aren't Aid Organisations Better Learners. *Learning in Development Cooperation, Stockholm, EGDI.*

Bergman, J., (1993) Evolution and the origins of the biological race theory. *Journal of Creation,* 7(2), pp.155-168.

Bergman, J., (2004) Darwinism and the Teaching of Racism and Eugenics in Biology Textbooks. *Pennsylvania State University.*

Blomstedt, P., (2014) "Orthopedic Surgery in Ancient Egypt." *Acta Orthopaedica* 85 (6), pp. 670-676.

Bloom, D.E., Canning, D., and Chan, K., (2006) *Higher Education and Economic Eevelopment in Africa* (Vol. 102). Washington, DC: World Bank.

Bompani, B., and Valois, C., (2017) "Sexualizing Politics: the Anti-Homosexuality Bill, Party-Politics and the New Political Dispensation in Uganda." *Critical African Studies* 9 (1), pp. 52-70.

Bond, P., (2006) Looting Africa: The Economics of Exploitation. Zed Books.

Bonilla-Silva, E., (2001) White Supremacy and Racism in the Post-Civil Rights Era. Lynne Rienner Publishers.

Bornman, E., (2012) "The Mobile Phone in Africa: Has it Become a Highway to the Information Society or Not." *Contemporary Educational Technology* 3 (4), pp. 278-292.

Bose, S., (2007) Contested Lands: Israel-Palestine, Kashmir, Bosnia, Cyprus, and Sri Lanka. Harvard University Press.

Bourguignon, F., and Sundberg. M., (2007) "Aid Effectiveness: Opening the Black Box." *The American Economic Review* 97 (2), pp. 316-321.

Bourke, J., (2014) "Rape as a Weapon of War." *The Lancet* *383.9934*, e19-e20.

Bräutigam, D. A., and Knack. S., (2004) "Foreign Aid, Institutions, and Governance in Sub- Saharan Africa." *Economic Development and Cultural Change 52* (2), pp. 255-285.

Bräutigam, D., and Xiaoyang, T., (2011) "African Shenzhen: China's Special Economic Zones in Africa." *The Journal of Modern African Studies 49* (1), pp. 27-54.

Bräutigam, D., and Zhang. H., (2013) "Green Dreams: Myth and Reality in China's Agricultural Investment in Africa." *Third World Quarterly 34* (9), pp. 1676-1696.

Brei, V., and Böhm. S., (2013) "'1L= 10L for Africa': Corporate Social Responsibility and the Transformation of Bottled Water into a 'Consumer Activist 'Commodity." Discourse & Society, 0957926513503536.

Brounéus, K., (2008) "Truth-Telling as Talking Cure? Insecurity and Retraumatization in the Rwandan Gacaca Courts." *Security Dialogue* 39 (1), pp. 55-76.

Bruce, J.W., (2014) "The Variety of Reform: A Review of Recent Experience with Land Reform and the Reform of Land Tenure, with Particular Reference to the African Experience." *Occasional Paper 9*, pp. 13-56.

Burgess, R., *et al.* (2010) "Our Turn to Eat: The Political Economy of Roads in Kenya." Manuscript, London, UK: London School of Economics and Political Science.

Burke, N., (2014) *Gender and Envy*. Routledge.

Burton, R. F., (1872) Zanzibar: City, Island, and Coast. Vol. 2. Tinsley Brothers.

Byrne, S., (2001) "Consociational and Civic Society Approaches to Peacebuilding in Northern Ireland." *Journal of Peace Research* 38 (3), pp. 327-352.

Byrne, S., and Irvin, C.L., (2001) "Reconcilable Differences: Turning Points in Ethnopolitical Conflict," *The Global Review of Ethnopolitics*, 87-109.

Campbell, C. J., (2013) "Gabon." Campbell's Atlas of Oil and Gas Depletion. Springer New York, pp. 43-45.

Campbell, H., (2007) "Regime Hegemony in Museveni's Uganda: Pax Musevenica." The International Journal of African Historical Studies 40 (3) 546.

Campbell, P. J., and Chavey, D.P., (1995) "Tchuka Ruma Solitaire." *UMAP Journal 16.4* (1995): 343-365.

Carroll, S.T., (1988) "Solomonic Legend: The Muslims and the Great Zimbabwe." *The International Journal of African Historical Studies 21*(2), *pp*-233-247.

Carter, J., Irani, G., and Volkan, V.D., (2009) Regional and Ethnic Conflicts: Perspectives from the Front Lines, Pearson Prentice Hall.

Chaliand, G., and Blin, A., (2007) The History of Terrorism: From Antiquity to al Qaeda. Univ of California Press.

Chapter 16 of the Laws (Revised), 1981 (Tanzania).

Chingono, M., (2016) "Violent Conflicts in Africa: Towards a Holistic Understanding." *World Journal of Social Science Research, 3* (2), p. 199.

Chinua, A., (1958) "Things Fall Apart." Ch. Achebe, pp. 1-117.

Chirikure, S., *et al.,* (2013) "A Bayesian chronology for Great Zimbabwe: re-threading the sequence of a vandalised monument." *Antiquity* 87 (337), pp. 854-872.

Chiu, C., Meng-Hsiang Hsu, M., and Wang, E.T.G., (2006) "Understanding Knowledge Sharing in Virtual Communities: An Integration of Social Capital and Social Cognitive Theories." *Decision Support Systems* 42 (3), pp. 1872-1888.

Christensen, J., (2009) "Africa's Bane: Tax Havens, Capital Flight and the Corruption Interface." *Documentos de Trabajo (Real Instituto Elcano de Estudios Internacionales y Estratégicos),* (1) 1.

Chukwuebuka, E.C., (2010) "Child Trafficking in Sub-Saharan Africa: Continuation of Slavery by Other Means." *African Renaissance* 7.3 (4), pp. 29-40.

Cikara, M., Botvinick, M.M., and Fiske, S.T., (2011) "Us versus Them Social Identity Shapes Neural Responses to Intergroup Competition and Harm." *Psychological Science.*

Cikara, M., Bruneau, E.G., and Saxe, R.R., (2011) "Us and Them Intergroup Failures of Empathy." *Current Directions in Psychological Science* 20 (3), pp. 149-153.

Clark, J. F., (1998) "Foreign Intervention in the Civil War of the Congo Republic." *Issue: A Journal of Opinion 26* (1), pp. 31-36.

Clemm, R. H., (2009) Delineating *Dominion: The Use of Cartography in the Creation and Control of German East Africa.* Diss. The Ohio State University.

Clover, J., (2003) "Food Security in Sub-Saharan Africa." *African Security Studies 12* (1), pp. 5-15.

CNN. 7 August.

Cohen, C., and Chollet, D., (2007) "When $10 Billion Is Not Enough: Rethinking US Strategy toward Pakistan." *Washington Quarterly,* pp. 7-19.

Collier, P., (2007) "The Bottom Billion." Economic Review-Deddington- 25 (1), p. 17.

Collier, P., Hoeffler, A., and Pattillo, C., (2001) "Flight Capital as a Portfolio Choice." *The World Bank Economic Review 15* (1), pp. 55-80.

Collier, R.B., (1982) Regimes in Tropical Africa: Changing Forms of Supremacy, 1945-1975. Univ of California Press.

Connor, J.M., and Lande, R.H., (2012) "Cartels as Rational Business Strategy: Crime Pays."

Cook, C.R., (2010) "American Policymaking in the Democratic Republic of the Congo 1996-1999: The Anti-Kabila Bias and the Crushing Neutrality of the Lusaka Accords." *African and Asian Studies* 9 (4), pp. 393-417.

Corbo, V., and Fischer, S., (1995) "Structural Adjustment, Stabilization and Policy Reform: Domestic and International Finance." *Handbook of Development Economics 3*, pp. 2845-2924.

Cosgel, M. M., *et al.* (2011) "Controlling Corruption in Law Enforcement: Incentives, Safeguards, and Institutional Change in the Ottoman Empire." Safeguards, and Institutional Change in the Ottoman Empire (December 19, 2011).

Cotula, L., (2009) Land Grab or Development Opportunity?: Agricultural Investment and International Land Deals in Africa. IIED.

Cotula, L., (2011) Land *Deals in Africa: What Is in the Contracts?* IIED.

Cotula, L., and Vermeulen, S., (2009) "Deal or No Deal: The Outlook for Agricultural Land Investment in Africa." *International Affairs* 85 (6), pp. 1233-1247.

Cox, W., and Love, J., (1998) The Best Investment a Nation Ever Made: A Tribute to the Dwight D. Eisenhower System of Interstate and Defense Highways. DIANE Publishing.

Cramer, C., Johnston, D., and Oya, C., (2009) "Africa and the Credit Crunch: From Crisis to Opportunity?" *African Affairs 108* (433), pp. 643-654.

Crush, J., Chikanda, A., and Skinner, C., (2015) "Migrant Entrepreneurship and Informality in South African Cities." Mean Streets: Migration, Xenophobia and Informality in South Africa, Cape Town: *SAMP, ACC and IDRC*, pp. 1-24.

d'Agostino, G., Dunne, J.P., and Pieroni, L., (2012) "Corruption, Military Spending and Growth." *Defence and Peace Economics 23* (6), pp. 591-604.

Dale, B. E., *et al.,* (2010) "Biofuels Done Right: Land Efficient Animal Feeds Enable Large Environmental and Energy Benefits." *Environmental Science & Technology 44* (22), pp. 8385-8389.

Darley, W. K., and Blankson, C., (2008) "African Culture and Business Markets: Implications for Marketing Practices." *Journal of Business & Industrial Marketing 23* (6), pp. 374-383.

De Maret, P., and Nsuka, F., (1977) "History of Bantu Metallurgy: Some Linguistic Aspects." *History in Africa* 4, pp. 43-65.

De Mesquita, E. B., (2008) "The Political Economy of Terrorism: A Selective Overview of Recent Work." *The Political Economist* 10 (1), pp. 1-12.

Defeis, E. F., (2008) "UN Peacekeepers and Sexual Abuse and Exploitation: An End to Impunity." *Wash. U. Global Stud. L. Rev.* 185.

Dennett, D. C., (1995) "Darwin's Dangerous Idea." *The Sciences 35* (3), pp. 34-40.

Dennis, R. M., (1995) "Social Darwinism, Scientific Racism, and the Metaphysics of Race." *Journal of Negro Education*, pp. 243-252.

Dizolele, M. P., (2010) "The Mirage of Democracy in the DRC." *Journal of Democracy 21* (3), pp. 143-157.

Dreher, A., (2006) "IMF and Economic Growth: The Effects of Programs, Loans, and Compliance with Conditionality." *World Development* 34 (5), pp. 769-788.

Dunne, P., and Perlo-Freeman, S., (2003) "The Demand for Military Spending in Developing Countries." *International Review of Applied Economics 17* (1), pp. 23-48.

Dzingirai, V., (2003) "The New Scramble for the African Countryside." Development and Change 34 (2), pp. 243-264.

Easterly, W., and Easterly, W.R., (2006) *The White Man's Burden: Why the West's Efforts to Aid the Rest Have Done So Much Ill and So Little Good.* Penguin.

Efobi, U., and Asongu, A., (2016) "Terrorism and Capital Flight from Africa." *International Economics* 148, pp. 81-94.

Ellis, W. J. D., (2011) "Social Darwinism in Nazi Family and Inheritance Law."

Eme, I. E. (2013) "Dependency Theory and Africa's Underdevelopment: A Paradigm Shift from Pseudo-Intellectualism. The Nigerian Perspective." *International Journal of African and Asian Studies. Vol* 1.

Emerson, S., (2004) "Lockerbie Terrorist Attack and Libya: A Retrospective Analysis, The." *Case W. Res. J. Int'l L.* 36, 487.

Englebert, P., (2000) "Pre-Colonial Institutions, Post-Colonial States, and Economic Development in Tropical Africa." *Political Research Quarterly* 53 (1), pp. 7-36.

Esty, D. C., (2006) "Good Governance at the Supranational Scale: Globalizing Administrative Law." *The Yale Law Journal*, pp. 1490-1562.

Excoffier, L., *et al.,* (1987) "Genetics and History of Sub-Saharan Africa." *American Journal of Physical Anthropology 30* (8), pp. 151-194.

Falola, T., and Achberger, J., (2013) *The Political Economy of Development and Underdevelopment in Africa.* Vol. 10. Routledge.

Fan, S., *et al.,* (2008) Investing *in African Agriculture to Halve Poverty by 2015.* Intl Food Policy Res Inst.

Fan, S., Nestorova, B., and Olofinbiyi, T., (2010) "China's Agricultural and Rural Development: Implications for Africa." *Grupo de Estudio del Comité de Asistencia de Desarrollo de China Sobre Agricultura, Seguridad Alimentaria y Desarrollo Rural 27.*

Fan, S., Omilola, B., and Lambert, M., (2009) "Public Spending for Agriculture in Africa: Trends and Composition." *Regional Strategic Analysis and Knowledge Support System* 5.

Fan, S., Yu. B., and Saurkar, A., (2008) "Public Spending in Developing Countries: Trends, Determination, and Impact." *Public Expenditures, Growth, and Poverty*, pp. 20-55.

Fennell, C. W., *et al.,* (2004) "Assessing African Medicinal Plants for Efficacy and Safety: Pharmacological Screening and Toxicology." *Journal of Ethnopharmacology 94* (2), pp. 205-217.

Fenske, J., (2014) "Ecology, Trade, and States in Pre- Colonial Africa." *Journal of the European Economic Association* 12 (3), pp. 612-640.

Ferguson, J., (2006) *Global Shadows: Africa in the Neoliberal World Order.* Duke University Press.

Fielding, M., and Moss, P., (2011) Radical Education and the Common School: A Democratic Alternative. London: Routledge.

Fombad, C.M., (2004) "The Dynamics of Record-Breaking Endemic Corruption and Political Opportunism in Cameroon." *The Leadership Challenge in Africa:* Cameroon under Paul Biya, pp. 357-394.

Franco, Jennifer C. "Global Land Grabbing and Trajectories of Agrarian Change: A Preliminary Analysis." *Journal of Agrarian Change 12*.1 (2012): 34-59.

Frankel, J. A., (2010) *The natural Resource Curse: A Survey.* No. W15836. National Bureau of Economic Research.

Frantz, E., (2016) "Capital Escape: How Developing Countries Lose Money in Election Years."

Freeman, C., (2015) *Egypt, Greece, and Rome: Civilizations of the Ancient Mediterranean.* Oxford University Press.

Frynas, J.F., and Paulo, M., (2006) "A New Scramble for African Oil? Historical, Political, and Business Perspectives." *African Affairs* 106 (423), pp. 229-251.

Gedecho, E.K., (2015) "Urban Tourism Potential of Hawassa City, Ethiopia." *American Journal of Tourism Research* 4 (1), pp. 25-36.

German, L., Schoneveld, G., and Mwangi, E., (2011) "Processes of Large-Scale Land Acquisition by Investors: Case Studies from Sub-Saharan Africa." *International Conference on Global Land Grabbing, University of Sussex.*

Gibbon, P., Bangura, Y., and Ofstad, A., (1992) Authoritarianism, Democracy, and Adjustment: The Politics of Economic Reform in Africa. Vol. 26. Nordic Africa Institute.

Giller, K. E., *et al.,* (2011) "Communicating Complexity: Integrated Assessment of Trade-Offs Concerning Soil Fertility Management within African Farming Systems to Support Innovation and Development." *Agricultural Systems 104* (2), pp. 191-203.

Giroux, J., Lanz, D., and Sguaitamatti, D., (2009) "The Tormented Triangle: The Regionalisation of Conflict in Sudan, Chad, and the Central African Republic."

Gisselquist, R. M., (2012) Good Governance as a Concept, and Why This Matters for Development Policy. Vol. 30. WIDER.

Goffman, E., (2009) *Stigma: Notes on the Management of Spoiled Identity.* Simon and Schuster.

Goldsmith, A. A., (2000) "Sizing Up the African State." *The Journal of Modern African Studies 38* (1), pp. 1-20.

Goldstein, A., Pinaud, N., and Reisen, H., (2006) "The Rise of China and India."

Goldstein, J. L., Rivers, D., and Tomz, M., (2007) "Institutions in International Relations: Understanding the Effects of the GATT and the WTO on World Trade." *International Organization* 61 (1), pp. 37-67

Goldstein, J., and Rotich, J., (2008) "Digitally Networked Technology in Kenya's 2007–2008 Post-Election Crisis." Berkman Center Research Publication.

Gow, D. D., (2008) *Countering Development: Indigenous Modernity and the Moral Imagination.* Duke University Press.

Grabel, I., (2011) "Not Your Grandfather's IMF: Global Crisis, 'Productive Incoherence' and Developmental Policy Space." *Cambridge Journal of Economics* 35 (5), pp. 805-830.

Grier, R. M., (1999) "Colonial Legacies and Economic Growth." *Public Choice 98 (3-4)*, pp. 317-335.

Grindle, M. S., (2007) "Good Enough Governance Revisited." *Development Policy Review 25* (5), pp. 533-574.

Gunaratna, R., (2002) Inside Al Qaeda: Global Network of Terror. Columbia University Press.

Gupta, S., Davoodi, H.R., and Tiongson, E., (2000) *Corruption and the Provision of Health Care and Education Services.* No. 2000-2116. International Monetary Fund.

Haber, S., and Menaldo, V., (2011) "Do Natural Resources Fuel Authoritarianism? A Reappraisal of the Resource Curse." *American political science Review 105* (1), pp. 1-26.

Habiyaremye, A., (2011) "Chinafrique, Africom, and African Natural Resources: A Modern Scramble for Africa." *Whitehead J. Dipl. & Int'l Rel.* (12), 79.

Hallam, D., (2009). "International Investments in Agricultural Production." *Land Grab.*

Hallam, D., (2011) "International Investment in Developing Country Agriculture—Issues and Challenges." *Food Security* 3 (1), pp. 91-98.

Harper, D. J., (1996) "Accounting for Poverty: From Attribution to Discourse." *Journal of Community & Applied Social Psychology* 6 (4), pp. 249-265.

Haugen, H.Ø., (2011) "Chinese Exports to Africa: Competition, Complementarity and Cooperation between Micro-Level Actors." *Forum for Development Studies. Vol. 38.* No. 2. Routledge.

Hayman, R., (2010) "Abandoned Orphan, Wayward Child: the United Kingdom and Belgium in Rwanda since 1994." *Journal of Eastern African Studies 4* (2), pp. 341-360.

Haynes, J., (2005) "Islamic Militancy in East Africa." Third World Quarterly 26 (8), pp. 1321-1339.

Hellsten, S., and Larbi, G.A., (2006) "Public Good or Private Good? The Paradox of Public and Private Ethics in the

Context of Developing Countries." *Public Administration and Development* 26 (2), pp. 135-145.

Hellström, J., and Tröften, P., (2010) *The Innovative Use of Mobile Applications in East Africa.* Swedish International Development Cooperation Agency (SIDA).

Henk, D. W., and Rupiya, M. R., (2001) *Funding Defense: Challenges of Buying Military Capability in Sub-Saharan Africa.* Army War Coll Strategic Studies Inst Carlisle Barracks PA.

Hestermeyer, H., (2007) Human Rights and the WTO: The Case of Patents and Access to Medicines. Oxford: Oxford University Press.

Hoeffler, A., (2008) "Dealing with the Consequences of Violent Conflicts in Africa." African Development Bank Report.

Hoffman, P. T., (2012) "Why Was It Europeans Who Conquered the World?" *The Journal of Economic History 72* (3), pp. 601-633.

Holslag, J., (2010) "China's Roads to Influence." Asian Survey 50 (4), pp. 641-662.

Hopkin, J., and Rodriquez-Pose, A., (2007) ""Grabbing Hand" or "Helping Hand"?: corruption and the economic role of the state." *Governance* 20 (2), pp. 187-208.

Hopkins, A. G., (2014) *An Economic History of West Africa.* Routledge.

Howard, R., and Hoffman, B., (2012) *Terrorism and Counterterrorism: Understanding the New Security Environment Readings and Interpretation.* McGraw Hill.

https://www.youtube.com/watch?v=0cTm9aJm8wA accessed 1st October, 2015.

Huffman, T. N., (2004) "Ancient Mining and Zimbabwe."

Hui, V. T., (2004) "Toward a Dynamic Theory of International Politics: Insights From Comparing Ancient China and Early Modern Europe." *International Organization 58* (1), pp. 175-205.

Hulme, D., (2009) "The Millennium Development Goals (MDGs): A Short History of the World's Biggest Promise."

Hung, H., (2008). "Normalized Collective Corruption in a Transitional Economy: Small Treasuries in Large Chinese Enterprises." *Journal of Business Ethics* 79 (1-2), pp. 69-83.

Huntington, S.P., (1996) "The West Unique, not Universal." *Foreign Affairs*, pp. 28-46.

Ifejirika, E.E., (2014) "The Image of Africa and Africans in Selected Anglophone Expatriate Novels." *AFRREV LALIGENS: An International Journal of Language, Literature and Gender Studies* 3 (2), pp. 47-65.

Island, R., (2011) "Jacob Gedleyihlekisa Zuma."

Izama, A., and Wilkerson, M., (2011) "Uganda: Museveni's Triumph and Weakness." *Journal of Democracy* 22 (3), pp. 64-78.

Jackson, S., (2006) "Sons of Which Soil? The language and Politics of Autochthony in Eastern DR Congo." *African Studies Review 49*. (02), pp. 95-124.

Jensen, M.F., and Gibbon, P., (2007) "Africa and the WTO DOHA Round: An Overview." *Development Policy Review 25* (1), pp. 5-24.

Jeong, H., (2000) *Peace and Conflict Studies: An Introduction.* Ashgate Pub Limited.

Juma, C., (2015) *The New Harvest: Agricultural Innovation in Africa.* Oxford University Press.

Kaarsholm, P., (1992) "The Past as Battlefield in Rhodesia and Zimbabwe." Collected Seminar Papers. Institute of Commonwealth Studies. Vol. 42. Institute of Commonwealth Studies.

Kanu, I. A., (n.d year) "African Traditional Democracy."

Kapteijns, L., (2001) "The Disintegration of Somalia: A Historical Essay." Bildhaan: *An International Journal of Somali Studies 1*, pp. 11-52.

Karsten, L., and Illa, H., (2005) "Ubuntu as a Key African Management Concept: Contextual Background and Practical Insights for Knowledge Application." *Journal of Managerial Psychology 20* (7), pp. 607-620.

Kaufman, S. J., (2006) "Escaping the Symbolic Politics Trap: Reconciliation Initiatives and Conflict Resolution in Ethnic Wars." *Journal of Peace Research* 43 (2), pp. 201-218.

Kaufmann, D., Kraay, A., and Mastruzzi, M., (2011) "The Worldwide Governance Indicators: Methodology and Analytical Issues." *Hague Journal on the Rule of Law* 3 (2), pp. 220-246.

Kennedy, G., (2011) "Adam Smith and the Role of the Metaphor of an Invisible Hand." *Economic Affairs* 31 (1), pp. 53-57.

Khan, Z., et al., (2011) "Push—Pull Technology: A Conservation Agriculture Approach for Integrated Management of Insect Pests, Weeds and Soil Health in Africa: UK Government's Foresight Food and Farming Futures Project." *International Journal of Agricultural Sustainability* 9 (1), pp. 162-170.

Kim, N. C., and Kusimba, C. M, (2008) "Pathways to Social Complexity and State Formation in the Southern Zambezian Region." *African Archaeological Review* 25 (3-4), pp. 131-152.

King, L.W., and Hall, H.R., (1906) History of Egypt, Chaldea, Syria, Babylonia, and Assyria in the Light of Recent Discovery. Vol. 13. Grolier Society.

Kirby, P., (2012) "How Is Rape a Weapon of War?: Feminist International Relations, Modes of Critical Explanation and the Study of Wartime Sexual Violence." *European Journal of International Relations*, 1354066111427614.

Kohn, R. H., (1997) "How Democracies Control the Military." *Journal of Democracy 8* (4), pp. 140-153.

Kroesen, O., and Rozendaal, A., (2010) "A Cross-Cultural Management System: The Ubuntu Company as Paradigm."

International Journal of Technology, Policy and Management 10 (3), pp. 284-298.

Lall, S., and Pietrobelli, C., (2005) "National technology Systems in Sub-Saharan Africa." International *Journal of Technology and Globalisation 1* (3-4), pp. 311-342.

Lamb, D., (1982) *The Africans.* Vintage.

Lambsdorff, J. G., (2003) "How Corruption Affects Productivity." *Kyklos* 56 (4), pp. 457-474.

Lawson, L., (2007) *US Africa policy since the Cold War.* Naval Postgraduate School Monterey CA Center for Contemporary Conflict.

Lederach, J.P., (1997) "Building Peace: Sustainable Reconciliation in Divided Societies." Washington DC, 4.

Lee, M.C., (2006) "The 21st Century Scramble for Africa." *Journal of Contemporary African Studies* 24 (3), pp. 303-330.

Levitsky, S., and Way, L.A., (2010) *Competitive Authoritarianism: Hybrid Regimes after the Cold War.* Cambridge University Press.

Lien, D., and Wang, Y., (2005) "Brain Drain or Brain Gain: A Revisit." *Journal of Population Economics 18* (1), pp. 153-163.

Lijphart, A., (1975) "Review Article: the Northern Ireland Problem; Cases, Theories, and Solutions." *British Journal of Political Science 5* (01), pp. 83-106.

Litwak, R.S., (2008) "Living with Ambiguity: Nuclear Deals with Iran and North Korea." *Survival* 50 (1), pp. 91-118.

Lodge, T., (n.d year) "From Apartheid to Democracy in South Africa." *Mediterranean Academy of Diplomatic Studies* (MEDAC): 34.

Lodhi, A. Y., (1994) "Muslims in Eastern Africa: Their Past and Present." *Nordic Journal of African Studies 3.1* (1994): 88-99.

Louw, D. J., (1998) "Ubuntu: An African Assessment of the Religious Other." Twentieth World Congress of Philosophy. Vol. 25.

Lumumba-Kasongo, T., (2011) "China-Africa Relations: A Neo-Imperialism or a Neo-Colonialism? A Reflection." *African and Asian Studies 10* (2-3), pp. 234-266.

Lyman, P. N., and Morrison J. S., (2004). "The Terrorist Threat in Africa." *Foreign Affairs,* pp. 75-86.

M'Baye, B., (2006) "Marcus Garvey and African Francophone Political Leaders of the Early Twentieth Century: Prince Kojo Tovalou Houénou Reconsidered." *The Journal of Pan African Studies* 1, pp. 2-19.

Machel, S.M., (1987) "Apartheid Must Be Eradicated." *The Black Scholar,* pp. 25-33.

Madrick, J., (2010) *The Case for Big Government.* Princeton University Press.

Maedl, A., (2011) "Rape as Weapon of War in the Eastern DRC?: The Victims' Perspective." *Human Rights Quarterly 33* (1) pp. 128-147.

Magosvongwe, R., (2017). "And God Saw that It Was Good? Poverty Disability and Dependency Demystified: Interrogating the Systemic Improvement, Disempowerment and Paralysis of African Communities Selected Fictional Narratives on Eastern and Southern Africa." *BOLESWA* 4 (3).

Malan, S., (2015) ""If You Don't Know Where You Are Going, Any Road Will Get You There"-Lewis Carroll: President's Message." *SA Pharmaceutical Journal* 82 (7), pp. 5-5.

Malik, S., Hayat, M.K., and Hayat, M.U., (2010). "External Debt and Economic Growth: Empirical Evidence from Pakistan." *International Research Journal of Finance and Economics* 44 (44), pp. 1450-2887.

Mamdani, M., (2005) "Political Identity, Citizenship and Ethnicity in Post-Colonial Africa." *Conference on New Frontiers of Social Policy.*

Mancke, E., (1999) "Early Modern Expansion and the Politicization of Oceanic Space." Geographical Review 89 (2), pp. 225-236.

Mandela, N., (1993) "South Africa's Future Foreign Policy." *Foreign Affairs*, pp. 86-97.

Mann, M., (2005) *The Dark Side of Democracy: Explaining Ethnic Cleansing.* Cambridge University Press.

Marchal, R., (2007) "Warlordism and Terrorism: How to Obscure an Already Confusing Crisis? The Case of Somalia." *International Affairs 83* (6), pp. 1091-1106.

Martin, G., (2013) *Understanding Terrorism: Challenges, Perspectives, and Issues.* Sage Publications.

Martin, J., (2013) "The Politics of Fear. "*Child & Youth Services* 34.1), pp. 5-8.

Masha, E. m., (2011) *Assessment of Technology Adoption for Free Range Local Chicken Improvement in Mzumbe ward Mvomero District Morogoro.* Diss. Sokoine University of Agriculture.

Masinge, K., (2011) "Factors Influencing the Adoption of Mobile Banking Services at the Bottom of the Pyramid in South Africa."

Massey, P., (2000) "Market Definition and Market Power in Competition Analysis: Some Practical Issues." *Economic and Social Review 31* (4), pp. 309-328.

Matunhu, J., (2011) "A Critique of Modernization and Dependency Theories in Africa: Critical Assessment."

Matyok, T., and Mendoza, H.R., (2014) "Deep Analysis: Designing Complexity into Our Understanding of Conflict." *InterAgency Journal* 5 (2), pp. 14-24.

Matyók, T., and Schmitz, C.L., (n.d year) "The Violence in Helping: Resisting the Neo-Colonialism of Humanitarian Action."

Mawere, M., (2014) "Divining the Future of Africa: Healing the Wounds, Restoring Dignity and Fostering Development." Langaa RPCIG Publishers: Cameroon.

Mawere, M., and Mubaya, T., (2016) "African Philosophy and Thought Systems: A Search for a Culture and Philosophy of Belonging." Langaa Publishers: Bamenda.

Max-Neef, M., Elizalde, A., and Hopenhayn, M., (1992) "Development and Human Needs," Real-life Economics: Understanding Wealth Creation, pp. 197-213.

Maxwell, D. G., Gelsdorf, K., and Santschi, M., (2012) Livelihoods, Basic Services and Social Protection in South Sudan. Secure Livelihoods Research Consortium; Overseas Development Institute.

Mbisso, D., (2011) "Petty Trading in Marketplaces: Space Generation, Use and Management at Temeke Stereo Marketplace in Dar es Salaam, Tanzania."

McMillan, M., Rodrik, D., and Verduzco-Gallo, I., (2014) "Globalization, Structural Change, and Productivity Growth, with an Update on Africa." *World Development 63* (1), pp. 11-32.

McSherry, B., (2006) "The Political Economy of Oil in Equatorial Guinea." *African Studies Quarterly 8* (3), pp. 23-45.

Meredith, M., (2005) "The Fate of Africa: A History of 50 Years of Independence." New York: Public Affairs.

Mhango, N. N., (2016) "Chapter Five Violence, Power, Politics and (Anti-) Development in Africa." *Violence, Politics and Conflict Management in Africa: Envisioning Transformation, Peace and Unity in the Twenty-First Century*, 117.

Mhango, N. N., (2016) *Africa Reunite or Perish*. Langaa RPCIG, Cameroon.

Mhango, N.N., (2016) *Africa's Best and Worst Presidents: How Neocolonialism and Imperialism Maintained Venal Rules in Africa*. Langaa RPCIG.

Mhango, N.N., (2017) "Chapter Nine History, Culture, Religion and [under-] Development in Africa." *Africa at the Crossroads: Theorising Fundamentalisms in the 21st Century*, 223.

Michalopoulos, S., and Papaioannou, E., (2013) "Pre- Colonial Ethnic Institutions and Contemporary African Development." *Econometrica* 81 (1), pp. 113-152.

Mideksa, T. K., (2013) "The Economic Impact of Natural Resources." *Journal of Environmental Economics and Management* 65 (2), pp. 277-289.

Miedema, M. J., (2010) *Ugandan President Museveni and the ICC Referral.* MS Thesis.

Mitchell, T., (1991) *Colonising Egypt: With a New Preface.* Univ. of California Press, 1991.

Montague, D., (2002) "Stolen Goods: Coltan and Conflict in the Democratic Republic of Congo." *Sais Review,* pp. 103-118.

Morapedi, W. G., (2007) "Post-Liberation Xenophobia in Southern Africa: The Case of the Influx of Undocumented Zimbabwean Immigrants into Botswana, c. 1995–2004." *Journal of Contemporary African Studies 25* (2), pp. 229-250.

Mosley, P., Subasat, T., and Weeks. J., (1995) "Assessing Adjustment in Africa." *World Development 23* (9), pp. 1459-1473.

Moss, T, J., Pettersson, G., and Van de Walle, N., (2006). "An Aid-Institutions Paradox? A Review Essay on Aid Dependency and State Building in Sub-Saharan Africa." *Center for Global Development Working Paper 74,* pp. 11-05.

Moyo, D., (2011) *Dead Aid: Why Aid Is Not Working and How There Is a Better Way for Africa.* Macmillan, 2009.

Muller, Ralf. "Project Governance." *Strategic Direction* 27 (1).

Munene, I. I., (2010) "No-Party Democracy? Ugandan Politics in Comparative Perspective, Giovanni Carbone," pp. 91-94.

Mupepi, M.G., (2016) "Developing Democratic Paradigms to Effectively Manage Business, Government, and Civil Society: The African Spring." *Handbook of Research on Sub-National Governance and Development,* 432.

Murphy, S.D., (2003) "Libyan Payment to Families of Pan Am Flight 103 Victims." *The American Journal of International Law 97* (4), 987.

Murshed, S. M., and Sen, S., (1995) "Aid Conditionality and Military Expenditure Reduction in Developing Countries: Models of Asymmetric Information." *The Economic Journal,* pp. 498-509.

Mwenda, A., (2006) *Foreign Aid and the Weakening of Democratic Accountability in Uganda.* Cato Institute.

Nadasdy, P., (2005) The Anti-Politics of TEK: The Institutionalization of Co-Management Discourse and Practice: *Anthropologica, Vol. 47, No. 2,* pp. 215-232, Canadian Anthropology Society.

Nafziger, E. W., and Auvinen, J., (2002) "Economic Development, Inequality, War, and State Violence." *World Development 30* (2), pp. 153-163.

Nathan, D., and Sarkar, S., (2011) "Blood on Your Mobile Phone? Capturing the Gains for Artisanal Miners, Poor Workers and Women, Capturing the Gains for Artisanal Miners, Poor Workers and Women.

Nathanson, J., (2013) "The Pornography of Poverty: Refraining the Discourse of International Aid's Representations of Starving Children." *Canadian Journal of Communication 38* (1), 103.

Ndulo, M., (2003) "The Democratization Process and Structural Adjustment in Africa." *Indiana Journal of Global Legal Studies 10* (1), pp. 315-368.

Newman, S., (1991) "Does Modernization Breed Ethnic Political Conflict?" *World Politics 43.* (03), pp. 451-478.

Nicolai, S., et al., (2014) "Unbalanced Progress."

Noman, A., and Stiglitz, J.E., (2015) "Economics and Policy: Some Lessons from Africa's Experience'." *The Oxford Handbook of Africa and Economics* (2), pp. 830-48.

234

Ntuli, P. P., (2002) "Indigenous Knowledge Systems and the African Renaissance." Indigenous Knowledge and the Integration of Knowledge Systems: *Towards a Philosophy of Articulation*, pp. 53-66.

Nunn, N., and Puga, D., (2012) "Ruggedness: The Blessing of Bad Geography in Africa." *Review of Economics and Statistics 94* (1), pp. 20-36.

Nyamnjoh, F. B., (2012) "'Potted Plants in Greenhouses': A Critical Reflection on the Resilience of Colonial Education in Africa." *Journal of Asian and African Studies*, 0021909611417240.

Nyerere, J. K., (1967) "Education for Self- reliance." *The Ecumenical Review 19* (4), pp. 382-403.

Ober, J., (2008) "The Original Meaning of "Democracy": Capacity to Do Things, not Majority Rule." *Constellations* 15 (1), pp. 3-9.

Ojo, E.O., (2016) "Underdevelopment in Africa: Theories and Facts." *The Journal of Social, Political, and Economic Studies* 41 (1), 89.

Ojo, Emmanuel O., (2015) "The Atlantic Slave Trade and Colonialism: Reasons for Africa's Underdevelopment?" *European Scientific Journal* 11 (17).

Olatunji, C.P., (2011) *A Philosophical Inquiry into the Problem of Democracy in Africa*. Diss.

Omorogbe, E.Y., (2011) "Club of Incumbents-The African Union and Coups d'états, A." *Vand. J. Transnat'l L. 44*, 123.

Orisakwe, O.E., and Frazzoli, C., (2010) "Electronic Revolution and Electronic Wasteland: the West/Waste Africa Experience." *Journal of Natural and Environmental Sciences 1*(1), pp. 43-47.

Ota, R., and Cas, S.M., (2008) Big *Government, High Debt, and Fiscal Adjustment in Small States (EPub)*. No. 8-39. International Monetary Fund.

Otsuka, K., and Kijima, Y., (2010) "Technology Policies for a Green Revolution and Agricultural Transformation in Africa." *Journal of African Economies 19* (2), pp. ii60-ii76.

Paarlberg, R., (2009) Starved for Science: How Biotechnology Is Being Kept out of Africa. Harvard University Press.

Page, J., (2012) "Can Africa Industrialise?" *Journal of African Economies 21* (2), pp. ii86-ii124.

Pati, R., (2008) "ICC and the Case of Sudan's Omar Al Bashir: Is Plea-Bargaining a Valid Option, The." *UC Davis J. Int'l L. & Pol'y 15*, 265.

Perlo-Freeman, S., Perdomo, C., and Sköns, E., (2010) "Military Expenditure." SIPRI Yearbook 2009, pp. 179-211.

Pinaud, C., (2014) "South Sudan: Civil War, Predation and the Making of a Military Aristocracy." *African Affairs 113* (451), pp. 192-211.

Plümper, T., and Martin, C.W., (2003) "Democracy, Government Spending, and Economic Growth: A Political-Economic Explanation of the Barro-Effect." *Public Choice 117* (1-2), pp. 27-50.

Porter, G., *et al.,* (2012) "Youth, Mobility and Mobile Phones in Africa: Findings from a Three-Country Study." *Information Technology for Development 18* (2), pp. 145-162.

Post, K. W.J., (1968) "Is There a Case for Biafra?" *International Affairs (Royal Institute of International Affairs* 1944-), pp. 26-39.

Przeworski, A., and Vreeland, J.R., (2000). "The Effect of IMF Programs on Economic Growth." *Journal of Development Economics* 62 (2), pp. 385-421.

Radelet, S., (2006) "A Primer on Foreign Aid." *Center for Global Development working paper* 92.

Rajan, R. G., and Subramanian, A., (2008) "Aid and Growth: What Does the Cross-Country Evidence Really Show?" *The Review of Economics and Statistics 90* (4), pp. 643-665.

Rakotoarisoa, M., Iafrate, M., and Paschali, M., (2011) Why Has Africa Become a Net food Importer. FAO.

Ralston, D. A., (2008) "The Crossvergence Perspective: Reflections and Projections." *Journal of International Business Studies* 39 (10), pp. 27-40.

Reij, C., Scoones, I., and Toulmin, C., (2013) Sustaining the Soil: Indigenous Soil and Water Conservation in Africa. Routledge.

Reinhart, C. M., and Rogoff, K.S., (2009) *This Time Is Different: Eight Centuries of Financial Folly.* Princeton University press.

Rice, C., (2008) "Rethinking the National Interest: American Realism for a New World." *Foreign Affairs*, pp. 2-26.

Richman, B. D., (2006) "How community Institutions Create Economic Advantage: Jewish Diamond Merchants in New York." *Law & Social Inquiry 31* (2), pp. 383-420.

Roberts, M. J., (2009) "Conflict Analysis of the 2007 Post-Election Violence in Kenya." Managing Conflicts in Africa's Democratic Transitions, pp. 141-55.

Robertson, B., and Pinstrup-Andersen, P., (2010) "Global land Acquisition: Neo-colonialism or Development Opportunity?" *Food Security* 2 (3), pp. 271-283.

Robinson, J. A., Torvik, R., and Verdier, T., (2006) "Political Foundations of the Resource Curse." *Journal of development Economics* 79 (2), pp. 447-468.

Rodney, W., (1972) "How Europe Underdeveloped Africa," Washington, DC: Howard, United States of America.

Rose-Ackerman, S., and Palifka, B.J., (2016) *Corruption and Government: Causes, Consequences, and Reform.* Cambridge University press.

Rothstein, B., (2011) "Anti-Corruption: The Indirect 'Big Bang' Approach." *Review of International Political Economy 18* (2) pp. 228-250.

Royster, D., (2003) Race and the Invisible Hand: How White Networks Exclude Black Men from Blue-Collar Jobs. Univ of California Press.

Ruetschlin, C., and Asante-Muhammad, D., (2013) "The Challenge of Credit Card Debt for the African American Middle Class." Demos and NAACP.

Scholz, A., (2015) "Hutu, Tutsi and the Germans: Racial Cognition in Rwanda under German Colonial Rule."

Selin, H., (Eds) (2013) *Encyclopaedia of the History of Science, Technology, and Medicine in Non-Western Cultures.* Springer Science & Business Media.

Seriki, H. T., Hoegl, M., and Parboteeah, K.P., (2010) "Innovative Performance in African Technical Projects—A Multi-Level Study." *Journal of World Business 45* (3), pp. 295-303.

Shankleman, J., (2011) "Oil and State Building in South Sudan." United States Institute of Peace. Special Report 282.

Skinner, E. P., (1998) "African Political Cultures and the Problems of Government." *African Studies Quarterly* 2 (3), pp. 17-25.

Sklar, R. L., (1983) "Democracy in Africa." *African Studies Review 26* (3/4), 11-24.

Sloan, L. M., et al., (2010) "A Story to Tell: Bullying and Mobbing in the Workplace." *International Journal of Business and Social Science* 1(3).

Smaldone, J. P., (2006) "African Military Spending: Defence versus Development?" *African Security Studies 15* (4), pp. 17-32.

Smith, M.C., (2012). "The Politics of Fear." *Torch* 32 (2), 8.

Špička, J., Boudný, J., and Janotová, B., (2009). "The Role of Subsidies in Managing the Operating Risk of Agricultural Enterprises." *Agricultural Economics–Czech 50* (4), pp. 169-179.

Staub, E., (2003) "Notes on Cultures of Violence, Cultures of Caring and Peace, and the Fulfilment of Basic Human Needs." *Political Psychology 24* (1), pp. 1-21.

Stolte, C., (2012) Brazil *in Africa: Just another BRICS country seeking resources?* London: Chatham House.

Sutton, K., and Fahmi, W., (2002) "The Rehabilitation of Old Cairo." *Habitat International 26* (1), pp. 73-93.

Taiwo, O., (2011) "Improving aid Effectiveness for Africa's Economic Growth." *Foresight Africa*, 16.

Tandon, Y., (2011) "Whose Dictator is Qaddafi? The Empire and its Neo-colonies." *Insight on Africa* 3 (1), pp. 1-21.

Tangri, R., and Mwenda, A.M., (2013) *The Politics of Elite Corruption in Africa: Uganda in Comparative African Perspective.* Vol. 3. Routledge.

Tan- Mullins, M., Mohan, G., and Power, M., (2010) "Redefining 'Aid' in the China–Africa Context." *Development and Change* 41 (5), pp. 857-881.

Tarman, C., and Sears, D.O., (2005) "The Conceptualization and Measurement of Symbolic Racism." *The Journal of Politics* 67(03), pp. 731-761.

Taylor, I., (2009) China's New Role in Africa. Boulder, CO: Lynne Rienner Publishers.

Telesetsky, A., (2011) "Resource Conflicts over Arable Land in Food Insecure States: Creating a United Nations Ombudsman Institution to Review Foreign Agricultural Land Leases." *Browser Download This Paper.*

Tencati, A., and Zsolnai, L., (2012) "Collaborative Enterprise and Sustainability: The Case of Slow Food." *Journal of Business Ethics* 110 (3), pp. 345-354.

Terheggen, A., (2011) "The Tropical Timber Industry in Gabon: A Forward Linkages Approach to Industrialisation."

Theletsane, K. I., (2012) "Ubuntu Management Approach and Service Delivery." *Journal of Public Administration* 47 (Special Issue 1), pp. 265-278.

Themnér, L., and Wallenstein, P., (2013) "Armed Conflicts, 1946–2012." *Journal of Peace Research 50* (4), pp. 509-521.

Thies, C. G., (2007) "The Political Economy of State Building in Sub-Saharan Africa." *Journal of Politics* 69 (3), pp. 716-731.

Thomson, A., (2016) An Introduction to African Politics. Routledge.

Tidemand, P., (2013) "The resistance Councils in Uganda: A Study of Rural Politics and Popular Democracy in Africa."

Truth, J.R.C., (2013) "TJRC Report (Abridged Version)."

Tull, D. M., (2006) "China's Engagement in Africa: Scope, Significance and Consequences." *The Journal of Modern African Studies* 44 (3), pp. 459-479.

Udeala, S.O., (2010) "Nigeria-China Economic Relations under the South-South Cooperation." *African Journal of International Affairs 13* (1-3), pp. 61-88.

Uduji, J. I., (2013) "Towards an Instrumentality Theory of Salesforce Motivation: A Pragmatic Model." *European Journal of Business and Management* 5 (20), pp. 213-225.

Union, A., (2006) "Status of Food Security and Prospects for Agricultural Development in Africa." Ethiopia, Addis Ababa.

US, D.O.J., (1998) Federal Bureau of Investigation, November 18.

Uzodike, U.O., and Maiangwa, B., (2012) "African Renaissance Vol 9, No 1, 2012."

Van der Ploeg, F., (2011) "Natural Resources: Curse or Blessing?" *Journal of Economic Literature,* 366-pp. 420.

Van der Ploeg, F., and Poelhekke, S., (2010) "The Pungent Smell of "Red Herrings": Subsoil Assets, Rents, Volatility and the Resource Curse." *Journal of Environmental Economics and Management 60* (1), pp. 44-55.

Vasudevan, P., (2010) "The Changing Nature of Nigeria–India Relations." London: Chatham House Programme Paper 2.

Vermeulen, S., and Cotula, L., (2010) "Over the Heads of Local People: Consultation, Consent, and Recompense in Large-

Scale Land Deals for Biofuels Projects in Africa." *The Journal of Peasant Studies 37* (4), pp. 899-916.

Viriri, A., and Mungwini, P., (2010) "African Cosmology and the Duality of Western Hegemony: The Search for an African Identity." *The Journal of Pan African Studies 3* (6), pp. 27-42.

Viviano, F., (2005) "China's Great Armada, Admiral Zheng He." National Geographic, July, 6.

Vlassenroot, K., and Huggins, C., (2005) "Land, Migration and Conflict in Eastern DRC." From the Ground up: Land Rights, *Conflict and Peace in Sub-Saharan Africa*, pp. 115-195.

West, D. M., and Dasgupta, S., (2011) *Creating a 'Brain Gain' for US Employers*: The Role of Immigration. Washington, DC: Brookings Institution.

Whitaker, B.E., (2010) "Compliance among Weak States: Africa and the Counter-Terrorism Regime." *Review of International Studies* 36 (03), pp. 639-662.

Wily, L.A., (2011) "The Law is to Blame': The Vulnerable Status of Common Property Rights in Sub- Saharan Africa." *Development and change* 42 (3), pp. 733-757.

Wimmer, A., Lars-Erik., and Min, B., (2009) "Ethnic politics and Armed Conflict: a Configurational Analysis of a New Global Data Set," *American Sociological Review 74.* (2), pp. 316-337.

Wiredu, K., (1995) "Democracy and Consensus in African Traditional Politics: A Plea for a Non-Party Polity." *The Centennial Review 39* (1), pp. 53-64.

Wodak, R., (2015) *The Politics of Fear: What Right-Wing Populist Discourses Mean.* Sage.

Wolf, E. R., and Eriksen, T.H., (2010) Europe and the People without History. Univ of California Press.

Wood, R. M., J.D., Kathman, and Gent, S.E., (2012) "Armed Intervention and Civilian Victimization in

Wright, J., (2007) *The Trans-Saharan Slave Trade.* Vol. 2. Routledge.

Wright, J., (2008) "To Invest or Insure? How Authoritarian Time Horizons Impact Foreign Aid Effectiveness." *Comparative Political Studies 41* (7), pp. 971-1000.

Xu, C., Ye, H., and Cao, S., (2011) "Constructing China's Greenways Naturally." *Ecological Engineering 37* (3), pp. 401-406.

Xu, Q., (2006) "Maritime Geostrategy and the Development of the Chinese Navy in the Early Twenty-First Century." *Naval War College Review 59* (4), 46.

Yakovlev, P., (2007) "Arms Trade, Military Spending, and Economic Growth." *Defence and Peace Economics 18* (4), pp. 317-338.

Young, C., and Godlee, F., (2007) "Reed Elsevier's Arms Trade." *BMJ 334* (7593), pp. 547-548.

Zartman, I. W., (1994) *International Multilateral Negotiation: Approaches to the Management of Complexity.* Jossey-Bass.

Zweig, D., Fung, C.S., and Han, D., (2008) "Redefining the Brain Drain China's 'Diaspora Option'." *Science Technology & Society 13* (1), pp. 1-33.

"'Racist' Indian Mob Attacks African Students." *Telegram*, October, 1 (2014).

"'The Donors' Dilemma' - Aid in Reverse: How Poor Countries Develop Rich Countries." *Global Policy*, December 12 (2013).

"Africa Focus: African Countries Invest Heavily in Education." Ministry of Foreign Affairs of the People's Republic of China, October 28 (2006).

"Anti-terror Tactics Targeting Muslim Leaders Provoking Tensions in Kenya." *Globe and Mail*, July 2 (2015).

"Cameroon Spends Millions of Euros on Medical Care for Highly Placed Government Officials Abroad." *Cameroon Concord*, October 22 (2015).

"Central African Republic Capital under Lockdown." *BBC*, September 30 (2015).

"Central African Republic's Seleka Rebels call For Secession amid Sectarian War." *Guardian*, 25 April, 2014.

"China Starts Emergency Food Aid Plan to Africa." *Xinhua*, February, 8 (2016).

"Dangote Announces Tanzania Investment Africa." *Africa Global Fund*, October 6 (2014).

"French Woman Kidnapped By Somali Militants Dies." *Guardian*, 19 October 19 (2011.

"Ghana: Searching for Opportunities at Home and Abroad." *Migration Policy Institute, MPI*, March 1 (2006).

"Hope, and Doubt, South of the Sahara." *Economics*, November 2 (2012).

"Jacob Zuma Accused of Corruption 'on a Grand Scale' in South Africa." *Guardian*, November 29 (2013).

"Khalid al-Fawwaz Convicted of 1998 U.S. Embassy Attacks." *Daily Nation*, February 26 (2015).

"Lack of Market for Farm Produces Impoverishing Africa, Banker says." *Daily Nation*, August 28 (2016).

"Magufuli Bans Foreign Travels For Senior Government Officials." *Daily Nation*, November 9 (2015).

"Mali Attack: Special Forces Storm Hotel to Free Hostages." *BBC*, November 20 (2015).

"Mapping Mediterranean Migration." *BBC*, September 15 (2014).

"Nigerian Students Patronise Foreign Schools." *Vanguard*, October, 22 (2015).

"Police Holding Boy, 14, Rescued From Al-Shabaab Training." *Daily Nation*, October 10 (2015).

"Police to Shut Down Radical Madrasas in Terror Clampdown." *Daily Nation*, September 24 (2014).

"South Africa -Gupta Files Sent to Hawks by ANC Whistleblower." *City Press*, June 10 (2016).

"South Africa President's Woes as Good-Time Nephew Mentioned in Panama Papers." *Telegraph*, April 4 (2016).

"Tanzania's Government Urges End to Donor Dependence as MCC Cancels Aid." *Guardian*, April 1 (2016).

"The 30m-strong Africa Diaspora Likely Sends $160bn Home Every Year: Where Does it Go?" *Mail and Guardian*, June 2 (2015).

"The Resource Nationalism in Africa: Wish You Were Mine." *Economist*, February 11 (2012).

"The singer Andy Brown Has died." *New Zimbabwe*, 16, March, 2012.

"The Tanzania: First Ever Heart Institute Opens in Dar." *Daily News*, September 6 (2015).

"Trainspotter: Panama Papers–How Zuma's Family is Implicated in the Greatest Corruption Data Dump of All Time." *Daily Maverick*, April 4 (2016).

"Two U.S. Embassies in East Africa Bombed." *New York Times*, August 8 (1998).

"Xi Announces 10 Major Programs to Boost China-Africa Cooperation in Coming 3 Years." *China Daily*, December 4 (2015).

"Zille: Gupta Executive Donated Money." *iol.co.za*, January 29 (2013).